T0192513

Machine Learning with R

Abhijit Ghatak

Machine Learning with R

Abhijit Ghatak
Consultant Data Engineer
Kolkata
India

ISBN 978-981-13-4950-8   ISBN 978-981-10-6808-9   (eBook)
DOI 10.1007/978-981-10-6808-9

Printed on acid-free paper

This Springer imprint is published by Springer Nature
The registered company is Springer Nature Singapore Pte Ltd.
The registered company address is: 152 Beach Road, #21-01/04 Gateway East, Singapore 189721, Singapore

I dedicate this book to my wife Sushmita, who has been my constant motivation and support.

Preface

My foray in machine learning started in 1992, while working on my Masters thesis titled *Predicting torsional vibration response of a marine power transmission shaft*. The model was based on an iterative procedure using the Newton–Raphson rule to optimize a continuum of state vectors defined by transfer matrices. The optimization algorithm was written using the *C* programming language and it introduced me to the power of machines in numerical computation and its vulnerability to floating point errors. Although the term "machine learning" came much later intuitively, I was using the power of an 8088 chip on my mathematical model to predict a response.

Much later, I started using different optimization techniques using computers both in the field of engineering and business. All through I kept making my own notes. At some point of time, I thought it was a good idea to organize my notes, put some thought on the subject, and write a book which covers the essentials of machine learning—linear algebra, statistics, and learning algorithms.

The Data-Driven Universe

Galileo in his *Discorsi* [1638] stated that data generated from natural phenomena can be suitably represented through mathematics. When the size of data was small, then, we could identify the obvious patterns. Today, a new era is emerging where we are "downloading the universe" to analyze data and identify more subtle patterns.

The Merriam Webster dictionary defines the word "cognitive", as *"relating to, or involving conscious mental activities like learning"*. The American philosopher of technology and founding executive editor of *Wired*, Kevin Kelly, defines "cognitize" as injecting intelligence to everything we do, through machines and algorithms. The ability to do so depends on data, where intelligence is a stowaway in the data cloud. In the data-driven universe, therefore, we are not just using data but constantly seeking new data to extract knowledge.

Causality—The Cornerstone of Accountability

Smart learning technologies are better at accomplishing tasks but they do not think. They can tell us "what" is happening but they cannot tell us "why". They may tell us that some stromal tissues are important in identifying breast cancer but they lack the cause behind why some tissues are playing the role. Causality, therefore, is the rub.

The Growth of Machines

For the most enthusiastic geek, the default mode just 30 years ago from today was offline. Moore's law has changed that by making computers smaller and faster, and in the process, transforming them from room-filling hardware and cables to slender and elegant tablets. Today's smartphone has the computing power, which was available at the MIT campus in 1950. As the demand continues to expand, an increasing proportion of computing is taking place in far-off warehouses thousands of miles away from the users, which is now called "cloud computing"—*de facto* if not *de jure*. The massive amount of cloud-computing power made available by Amazon and Google implies that the speed of the chip on a user's desktop is becoming increasingly irrelevant in determining the kind of things a user can do.

Recently, AlphaGo, a powerful artificial intelligence system built by Google, defeated Lee Sedol, the world's best player of Go. AlphaGo's victory was made possible by clever machine intelligence, which processed a data cloud of 30 million moves and played thousands of games against itself, "learning" each time a bit more about how to improve its performance. A learning mechanism, therefore, can process enormous amounts of data and improve their performance by analyzing their own output as input for the next operation(s) through **machine learning**.

What is Machine Learning?

This book is about data mining and machine learning which helps us to discover previously unknown patterns and relationships in data. Machine learning is the process of automatically discovering patterns and trends in data that go beyond simple analysis. Needless to say, sophisticated mathematical algorithms are used to segment the data and to predict the likelihood of future events based on past events, which cannot be addressed through simple query and reporting techniques.

There is a great deal of overlap between learning algorithms and statistics and most of the techniques used in learning algorithms can be placed in a statistical framework. Statistical models usually make strong assumptions about the data and, based on those assumptions, they make strong statements about the results.

However, if the assumptions in the learning model are flawed, the validity of the model becomes questionable. Machine learning transforms a small amount of input knowledge into a large amount of output knowledge. And, the more knowledge from *(data)* we put in, we get back that much more knowledge out. Iteration is therefore at the core of machine learning, and because we have constraints, the driver is optimization.

If the knowledge and the data are not sufficiently complete to determine the output, we run the risk of having a model that is not "real", and is a foible known as *overfitting* or *underfitting* in machine learning.

Machine learning is related to artificial intelligence and deep learning and can be segregated as follows:

- **Artificial Intelligence** (AI) is the broadest term applied to any technique that enables computers to mimic human intelligence using logic, if-then rules, decision trees, and machine learning (including deep learning).
- **Machine Learning** is the subset of AI that includes abstruse statistical techniques that enable machines to improve at tasks with the experience gained while executing the tasks. If we have input data x and want to find the response y, it can be represented by the function $y = f(x)$. Since it is impossible to find the function f, given the data and the response (due to a variety of reasons discussed in this book), we try to approximate f with a function g. The process of trying to arrive at the best approximation to f is through a process known as machine learning.
- **Deep Learning** is a scalable version of machine learning. It tries to expand the possible range of estimated functions. If machine learning can learn, say 1000 models, deep learning allows us to learn, say 10000 models. Although both have infinite spaces, deep learning has a larger viable space due to the math, by exposing multilayered neural networks to vast amounts of data.

Machine learning is used in web search, spam filters, recommender systems, credit scoring, fraud detection, stock trading, drug design, and many other applications. As per Gartner, AI and machine learning belong to the top 10 technology trends and will be the driver of the next big wave of innovation.[1]

Intended Audience

This book is intended both for the newly initiated and the expert. If the reader is familiar with a little bit of code in R, it would help. R is an open-source statistical programming language with the objective to make the analysis of empirical and simulated data in science reproducible. The first three chapters lay the foundations of machine learning and the subsequent chapters delve into the mathematical

---

[1] http://www.gartner.com/smarterwithgartner/gartners-top-10-technology-trends-2017/.

interpretations of various algorithms in regression, classification, and clustering. These chapters go into the detail of supervised and unsupervised learning and discuss, from a mathematical framework, how the respective algorithms work. This book will require readers to read back and forth. Some of the difficult topics have been cross-referenced for better clarity. The book has been written as a first course in machine learning for the final-term undergraduate and the first-term graduate levels. This book is also ideal for self-study and can be used as a reference book for those who are interested in machine learning.

Kolkata, India   Abhijit Ghatak
August 2017

Acknowledgements

In the process of preparing the manuscript for this book, several colleagues have provided generous support and advice. I gratefully acknowledge the support of Edward Stohr, Christopher Asakiewicz and David Belanger from Stevens Institute of Technology, NJ for their encouragement.

I am indebted to my wife, Sushmita for her enduring support to finish this book, and her megatolerance for the time to allow me to dwell on a marvellously 'confusing' subject, without any complaints.

August 2017   Abhijit Ghatak

Contents

About the Author

Abhijit Ghatak is a Data Engineer and holds an ME in Engineering and MS in Data Science from Stevens Institute of Technology, USA. He started his career as a submarine engineer officer in the Indian Navy and worked on multiple data-intensive projects involving submarine operations and construction. He has worked in academia, technology companies, and as research scientist in the area of Internet of Things (IoT) and pattern recognition for the European Union (EU). He has authored scientific publications in the areas of engineering and machine learning, and is presently consultant in the area of pattern recognition and data analytics. His areas of research include IoT, stream analytics, and design of deep learning systems.

Chapter 1
Linear Algebra, Numerical Optimization, and Its Applications in Machine Learning

The purpose of computing is insight, not numbers.

-R.W. Hamming

Linear algebra is a branch of mathematics that lets us concisely describe the data and its interactions and performs operations on them. Linear algebra is therefore a strong tool in understanding the logic behind many machine learning algorithms and as well as in many branches of science and engineering. Before we start with our study, it would be good to define and understand some of its key concepts.

1.1 Scalars, Vectors, and Linear Functions

Linear algebra primarily deals with the study of vectors and linear functions and its representation through matrices. We will briefly summarize some of these components.

1.1.1 Scalars

A scalar is just a single number representing only magnitude (defined by the unit of the magnitude). We will write scalar variable names in lower case.

1.1.2 Vectors

An ordered set of numbers is called a vector. Vectors represent both magnitude and direction. We will identify vectors with lower case names written in **bold**, i.e., **y**. The elements of a vector are written as a column enclosed in square brackets:

© Springer Nature Singapore Pte Ltd. 2017
A. Ghatak, *Machine Learning with R*, DOI 10.1007/978-981-10-6808-9_1

$$\mathbf{x} = \begin{bmatrix} x_1 \\ x_2 \\ \vdots \\ x_m \end{bmatrix} \tag{1.1.1}$$

These are called column vectors. Column vectors can be represented in rows by taking its transpose:

$$\mathbf{x}^\top = [x_1, x_2, \ldots, x_m] \tag{1.1.2}$$

1.1.2.1   Multiplication of Vectors

Multiplication by a vector $\mathbf{u}$ to another vector $\mathbf{v}$ of the same dimension may result in different types of outputs. Let $\boldsymbol{u} = (u_1, u_2, \cdots, u_n)$ and $\boldsymbol{v} = (v_1, v_2, \cdots, v_n)$ be two vectors:

- The **inner** or **dot product** of two vectors with an angle θ between them is a **scalar** defined by

$$\begin{aligned} \boldsymbol{u} . \boldsymbol{v} &= u_1 v_1 + u_2 v_2 + \cdots + u_n v_n \\ &= \|u\| \, \|v\| \, cos(\theta) \\ &= \boldsymbol{u}^\top \boldsymbol{v} \\ &= \boldsymbol{v}^\top \boldsymbol{u} \end{aligned} \tag{1.1.3}$$

- **Cross product** of two vectors is a vector, which is perpendicular to both the vectors, i.e., if $\boldsymbol{u} = (u_1, u_2, u_3)$ and $\boldsymbol{v} = (v_1, v_2, v_3)$, the cross product of $\mathbf{u}$ and $\mathbf{v}$ is the vector $\boldsymbol{u} \times \boldsymbol{v} = (u_2 v_3 - u_3 v_2, u_3 v_1 - u_1 v_3, u_1 v_2 - u_2 v_1)$.
  NOTE: The cross product is only defined for vectors in $\mathbb{R}^3$

$$\boldsymbol{u} \times \boldsymbol{v} = \|u\| \, \|v\| \, sin(\theta) \tag{1.1.4}$$

Let us consider two vectors $\boldsymbol{u} = (1, 1)$ and $\boldsymbol{v} = (-1, 1)$ and calculate (a) the angle between the two vectors, (b) their inner product

```
u <- c(1, 1)
v <- c(-1, 1)
theta <- acos(sum(u * v) / (sqrt(sum(u * u)) * sqrt(sum(v * v))))*180/pi
theta
```

```
[1] 90
```

```
inner_product <- sum(u * v)
inner_product
```

```
[1] 0
```

The cross product of a three-dimensional vector can be calculated using the function "crossprod" or the multiplication of the two vectors:

```
u <- c(3, -3, 1)
v <- c(4, 9, 2)
cross_product <- crossprod(u,v)
cross_product
```

```
       [,1]
[1,]   -13
```

```
t(u) %*% v
```

```
       [,1]
[1,]   -13
```

1.1.2.2 Orthogonal Vectors

The two vectors are orthogonal if the angle between them is 90°, i.e., when $x^\top y = 0$. Figure 1.1 depicts two orthogonal vectors $u = (1, 1)$ and $v = (-1, 1)$.

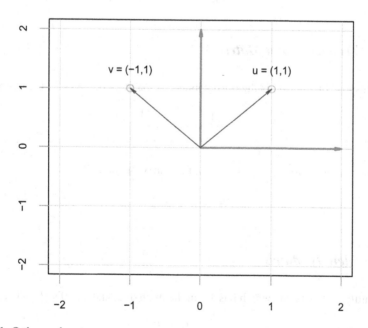

Fig. 1.1 Orthogonal vectors

1.2   Linear Functions

Linear functions have **vectors** as both **inputs** and **outputs**. A system of linear functions can be represented as

$$\mathbf{y}_1 = a_1\mathbf{x}_1 + a_2\mathbf{x}_2 + \cdots + a_n\mathbf{x}_n$$
$$\mathbf{y}_2 = b_1\mathbf{x}_1 + b_2\mathbf{x}_2 + \cdots + b_n\mathbf{x}_n$$

1.3   Matrices

Matrices help us to compact and organize the information present in vectors and linear functions. A matrix is a two-dimensional array of numbers, where each element is identified by two indices—the first index is the row and the second index is the column and is represented by bold upper case variable names.

$$\mathbf{X} = \begin{bmatrix} x_{1,1} & x_{1,2} & x_{1,3} \\ x_{2,1} & x_{2,2} & x_{2,3} \\ x_{3,1} & x_{3,2} & x_{3,3} \end{bmatrix} \tag{1.3.1}$$

1.3.1   Transpose of a Matrix

The transpose of a matrix is the mirror image of the main diagonal of the matrix:

$$\mathbf{X}^\top = \begin{bmatrix} x_{1,1} & x_{2,1} & x_{3,1} \\ x_{1,2} & x_{2,2} & x_{3,2} \\ x_{1,3} & x_{2,3} & x_{3,3} \end{bmatrix} \tag{1.3.2}$$

In mathematical form, the transpose of a matrix can be written as

$$(\mathbf{X}^\top)_{i,j} = (\mathbf{X})_{j,i}$$

1.3.2   Identity Matrix

An identity matrix is one which has 1's in the main diagonal and 0's elsewhere:

$$I = \begin{bmatrix} 1 & 0 & \cdots & 0 \\ 0 & 1 & \cdots & 0 \\ \vdots & \vdots & \ddots & \vdots \\ 0 & 0 & \cdots & 1 \end{bmatrix} \tag{1.3.3}$$

Any matrix $\mathbf{X}$ multiplied by the identity matrix $\mathbf{I}$ does not change $\mathbf{X}$:

$$\mathbf{X}I = \mathbf{X}$$

1.3.3 Inverse of a Matrix

Matrix inversion allows us to analytically solve equations. The inverse of a matrix A is denoted as A^{-1}, and it is defined as

$$A^{-1}A = I \tag{1.3.4}$$

Consider the matrix A defined as

$$A = \begin{bmatrix} 1 & 3 \\ 2 & 4 \end{bmatrix}$$

The inverse of a matrix in R is computed using the "solve" function:

```
solve(A)
```

```
       [,1]  [,2]
[1,]    -2   1.5
[2,]     1  -0.5
```

The matrix inverse can be used to solve the general equation $Ax = b$

$$A^{-1}Ax = A^{-1}b$$
$$Ix = A^{-1}b \tag{1.3.5}$$

1.3.4 Representing Linear Equations in Matrix Form

Consider the list of linear equations represented by

$$y_1 = \mathbf{A}_{(1,1)}x_1^1 + \mathbf{A}_{(1,2)}x_2^1 + \ldots + \mathbf{A}_{(1,n)}x_n^1$$
$$y_2 = \mathbf{A}_{(2,1)}x_1^2 + \mathbf{A}_{(2,2)}x_2^2 + \ldots + \mathbf{A}_{(2,n)}x_n^2$$
$$\vdots$$
$$y_m = \mathbf{A}_{(m,1)}x_1^m + \mathbf{A}_{(m,2)}x_2^m + \ldots + \mathbf{A}_{(m,n)}x_n^m \tag{1.3.6}$$

The above linear equations can be written in matrix form as

$$\begin{bmatrix} y_1 \\ y_2 \\ \vdots \\ y_m \end{bmatrix} = \begin{bmatrix} A_{1,1} & A_{1,2} & \cdots & A_{1,n} \\ A_{2,1} & A_{2,2} & \cdots & A_{2,n} \\ \vdots & \vdots & \vdots & \vdots \\ A_{m,1} & A_{m,2} & \cdots & A_{m,n} \end{bmatrix} \begin{bmatrix} x_1^1 & x_2^1 & \cdots & x_n^1 \\ x_1^2 & x_2^2 & \cdots & x_n^2 \\ \vdots & \vdots & \cdots & \vdots \\ x_1^m & x_2^m & \cdots & x_n^m \end{bmatrix} \qquad (1.3.7)$$

1.4   Matrix Transformations

Matrices are often used to carry out transformations in the vector space. Let us consider two matrices A_1 and A_2 defined as

$$A_1 = \begin{bmatrix} 1 & 3 \\ -3 & 2 \end{bmatrix}$$

$$A_2 = \begin{bmatrix} 3 & 0 \\ 0 & 2 \end{bmatrix}$$

When the points in a circle are multiplied by A_1, it **stretches** and **rotates** the unit circle, as shown in Fig. 1.2. The matrix A_2, however, only stretches the unit circle as shown in Fig. 1.3. The property of rotating and stretching is used in singular value decomposition (SVD), described in Sect. 1.11.

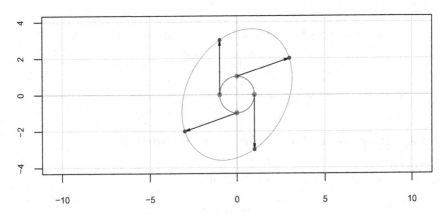

Fig. 1.2 Matrix transformation—rotate and stretch

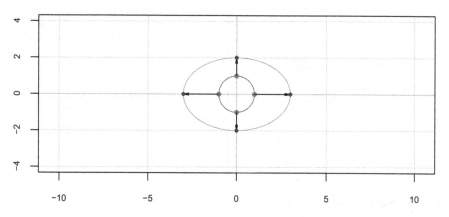

Fig. 1.3 Matrix transformation—stretch

1.5 Norms

In certain algorithms, we need to measure the size of a vector. In machine learning, we usually measure the size of vectors using a function called a **norm**. The ℓ_p norm is represented by

$$\|x\|_p = \left(\sum_i |x_i|^p\right)^{\frac{1}{p}} \tag{1.5.1}$$

Let us consider a vector $\mathbf{X}$, represented as $(x_1, x_2, \cdots, x_n)^\top$
Norms can be represented as

$$
\begin{aligned}
\ell_1 \; norm &= \|x\|_1^1 = |x_1| + |x_2| + \ldots \cdots + |x_n| \\
\ell_2 \; norm &= \|x\|_2^2 = \sqrt{x_1^2 + x_2^2 + \cdots + x_n^2}
\end{aligned}
\tag{1.5.2}
$$

The ℓ_1 norm (*Manhattan norm*) is used in machine learning when the difference between zero and nonzero elements in a vector is important. Therefore, ℓ_1 norm can be used to compute the magnitude of the differences between two vectors or matrices, i.e., $\|x_1 - x_2\|_1^1 = \sum_{i=0}^n |x_{1i} - x_{2i}|$.

The ℓ_2 norm (*Euclidean norm*) is the Euclidean distance from the origin to the point identified by x. Therefore, ℓ_2 norm can be used to compute the size of a vector, measured by calculating $\mathbf{x}^\top \mathbf{x}$. The Euclidean distance is $\sum_{i=1}^n \sqrt{(x_{1i} + x_{2i})^2}$.

A vector is a **unit vector** with unit norm if $\|x\|_2^2 = 1$.

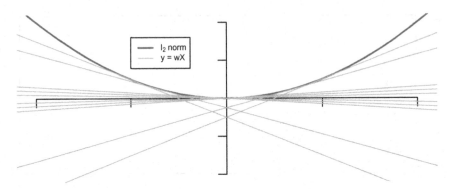

Fig. 1.4 Optimizing using the $\ell_2\ norm$

1.5.1 ℓ_2 Optimization

The ℓ_2 optimization requirement can be represented as, minimizing ℓ_2 norm,

$$\text{find } \{min\}\|w\|_2^2 \text{ subject to}$$
$$\mathbf{y} = w\mathbf{X} \tag{1.5.3}$$

$\mathbf{y} = w\mathbf{X}$ has infinite solutions. ℓ_2 optimization is finding the minimum value of the ℓ_2 norm, i.e., $\|w\|_2^2$ from $\mathbf{y} = w\mathbf{X}$ (Fig. 1.4).

This could be computationally very expensive, however, Lagrange multipliers can ease the problem greatly:

$$\mathcal{L}(w) = \|w\|_2^2 + \lambda^{\top}(wX - y) \tag{1.5.4}$$

λ is the Lagrange multiplier.

Equating the derivative of Eq. 1.5.4 to zero gives us the optimal solution:

$$\hat{w}_{opt} = \frac{1}{2}X^{\top}\lambda \tag{1.5.5}$$

Substituting this optimal estimate of w in Eq. 1.5.3, we get the value of λ:

$$y = \frac{1}{2}XX^{\top}\lambda$$
$$\lambda = 2(XX^{\top})^{-1}y \tag{1.5.6}$$

This gives us $\hat{w}_{opt} = X^{\top}(XX^{\top})^{-1}y$, which is known as the *Moore–Penrose Pseudoinverse* and more commonly known as the **Least Squares** (LS) solution. The downside of the LS solution is that even if it is easy to compute, it is not necessarily the best solution.

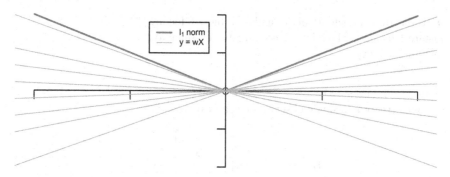

Fig. 1.5 Optimizing using the $\ell_1 norm$

The ℓ_1 optimization can provide a much better result than the above solution.

1.5.2 ℓ_1 *Optimization*

The ℓ_1 optimization requirement can be represented as, minimizing ℓ_1 norm,

$$\text{find } \{min\} \|w\|_1^1 \text{ subject to:}$$
$$\mathbf{y} = w\mathbf{X} \tag{1.5.7}$$

ℓ_1 norm is not differentiable with respect to the coordinate when it is zero. Elsewhere, the partial derivatives are the constants, ± 1 ($\frac{d\|X\|_1}{dX} = sign(X)$).

From Fig. 1.5, it can be seen that the optimal solution occurs when ℓ_1 norm $= 0$, where it is not differentiable, i.e., it does not have a closed-form solution. The only way left is to compute every possible solution and then find the best solution.

The usefulness of ℓ_1 optimization was limited for decades until the advent of high computational power. It now allows us to "sweep" through all the solutions using the convex optimization algorithm. This is further discussed in Sect. 4.9.

1.6 Rewriting the Regression Model in Matrix Notation

The general basis expansion of the linear regression equation for observation i is

$$y_i = w_0 h_0(x_i) + w_1 h_1(x_i) + w_2 h_2(x_i) + \ldots + w_n h_n(x_i) + \epsilon_i$$
$$= \sum_{j=0}^{n} w_j h_j(x_i) + \epsilon_i \tag{1.6.1}$$

w_j is the jth parameter (weight) and h_j is the jth feature.
feature $1 = h_0(x)$, which is a constant and often equal to 1
feature $2 = h_1(x)$
$\vdots$

feature $(n + 1) = h_n(x)$

In matrix form, a single observation can be represented as

$$y_i = [w_0, w_1, \ldots, w_n] \begin{bmatrix} h_0(x_i) \\ h_1(x_i) \\ \vdots \\ h_n(x_i) \end{bmatrix} + \epsilon_i$$

$$= [h_0(x_i), h_1(x_i), \ldots, h_n(x_i)] \begin{bmatrix} w_0 \\ w_1 \\ \vdots \\ w_n \end{bmatrix} + \epsilon_i \tag{1.6.2}$$

$$= w^\mathsf{T} h(x_i) + \epsilon_i$$

For all observations,

$$\begin{bmatrix} y_1 \\ y_2 \\ \vdots \\ y_m \end{bmatrix} = \begin{bmatrix} h_0(x_1) & h_1(x_1) & \ldots & h_n(x_1) \\ h_0(x_2) & h_1(x_2) & \ldots & h_n(x_2) \\ \vdots & \vdots & \vdots & \vdots \\ h_0(x_m) & h_1(x_m) & \ldots & h_n(x_m) \end{bmatrix} \begin{bmatrix} w_0 \\ w_1 \\ \vdots \\ w_n \end{bmatrix} + \begin{bmatrix} \epsilon_1 \\ \epsilon_2 \\ \vdots \\ \epsilon_m \end{bmatrix} \tag{1.6.3}$$

Equation (1.6.3) can be written as

$$y = Hw + \epsilon \tag{1.6.4}$$

1.7   Cost of a n-Dimensional Function

The estimate of the ith observation from the regression equation (Eq. 1.6.2) y_i is
represented as $\hat{y}_i$, which is

$$\hat{y}_i = [h_0(x_i), h_1(x_i), \ldots, h_n(x_i)] \begin{bmatrix} w_0 \\ w_1 \\ \vdots \\ w_n \end{bmatrix} + \epsilon_i \tag{1.7.1}$$

The cost or residual sum of squares (RSS) of a regression equation is defined as
the squared difference between the actual value y_i and the estimate $\hat{y}_i$, which is

$$RSS(w) = \sum_{i=1}^{m}(y_i - \hat{y}_i)^2$$

$$= \sum_{i=1}^{m}(y_i - h(\boldsymbol{x}_i)^{\top}w_i)^2 \tag{1.7.2}$$

$$= (y - \boldsymbol{H}w)^T(y - \boldsymbol{H}w)$$

As $\hat{y} = \mathbf{H}w$ and the **residuals** ϵ is the difference between $\hat{y}$ and y, we can write Eq. (1.7.2) as

$$RSS(w) = [\epsilon_1, \epsilon_2, \ldots, \epsilon_m] \begin{bmatrix} \epsilon_1 \\ \epsilon_2 \\ \vdots \\ \epsilon_m \end{bmatrix}$$

$$= (\epsilon_1^2 + \epsilon_2^2 + \cdots + \epsilon_m^2) \tag{1.7.3}$$

$$= \sum_{i=1}^{m}\epsilon_i^2$$

1.8 Computing the Gradient of the Cost

The gradient of a vector is a generalization of the derivative and is represented by the vector operator Δ. The gradient of the RSS in Eq. (1.7.2) can be computed as

$$\Delta RSS(w) = \Delta[(y - \boldsymbol{H}w)^T(y - \boldsymbol{H}w)]$$

$$\text{Ref:} \frac{d}{dw}(y - hw)(y - hw) = -2h(y - hw) \tag{1.8.1}$$

$$= -2\boldsymbol{H}^T(y - \boldsymbol{H}w)$$

1.8.1 Closed-Form Solution

$$\text{Set gradient } = 0$$

$$\Delta RSS(\hat{w}) = -2H^{\top}(y - H\hat{w}) = 0$$

$$H^{\top}H\hat{w} = H^{\top}y$$

$$\text{multiplying both sides by}(H^{\top}H)^{-1} \tag{1.8.2}$$

$$(H^{\top}H)^{-1}(H^{\top}H)\hat{w} = (H^{\top}H)^{-1}(H^{\top})y$$

$$\hat{w} = (H^{\top}H)^{-1}(H^{\top})y$$

The following caveats apply to Eq. (1.8.2):

- $H^\top H$ is invertible if $n > m$.
- Complexity of the inverse is of the order, $O(n^3)$, implying that if the number of features is high, it can become computationally very expensive.

Imagine we have a high-dimensional cloud of data points consisting of 10^5 features and 10^6 observations represented by H. Storing a dense $H^\top H$ matrix would require 10^{10} floating point numbers, which at 8 bytes per number would require 80 gigabytes of memory, which is impractical. Fortunately, we have an iterative method to estimate the parameters (weights), which is the gradient descent method, described below.

1.8.2   Gradient Descent

Gradient descent is an iterative optimization algorithm where we try to obtain a minimum value of the RSS. The general algorithm can be written as

$$init \; w^{(t=0)} = 0$$
$$\textbf{while} \; \|\Delta RSS(w^{(t)})\| > v$$
$$w^{(t+1)} \leftarrow w^{(t)} - \eta \Delta RSS(w^{(t)}) \tag{1.8.3}$$
$$w^{(t+1)} \leftarrow w^{(t)} + 2\eta H^T(y - Hw^{(t)})$$
$$\eta \text{ is the step size}$$

Feature-by-feature update:

$$RSS(\mathbf{w}) = \sum_{i=1}^{m}(y_i - h(\mathbf{x}_i)^\top w)^2$$
$$= \sum_{i=1}^{m}(y_i - w_0 h_o(x_i) - w_1 h_1(x_i) - \cdots - w_n h_n(x_i))^2 \tag{1.8.4}$$

$$\frac{\partial(RSS(w_j))}{\partial w_j} = \sum_{i=1}^{m} 2(y_i - w_0 h_o(x_i) - w_1 h_1(x_i) - \cdots - w_n h_n(x_i))(-h_j(x_i))$$

$$= -2\sum_{i=1}^{m} h_j(x_i)(y_i - h(\mathbf{x}_i)^\top w) \tag{1.8.5}$$

The general algorithm for all the features is

$$init \ w^{(t=0)}$$

while $\| \Delta RSS(w_j^{(t)}) \| > v$

for $j = 0, 1, 2, \cdots, n$

$$w_j^{(t+1)} \leftarrow w_j^t - \eta(-2 \sum_{i=1}^{m} h_j(x_i)(y_i - h(x_i)^\top w^{(t)})) \qquad (1.8.6)$$

$$w_j^{(t+1)} \leftarrow w_j^{(t)} + \eta(\sum_{i=1}^{m} h_j(x_i)(y_i - \hat{y}_i w^{(t)}))$$

Equation (1.8.6) can be understood as follows:
A very small value of $\hat{w}_j^{(t)}$ implies that the feature x_j in the regression equation is being underestimated. This makes the value of $(y_i - \hat{y}_i w_j^{(t)})$ in the jth feature, positive. Therefore, the need is to increase the value of $w_j^{(t+1)}$.

1.9 An Example of Gradient Descent Optimization

Our objective here is to optimize the cost of our arbitrary function defined as $f(\beta_1) = 5 + \beta_1^3 - 3\beta_1^2$.

We will use the closed-form solution to find the **minimum absolute** value of $f(\beta_1)$.

The derivative of the function is

$$\frac{df(\beta_1)}{d\beta_1} = 3\beta_1^2 - 6\beta_1 \qquad (1.9.1)$$

Equating the derivative to 0, we obtain the estimate of β_1

$$\hat{\beta}_1 = 2 \qquad (1.9.2)$$

The plot in Fig. 1.6 shows the minimum absolute value of the function at $\hat{\beta}_1 = 2$ (blue line in the plot).

Let us try to find the minimum value of β_1 using the gradient descent optimization algorithm described in Eq. (1.8.6):

$$Initialize \ \beta_1^{(t)}, \ at \ t = 0$$

while $\| \beta_1^t - \beta_1^{t+1} \| > v$ $\qquad (1.9.3)$

$$\beta_1^{(t+1)} \leftarrow \beta_1^{(t)} - \eta \nabla f(\beta^{(t)})$$

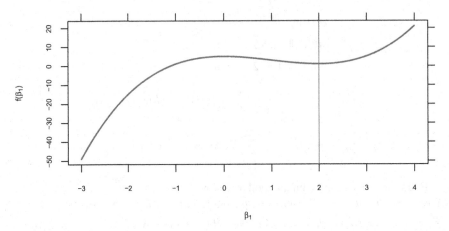

Fig. 1.6 Plot of $5 + \beta_1^3 - 3\beta_1^2$ vs. β_1

$\nabla f(\beta_1^{(t)})$ is the gradient of the cost function, η is the learning rate parameter of the algorithm, and ν is the precision parameter.

If our initial guess $\hat{\beta}_1^{(t=0)} = 3$ and we consider step size $\eta = 0.001$ and tolerance $\nu = 0.0001$,

$$\nabla f(\hat{\beta}_1^{(t=0)}) = 9$$
$$\hat{\beta}_1^{(t=0+1)} = \hat{\beta}_1^{(t=0)} - 0.001 \times 9 = 2.991$$
$$\|\hat{\beta}_1^{(t=1)} - \hat{\beta}_1^{(t=0)}\| = 0.009 > \nu$$

We repeat the process till at some time step t, $\|\hat{\beta}_1^{(t+1)} - \hat{\beta}_1^{(t)}\| \not> \nu$

It turns out that $\hat{\beta}^{(t=617)} = 2.016361$ and $\hat{\beta}^{(t=616)} = 2.016461$. As the difference between the consecutive β estimates is less than the defined tolerance, our application stops.

The plot in Fig. 1.7 shows how the gradient descent algorithm converges to $\beta_1 = 2.0164$ with a starting initial value of $\beta_1 = 3$.

1.10   Eigendecomposition

We know from Sect. 1.7 that a vector can be either rotated, stretched, or both by a matrix. Let us consider a matrix A which when used to transform a vector v, we get the transformed vector represented by the matrix Av. It turns out that most square matrices have a list of vectors within them known as **eigenvectors** v, which when

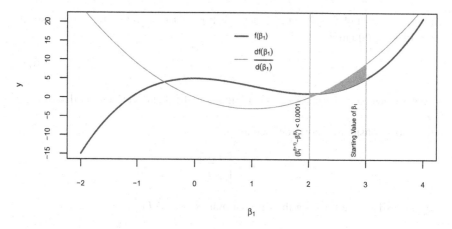

Fig. 1.7 Plot of β_1 and its derivative. Starting gradient descent with an initial value of $\beta_1 = 3$, it converges after 617 iterations at $\beta_1 = 2.01$

multiplied by the matrix **alters the magnitude of the vector** v, by a scalar amount λ. The scalar λ is called the **eigenvalues** of A.

The eigendecomposition problem is to find the set of eigenvectors v and the corresponding set of eigenvalues λ, for the matrix A. The transformation of the eigenvector can be written as

$$Av = \lambda v \tag{1.10.1}$$

Our objective is twofold, find the eigenvectors and eigenvalues of a square matrix A, and understand how we can use them in different applications.

Let us consider the following matrix:

$$A = \begin{bmatrix} 0 & 1 \\ 1 & 0 \end{bmatrix}$$

It is evident that there exists two sets of eigenvalues $\lambda_1 = 1$ and $\lambda_2 = -1$ with corresponding eigenvectors $v_1 = [1, 1]$ and $v_2 = [-1, 1]$, such that

$$A \begin{bmatrix} 1 \\ 1 \end{bmatrix} = 1 \begin{bmatrix} 1 \\ 1 \end{bmatrix}$$

and

$$A \begin{bmatrix} -1 \\ 1 \end{bmatrix} = -1 \begin{bmatrix} -1 \\ 1 \end{bmatrix}$$

For the matrix A, v_1 and v_2 are the eigenvectors and 1 and -1 are the eigenvalues, respectively.

To find the two unknowns, let us rearrange Eq. 1.10.1, such that for some nonzero value of v the equation is true:

$$(\mathbf{A} - \lambda I)\mathbf{v} = 0 \tag{1.10.2}$$

If $\mathbf{v}$ is nonzero, the term $(A - \lambda I)$ is a singular matrix[1] and therefore, its determinant is zero.

Let us now consider a matrix defined as

$$A = \begin{bmatrix} 3 & 2 \\ 1 & 2 \end{bmatrix}$$

We can easily solve for λ for the singular matrix $(A - \lambda I)$ as

$$det \begin{bmatrix} 3 - \lambda & 2 \\ 1 & 2 - \lambda \end{bmatrix} = 0$$

$$(3 - \lambda)(2 - \lambda) - 2 = 0 \tag{1.10.3}$$

$$\lambda^2 - 5\lambda + 4 = 0$$

$$\lambda_1 = 4, \; \lambda_2 = 1$$

With some algebraic manipulation, it can be easily established that the eigenvectors corresponding to the eigenvalue $\lambda_1 = 4$ is $v_1 = [2, 1]$ and that corresponding to the eigenvalue $\lambda_2 = 1$ is $v_2 = [1, 1]$.

It is also to be noted:

- An eigendecomposition of an n-dimensional matrix will always have n eigenvectors.
- The sum of the eigenvalues is the sum of the diagonals (trace) of the matrix.
- The product of the eigenvalues is the determinant of the matrix.
- Eigendecomposition does not work with all square matrices—it works with symmetric/near-symmetric matrices (symmetric matrices are ones where $A = A^\top$), or else we can end up with complex imaginary eigenvalues.

You may want to check these axioms from the examples above

To summarize, an eigenvector of a **square matrix** A is a nonzero vector v such that multiplication by A alters only the scale of $\mathbf{v}$ and which can be represented by the general equation:

$$\mathbf{Av} = \lambda\mathbf{v} \tag{1.10.4}$$

Eigenvectors and eigenvalues are also referred to as **characteristic vectors** and **latent roots** and **eigendecomposition**, is a method where the matrix is decomposed into a set of eigenvectors and eigenvalues.

---

[1]A matrix is singular if it's determinant is 0.

Having understood and derived the eigenvalues and their corresponding eigenvectors, we will use the strength of eigendecomposition to work for us in two different ways.

First, let us look how the eigenvalue problem can be used to solve differential equations. Consider there are two data populations x and y, for which their respective rates of change are dependent on each other (i.e., *coupled differential equations*):

$$\frac{dx}{dt} = 5x + 3y$$
$$\frac{dy}{dt} = -6x + 2y \tag{1.10.5}$$

Writing the above in matrix form, we get

$$\begin{bmatrix} \frac{dx}{dt} \\ \frac{dy}{dt} \end{bmatrix} = \begin{bmatrix} 5 & 3 \\ -6 & 2 \end{bmatrix} \begin{bmatrix} x \\ y \end{bmatrix} \tag{1.10.6}$$

The eigenvalues and eigenvectors of the matrix in Eq. 1.10.6 are $\lambda_1 = -1, \lambda_2 = 8$ and $v_1 = [1, 2], v_2 = [1, -1]$, respectively.

The solution of the differential equations then reduces to (a linear combination of the variables)

$$\begin{bmatrix} x(t) \\ y(t) \end{bmatrix} = k_1 e^{\lambda_1 t} v_1 + k_2 e^{\lambda_2 t} v_2$$
$$= k_1 e^{-t} \begin{bmatrix} 1 \\ 2 \end{bmatrix} + k_2 e^{8t} \begin{bmatrix} 1 \\ -1 \end{bmatrix} \tag{1.10.7}$$
$$x(t) = k_1 e^{-t} + k_2 e^{8t}$$
$$y(t) = 2k_1 e^{-t} - k_2 e^{8t}$$

If we know the end conditions, we can find the constant values k_1 and k_2 and thus have a complete solution.

In our second application, we will see how eigendecomposition is enormously helpful in matrix multiplication.

From Eq. 1.10.4,

$$\mathbf{Av} = \lambda \mathbf{v}$$
$$\mathbf{AAv} = \mathbf{A}\lambda \mathbf{v}$$
$$= \lambda \mathbf{Av} \tag{1.10.8}$$
$$= \lambda \lambda \mathbf{v}$$
$$\mathbf{A^2 v} = \lambda^2 \mathbf{v}$$

This is the power of eigendecomposition—complex matrix multiplications to any exponent have been reduced to multiplying the eigenvalues matrix to the same exponent. Let us find the 100th power of a matrix, defined as

$$A = \begin{bmatrix} 2 & 3 \\ 2 & 1 \end{bmatrix}$$

$$A^{100} = v\lambda^{100}v^{-1} \tag{1.10.9}$$

$$A^{100} = \begin{bmatrix} 0.832 & -0.707 \\ 0.554 & 0.707 \end{bmatrix} \begin{bmatrix} 4 & 0 \\ 0 & -1 \end{bmatrix}^{100} \begin{bmatrix} 0.721 & 0.721 \\ -0.565 & 0.848 \end{bmatrix}$$

Finding A^{100} now reduces to a simple R application. Recall the "solve" function calculates the inverse.

```
matrixMult <- function(A, n) {
  e <- eigen(A)
  v <- e$vectors
  d <- e$values
  return(v %*% diag(d^n) %*% solve(v))
}
matrixMult(A,100)
```

```
            [,1]            [,2]
[1,]  9.641628e+59  9.641628e+59
[2,]  6.427752e+59  6.427752e+59
```

Eigendecomposition plays a big role in many machine learning algorithms—the order in which search results appear in *Google* is determined by computing an eigenvector (called the PageRank algorithm). Computer vision, which automatically recognize faces, does so by computing eigenvectors of the images. As discussed above, eigendecomposition does not work with all matrices. A similar decomposition called the SVD is guaranteed to work on all matrices.

1.11   Singular Value Decomposition (SVD)

You may read this in conjunction with the discussion on variance and covariance in Sect. 2.8.

Decomposing a matrix helps us to analyze certain properties of the matrix. Much like decomposing an integer into its prime factors can help us understand the behavior of the integer, decomposing matrices gives us information about their functional properties that would not be very obvious otherwise. In Sect. 1.5 on matrix transformations, we had seen that a matrix multiplication either stretches/compresses and rotates the vector or just stretches/compresses it. This is the idea in an SVD.

In Fig. 1.8, we multiply a circle with unit radius by the matrix

$$A = \begin{bmatrix} 1 & 3 \\ -3 & 2 \end{bmatrix} \tag{1.11.1}$$

With the matrix multiplication, the unit circle (2-dimensional vector) having orthonormal vectors v_1 *and* v_2 rotates the circle by a certain amount and stretches it by a

Fig. 1.8 Stretching and rotating due to matrix transformation

certain amount, thereby giving us a vector represented by the ellipse, having a major axis $\sigma_1 u_1$ and a minor axis $\sigma_2 u_2$, where σ_1 *and* σ_2 is the stretch factor, also known as **singular values**, and u_1 *and* u_2 are orthonormal unit vectors.

More generally, if we have a n-dimensional sphere, multiplying that with A would give us a n-dimensional hyper-ellipse. Intuitively, we can write the following equation

$$Av_j = \sigma_j u_j \quad \{\text{for } j = 1, 2, ..., n\} \tag{1.11.2}$$

In the above equation, we are mapping each of the n directions in v to, n directions in u with a scaling factor σ. Equation 1.11.2 is also similar to the eigendecomposition Eq. 1.10.1, with which it shares an intimate relationship.

For all vectors in Eq. 1.11.2, the matrix form is

$$\begin{bmatrix} A_{m \times n} \end{bmatrix} \begin{bmatrix} v_{1,1} & v_{1,2} & \cdots & v_{1,n} \\ v_{2,1} & v_{2,2} & \cdots & v_{2,n} \\ \vdots & \vdots & \cdots & \vdots \\ v_{n,1} & v_{n,2} & \cdots & v_{n,n} \end{bmatrix} = \begin{bmatrix} u_{1,1} & u_{1,2} & \cdots & u_{1,n} \\ u_{2,1} & u_{2,2} & \cdots & u_{2,n} \\ \vdots & \vdots & \cdots & \vdots \\ u_{m,1} & u_{m,2} & \cdots & u_{m,n} \end{bmatrix} \begin{bmatrix} \sigma_1 & 0 & \cdots & 0 \\ 0 & \sigma_2 & \cdots & 0 \\ \vdots & \vdots & \cdots & \vdots \\ 0 & 0 & \cdots & \sigma_n \end{bmatrix} \tag{1.11.3}$$

or

$$AV = U\Sigma \tag{1.11.4}$$

Equation 1.11.3 is called a **unitary transformation**, which by definition, implies $V^{-1} = V^{\top}$ and $U^{-1} = U^{\top}$.

Multiplying both sides of Eq. 1.11.4 by V^{-1}, we get

$$AVV^{-1} = U\Sigma V^{-1}$$

$$AI = U\Sigma V^{\top} \tag{1.11.5}$$

$$A = U\Sigma V^{\top}$$

Equation 1.11.5 is called the SVD of matrix A represented by three matrices—V^T (an $n \times n$ matrix) rotates the matrix A, the Σ (a diagonal $n \times n$ matrix) stretches the matrix A and, U (an $m \times n$ matrix) once again rotates the matrix A:

$$\begin{bmatrix} A_{m \times n} \end{bmatrix} = \begin{bmatrix} u_{1,1} & u_{1,2} & \cdots & u_{1,n} \\ u_{2,1} & u_{2,2} & \cdots & u_{2,n} \\ \vdots & \vdots & \cdots & \vdots \\ u_{m,1} & u_{m,2} & \cdots & u_{m,n} \end{bmatrix} \begin{bmatrix} \sigma_1 & 0 & \cdots & 0 \\ 0 & \sigma_2 & \cdots & 0 \\ \vdots & \vdots & \cdots & \vdots \\ 0 & 0 & \cdots & \sigma_n \end{bmatrix} \begin{bmatrix} v_{1,1} & v_{2,1} & \cdots & v_{n,1} \\ \vdots & \vdots & \cdots & \vdots \\ v_{1,n} & v_{2,n} & \cdots & v_{n,n} \end{bmatrix}$$

$$(1.11.6)$$

SVD tries to reduce a rank R matrix to a rank K matrix. What that means is that we can take a list of R unique vectors and approximate them as a linear combination of K unique vectors. This intuitively implies that we can find some of the "best" vectors that will be a good representation of the original matrix. Every real matrix has an SVD, but its eigenvalue decomposition may not always be possible if it is not a square matrix.

Now, how do we find out the composition of these three matrices?

$$\begin{aligned} A^{\top}AV &= (U\Sigma V^{\top})^{\top}(U\Sigma V^{\top})V \\ &= (V\Sigma U^{\top})(U\Sigma V^{\top})V \\ &= V\Sigma^2 V^{\top}V \qquad \text{(for unitary matrices, } V^{\top}V = I) \\ &= V\Sigma^2 \end{aligned} \tag{1.11.7}$$

The beauty of linear algebra now unfolds as Eq. 1.11.7 is an eigenvalue problem and can be written as

$$Ax = \lambda x$$

In Eq. 1.11.7, the matrix V is the eigenvectors of $A^{\top}A$ and Σ^2 is the squared eigenvalues of $A^{\top}A$. Similarly,

$$\begin{aligned} AA^{\top}U &= (U\Sigma V^{\top})(U\Sigma V^{\top})^{\top}U \\ &= (U\Sigma V^{\top})(V\Sigma U^{\top})U \\ &= U\Sigma^2 U^{\top}U \qquad \text{(for unitary matrices, } U^{\top}U = I) \\ &= U\Sigma^2 \end{aligned} \tag{1.11.8}$$

Equation 1.11.8 is the same eigenvalue problem and can be written as

$$Ax = \lambda x$$

The matrix U is the eigenvectors of $AA^\top$ and Σ^2 is the squared eigenvalues of $AA^\top$.

Both $AA^\top$ and $A^\top A$ are **Hermitian matrices**,[2] which guarantees that the eigenvalues of these matrices are real, positive, and distinct.

From Eq. 1.11.4, we can now write the SVD of a matrix **A** and decompose it as the product of three matrices:

$$A_{m \times n} = U_{m \times n} \Sigma_{n \times n} V^\top_{n \times n}, \qquad (1.11.9)$$

where

- **U** is the eigenvectors of the matrix $\mathbf{A}A^\top$
- **V** is the eigenvectors of the matrix $\mathbf{A}^\top A$
- **D** is a diagonal matrix consisting of the squared eigenvalues (also called singular values) of $AA^\top or A^\top A$.

Intuitively, the matrix **A** is rotated by $\mathbf{V}^\top$, stretched by the diagonal matrix **D**, and again rotated by **U**. All the singular values in the diagonal matrix are ordered from largest to the smallest such that
$\sigma_1^2 \geq \sigma_2^2 \geq \cdots \geq \sigma_n^2 \geq 0$.

U and **V** are orthogonal matrices, i.e., their dot product (covariance) is 0, which means **U** and **V** are statistically independent and have nothing to do with each other.

The columns of matrix **U** are the **left-singular vectors** and the columns of matrix **V** are the **right-singular vectors**.

SVD is particularly useful when we have to deal with large dimensions in the data. The eigenvalues in SVD help us to determine which variables are most informative, and which ones are not. Using SVD, we may select a subset of the original n features, where each feature is a linear combination of the original n features.

1.12 Principal Component Analysis (PCA)

Principal component analysis (PCA) follows from SVD.

One of the problems of multivariate data is that there are too many variables. And the problem of having too many variables is sometimes known as the *curse of dimensionality*.[3] This brings us to *PCA*, a technique with the central aim of reducing the dimensionality of a multivariate data set while accounting for as much of the original variation as possible which was present in the data set.

---

[2]A Hermitian matrix (or self-adjoint matrix) is a square matrix that is equal to its own transpose, i.e., $A = A^\top$.

[3]The expression was coined by Richard E. Bellman in 1961.

This is achieved by transforming to a new set of variables known as the *principal components* that are *linear combinations* of the original variables, which are uncorrelated and are ordered such that the first few of them account for most of the variation in all the variables. The first principal component is that linear combination of the original variables whose variance is greatest among all possible linear combinations. The second principal component is that linear combination of the original variables that account for a maximum proportion of the remaining variance subject to being uncorrelated with the first principal component. Subsequent components are defined similarly.

Let us consider a cloud of data points represented by m observations and n features as matrix $\mathbf{X}$ where not all features n are independent, i.e., there are some correlated features in $\mathbf{X}$.

PCA is defined as the eigendecomposition of the covariance matrix of $\mathbf{X}$, i.e., the eigendecomposition of $\mathbf{X}^\top X$. The eigendecomposition of $\mathbf{X}^\top X$ will result in a set of eigenvectors say, $\mathbf{W}$ and a set of eigenvalues represented by λ. We will therefore be using $\mathbf{W}$ and λ to describe our data set.

If $\mathbf{W}$ are the eigenvectors of $\mathbf{X}^\top X$, represented by a $n \times n$ matrix, then each column of $\mathbf{W}$ is a principal component called *loadings*. The columns of $\mathbf{W}$ are **ordered by the magnitude of the eigenvalues** λ, i.e., the principal component corresponding to the largest eigenvalue will be the first column in $\mathbf{W}$ and so forth. Also, each principal component is orthogonal to each other, i.e., the principal components are uncorrelated.

We can now represent the high-dimensional cloud of data points represented by $\mathbf{X}$ by turning them into the $\mathbf{W}$ space represented as

$$\mathbf{T} = \mathbf{XW} \tag{1.12.1}$$

Multiplying $\mathbf{X}$ by $\mathbf{W}$, we are simply rotating the data matrix $\mathbf{X}$ and representing it by the matrix $\mathbf{T}$ called *Scores*, having the dimension $m \times n$.

Since the columns in $\mathbf{W}$ are ordered by the magnitude of the eigenvalues, it turns out that most of the variance present in $\mathbf{X}$ is explained by the first few columns in $\mathbf{W}$. Since $\mathbf{W}$ is a $n \times n$ matrix, we can afford to choose the first r columns of $\mathbf{W}$, which define most of the variance in $\mathbf{X}$ and disregard $n - r$ columns of $\mathbf{W}$. $\mathbf{T}$ will now represent a truncated version of our data set, but is good enough to explain most of the variance present in our data set.

Therefore, PCA does not change our data set but only allows us to look at the data set from a different frame of reference.

1.12.1 PCA and SVD

PCA is mathematically quite identical to SVD.

If we have a data set represented by the matrix $\mathbf{X}$, from Eq. 1.11.8, it follows that $\mathbf{XX}^\top = \mathbf{U\Sigma U}^{-1}$, where Σ is the squared eigenvalues of $\mathbf{XX}^\top$.

We have seen that a data matrix $\mathbf{X}$ can be represented as

$$\mathbf{X} = \mathbf{U}\mathbf{\Sigma}\mathbf{V}^{\top}$$

Σ has singular values in its diagonal and the other elements are 0. Matrix $\mathbf{V}$ from SVD is also called the *loadings* matrix in PCA. If we transform $\mathbf{X}$ by the loadings matrix $\mathbf{V}$

Equation 1.12.1 can now be written as

$$\begin{aligned} \mathbf{T} &= \mathbf{X}\mathbf{V} \\ &= \mathbf{U}\mathbf{\Sigma}\mathbf{V}^{\top}V \\ &= \mathbf{U}\mathbf{\Sigma} \\ \mathbf{T}_r &= \mathbf{U}_r\mathbf{\Sigma}_r \end{aligned} \qquad (1.12.2)$$

In PCA, we should be using the covariance matrix if the variables have the same scale. However, in the contrary, we should use the correlation matrix.

PCA is equivalent to performing SVD on the **centered data**, where the centering occurs on the columns.

Let us go through the following self-explanatory code to find common ground between SVD and PCA. We use the sweep function on the rows and columns of the matrix. The second argument in sweep specifies that we want to operate on the columns, and the third and fourth arguments specify that we want to subtract the column means.

```
# Generate a scaled 4x5 matrix
set.seed(11)
data_matrix <- matrix(rnorm(20), 4, 5)
mat <- sweep(data_matrix, 2, colMeans(data_matrix), "-")

# By default, prcomp will retrieve the minimum of (num rows
# and num features) components. Therefore we expect four
# principal components. The SVD function also behaves the
# same way.

# Perform PCA
PCA <- prcomp(mat, scale. = F, center = F)
PCA_loadings <- PCA$rotation  # loadings
PCA_Scores <- PCA$x  # scores
eigenvalues <- (PCA$sdev)^2

# Perform SVD
SVD <- svd(mat)
svd_U <- SVD$u
svd_V <- SVD$v
svd_Sigma <- diag(SVD$d)  # sigma is now our true sigma matrix

# The columns of V from SVD, correspond to the principal
# components loadings from PCA.
all(round(PCA_loadings, 5) == round(svd_V, 5))  # TRUE
```

```
[1] TRUE
```

```
# Show that SVD's U*Sigma = PCA scores (refer Eqn 1.11.2)
all(round(PCA_Scores, 5) == round(svd_U %*% svd_Sigma, 5))
```

[1] TRUE

```
# Show that data matrix == U*Sigma*t(V)
all(round(mat, 5) == round(svd_U %*% svd_Sigma %*% t(svd_V),
    5))
```

[1] TRUE

```
# Show that data matrix == scores*t(loadings)
all(round(mat, 5) == round(PCA_Scores %*% t(PCA_loadings), 5))
```

[1] TRUE

```
# Show that eigenvalues of PCA are the same as Sigma^2/(m-1)
# from SVD
eigenvalues
```

[1] 2.081273e+00 5.809988e-01 1.582894e-01 1.839700e-32

```
svd_Sigma^2/(nrow(mat) - 1)
```

```
            [,1]        [,2]        [,3]        [,4]
[1,]  2.081273  0.0000000  0.0000000  0.0000e+00
[2,]  0.000000  0.5809988  0.0000000  0.0000e+00
[3,]  0.000000  0.0000000  0.1582894  0.0000e+00
[4,]  0.000000  0.0000000  0.0000000  1.8397e-32
```

```
# Variances in percentage
variance <- eigenvalues * 100/sum(eigenvalues)
variance
```

[1] 7.378933e+01 2.059869e+01 5.611980e+00 6.522459e-31

```
# Cumulative variances
cumvar <- cumsum(variance)
cumvar
```

[1]   73.78933   94.38802 100.00000 100.00000

Let us now go through an example of dimensionality reduction and see how an "xgboost" algorithm improves its accuracy after reducing a high-dimensional data set by using PCA (Fig. 1.9).

We will use the *Arrythmia* data set from the *UCI Machine Learning Repository*.[4]

This data set contains 279 attributes and its aim is to distinguish between the presence and absence of cardiac arrhythmia so as to classify it in one of the 16

---

[4]http://archive.ics.uci.edu/ml/datasets/arrhythmia, downloaded on Jul 10, 2017, 11:24 am IST.

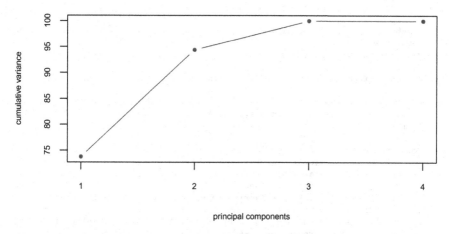

Fig. 1.9 The explained variance increase as the number of principal components increase; however, the first two principal components explain 95% of the variance present in the original data matrix

groups—class 01 refers to "normal ECG", classes 02 to 15 refer to different classes of arrhythmia, and class 16 refers to the rest of unclassified ones.

We will see how well the data set performs, using XGBoost (a boosting algorithm for classification/regression), so as to use the classification error and the AUC (*refer* Sect. 5.4) score as a basis for comparing the scores with the reduced feature data set, with the transformed PCA features.

We first remove the features which have variance less than 50 (which account for 213 features). It can then be seen that reducing the remaining 86 features to just 10 components improves our model accuracy scores.

If the details of the code below are not understood it is fine, because the objective here is to illustrate how dimensionality reduction works and therefore it is recommended to focus on the PCA portion of the code. Classification algorithms are discussed in Chap. 5.

```
data <- read.csv(paste(file_path, "arrythmia.csv", sep = ""))
```

```
[1] "The number of features in the data set is:   280"
```

```
data[data == "?"] <- NA
data[-280] <- lapply(data[-280], as.numeric)

colnames(data)[280] <- "class"
data$diagnosis <- (ifelse(data$class == 1, 1, 0))
data$diagnosis <- as.numeric(data$diagnosis)

library(matrixStats)
colvars <- data.frame(feature = colnames(data[-c(280, 281)]),
    variance = colVars(as.matrix(data[-c(280, 281)])))

data_subset <- cbind(data["diagnosis"], data[, which(colvars$variance >
    50)])
```

```r
model_xgboost <- function(data) {
    require(xgboost)
    require(Metrics)
    CV <- 5
    cv_Set <- floor(nrow(data)/(CV + 1))
    indexCount <- 1
    response <- "diagnosis"
    predictors <- names(data)[!names(data) %in% response]
    clErr <- AUC <- c()

    for (cv in seq(1:CV)) {
        testIndex <- c((cv * cv_Set):(cv * cv_Set + cv_Set))
        test_data <- data[testIndex, ]
        train_data <- data[-testIndex, ]
        bst <- xgboost(data = as.matrix(train_data[, predictors]),
            label = train_data[, response], max.depth = 6, eta = 1,
            verbose = 0, nround = 5, nthread = 4, objective = "binary:logistic")
        predictions <- predict(bst, as.matrix(test_data[, predictors]))
        pred = ifelse(predictions > 0.5, 1, 0)
        err <- length(which(pred != test_data[, response]))/length(test_data[,
            response])
        auc <- auc(test_data[, response], predictions)

        clErr <- c(clErr, err)
        AUC <- c(AUC, auc)
        gc()
    }
    print(paste("Mean Error:", mean(clErr)))
    print(paste("Mean AUC:", mean(AUC)))
}
```

[1] "Evaluating model with 86 features"

```r
model_xgboost(data_subset)
```

[1] "Mean Error: 0.310526315789474"
[1] "Mean AUC: 0.750990439559521"

```r
pca_matrix <- scale(data_subset[, -1])
pca <- prcomp(pca_matrix)

components <- 1
df_components <- predict(pca, newdata = pca_matrix)[, 1:components]
data_1 <- cbind(as.data.frame(df_components),
                diagnosis = data_subset['diagnosis'])
```

[1] "Evaluating model with 1 component"

```r
model_xgboost(data_1)
```

[1] "Mean Error: 0.476315789473684"
[1] "Mean AUC: 0.527447538739651"

```r
components <- 2
df_components <- predict(pca, newdata = pca_matrix)[, 1:components]
data_2 <- cbind(as.data.frame(df_components),
                diagnosis = data_subset['diagnosis'])
```

```
[1] "Evaluating model with 2 components"
```

model_xgboost(data_2)

```
[1] "Mean Error: 0.455263157894737"
[1] "Mean AUC: 0.556424505478193"
```

```
components <- 10
df_components <- predict(pca, newdata = pca_matrix)[, 1:components]
data_10 <- cbind(as.data.frame(df_components),
                 diagnosis = data_subset['diagnosis'])
```

```
[1] "Evaluating model with 10 components"
```

model_xgboost(data_10)

```
[1] "Mean Error: 0.286842105263158"
[1] "Mean AUC: 0.794573884113219"
```

In the above example, we have transformed a high-dimensional data set into a reduced data set having only 10 components using PCA. The reduced data set also returns a higher accuracy with respect to classification error and AUC as compared to the original data set consisting of 86 features.

It is time now to look into the sources of computational errors and how we can tackle them.

1.13 Computational Errors

In any applied numerical computation, there are four key sources of error:

- Inexactness of the mathematical model for the underlying physical phenomenon.
- Measurement errors of parameters entering the model.
- Round-off errors in computer arithmetic.
- Approximations used to solve the full mathematical system.

Of the above, the first is the domain of mathematical modeling and the second is about correct model parameter estimation. The third arises due to the finite numerical precision imposed by the computer and the last is the domain of numerical analysis and refers to the fact that most systems of equations are too complicated to solve explicitly.

Learning algorithms usually involve a high amount of **numerical computation**, by the way of solving mathematical problems that update estimates iteratively, **optimization** (maximize or minimize the function), and solving systems of linear equations.

The challenge in performing numerical computations on a machine (computer) is that we need to represent infinitely many real numbers with a finite number of bits. This means that for almost all real numbers, we incur some approximation error when we represent the number in the computer.

1.13.1   Rounding—Overflow and Underflow

The fundamental difficulty in performing mathematical operations is that we incur approximation errors. These could be simple rounding errors which have the potential to get magnified (when some x_i is either too big or too small), across many operations, and can cause errors in otherwise flawless algorithms. One form of rounding error is **underflow**, which occurs when numbers near zero are rounded to zero. This could cause a problem, for instance, if it happens to be a denominator or we have to take the logarithm of the number. Another form of error is its counterpart, **overflow**, which occurs when large numbers are approximated to ∞ or $-\infty$.

Avoiding Overflow/Underflow: Computing the length of a vector **x** (which has some x_i, which is either too big or too small) and by taking its ℓ_2 *norm*, has the potential of overflow or underflow. However, if we normalize the vector and then compute its ℓ_2 *norm*, this problem can be avoided. Another possible rectification is to transform the variable into a log space. Also, compensated summation approaches like **Kahan summation** reduce the numerical error in the total obtained by adding a sequence of finite precision floating point numbers.

1.13.2   Conditioning

Conditioning refers to how sensitive a function is when their inputs are perturbed slightly. It measures the ratio of relative change in $f(x)$ to relative changes in x. Conditioning is measured by the relative condition number defined as

$$\kappa = \frac{||\delta f||}{||f(x)||} \bigg/ \frac{||\delta x||}{||x||} \tag{1.13.1}$$

To get a better understanding, let us consider a simultaneous equation problem,

$$2x + y = 4$$
$$2x + 1.01y = 4.02$$

which has the solution $x = 1$ and $y = 2$.
By altering the coefficients of the second equation by 1% and the constant of the first equation by 5%, we get

$$2x + y = 3.8$$
$$2.02x + y = 4.02,$$

which has the solution $x = 11$ and $y = -18.2$

A slight perturbation has resulted in a huge difference in output. This is a poorly conditioned system and has the potential to amplify pre-existing errors.

1.14 Numerical Optimization

Numerical optimization is at the core of much of machine learning. Once we define our model and have a deployable dataset, estimating the parameters of the model typically involves minimizing some multivariate function $f(x)$, where the input x belongs to some high-dimensional space. In other words, if we solve

$$\{\arg\min_x f(x)\}, \tag{1.14.1}$$

then $\hat{x}$ is the "best" choice for our model's parameters.

Numerical optimization algorithms are mostly iterative in nature, i.e., we start with an initial guess of $x^{(timestep,\ t=0)}$ and the optimization algorithm iteratively converges to $\hat{x}$, which happens to be the global minimum of our function $f(x)$. The convergence is decided by a small number, which is called tolerance and identified by ϵ, such that

$$f(x^{t+1}) - f(x^t) < \epsilon$$
$$f(x^t + \Delta x^t) - f(x^t) < \epsilon \tag{1.14.2}$$

Using **Taylor's expansion** in Eq. 1.14.2, we get

$$f(x^t + \Delta x^t) \approx f(x^t) + \Delta x^t \left.\frac{\partial f}{\partial x}\right|_{x^t} + \frac{\Delta(x^t)^2}{2} \left.\frac{\partial^2 f}{\partial x^2}\right|_{x^t} \tag{1.14.3}$$

Equation 1.14.3 is a quadratic approximation, where $\left.\frac{\partial f}{\partial x}\right|_{x^t}$ and $\left.\frac{\partial^2 f}{\partial x^2}\right|_{x^t}$ are called the **gradient** and **Hessian** of the function f at time step x^t.

Since $x^{t+1} = x^t + \Delta x^t$, we can rewrite Eq. 1.14.3 as a function of Δx^t. Representing the gradient and the Hessian by $\mathbf{g_t}$ and $\mathbf{H_t}$, we can write

$$h_t(\Delta x^t) = f(x^t) + \Delta x^t \mathbf{g_t} + \frac{1}{2}\Delta(x^t)^2 \mathbf{H_t} \tag{1.14.4}$$

Since our intent, as stated in the beginning, is to minimize $f(x)$, we can do that by differentiating Eq. 1.14.4 and setting it to zero:

$$\frac{\partial h_t(\Delta x^t)}{\partial \Delta x^t} = \mathbf{g_t} + \Delta x^t \mathbf{H_t} \tag{1.14.5}$$

Solving for Δx^t, we get

$$\Delta x^t = -\mathbf{g_t} \mathbf{H_t^{-1}} \tag{1.14.6}$$

Since $x^{t+1} = x^t + \Delta x^t$, we can write

$$x^{t+1} = x^t - \mathbf{g_t} \mathbf{H_t^{-1}} \tag{1.14.7}$$

To make the iterative step small (we need to do this to control the convergence, or else we can easily overshoot the global minimum), we consider a step size α, so that $f(x^{t+1})$ is "sufficiently smaller" than x^t. Therefore, Eq. 1.14.7 is rewritten as

$$x^{t+1} = x^t - \alpha \mathbf{g_t} \mathbf{H_t}^{-1} \tag{1.14.8}$$

Newton Raphson is a powerful method for better approximations (in our case, the quadratic approximation of Eq. 1.14.4) in an iterative manner, to find the global minimum. The Newton Raphson algorithm to find $\{\arg \min_x f(x)\}$ can be written as

$$
\begin{aligned}
&\text{for } t = 0, 1, \cdots \text{till converged} \\
&\text{compute } \mathbf{g_t} \text{ and } \mathbf{H_t} \\
&\text{choose step size } \alpha \\
&x^{(t+1)} \leftarrow x^{(t)} - \alpha \mathbf{g_t} \mathbf{H_t}
\end{aligned}
\tag{1.14.9}
$$

One of the drawbacks in the above method is while dealing with large number of parameters. This would make the computation of the inverse of the Hessian very expensive and often impractical. Also, for some functions, the inverse of the Hessian may not be computable.

In such cases, we can use many other optimization methods. The *glm* function in R uses the IRWLS (Iteratively Reweighted Least Squares) algorithm.

Another optimization algorithm is {BFGS} (Broyden, Fletcher, Goldfarb, Shanno) update, named after the authors of this algorithm. A discussion on the BFGS update is beyond the scope of this book; however, we will be using it in Sect. 5.2.8 to optimize the log-likelihood function in logistic regression.

This concludes a preliminary introduction to linear algebra, optimization techniques, and its relevance to certain mathematical applications in machine learning.

Chapter 2
Probability and Distributions

Suam habet fortuna rationem (Chance has its reason).
–Petronius

David Hume, the renowned philosopher in his *Treatise of Human Nature*, describes probability as the amount of evidence that accompanies uncertainty, a reasoning from conjecture. Probability theory is the branch of mathematics dealing with the study of uncertainty. It provides a means of quantifying uncertainty.

Since machine learning relies on the probabilistic nature of data, probability theory has an important role to play in the design of learning algorithms.

While the evidence associated with uncertainty may allow us to reason about uncertain statements, information theory allows to measure the uncertainty or randomness of a probability distribution by a mathematical parameter known as *entropy*.

If an event is unpredictable because of a random variable, it is called a *stochastic* (nondeterministic) event. In a *deterministic* event, there is no presence of randomness and the outcomes can be precisely determined. Randomness and uncertainty are intrinsic to machine learning and may arise from different sources.

2.1 Sources of Uncertainty

The possible sources of uncertainty in machine learning are:

- Randomness inherent in the data, resulting in different learning models because models train differently with different data sets.
- A deterministic data set, which may appear stochastic if its observations are incomplete/missing, will result in an uncertain model.

© Springer Nature Singapore Pte Ltd. 2017
A. Ghatak, *Machine Learning with R*, DOI 10.1007/978-981-10-6808-9_2

- Randomness present in the learning model itself, i.e., initializing a set of weights specific to a model could induce randomness in the model. The *k-means* algorithm used in clustering is particularly vulnerable in this regard.

2.2 Random Experiment

A **random experiment** is one where we cannot predict the outcome with certainty before the experiment is conducted. Frequency-based probability (*frequentist*) theory assumes that the experiment can be indefinitely repeated, while the conditions of the experiment remain unchanged. The repetitions may be in time domain (repeatedly tossing a single coin) or in the space domain (tossing a bunch of similar coins all at once). Since we are concerned with the long-term behavior of the outcomes of the experiment, the "repeatability" aspect of a random experiment assumes importance. Therefore, a random experiment should clearly state, what constitutes an outcome.

The **sample space** of a random experiment constitutes the set **S**, which includes all the possible outcomes of a random experiment.

The **parameter** of a model refers to a non-random quantity which does not change once its value is chosen.

A **random variable** is the function defining the outcome of a random experiment. It is a description of the states that it can possibly take. Depending on the possible values of the outcome, a random variable may be defined to be **discrete** or **continuous**. A discrete random variable has a finite or countably infinite[1] number of states. A continuous random variable is associated with an infinite number of possible values and is defined over an interval.

2.3 Probability

The probability P of a success is defined by the frequency of that event based over past observations. Therefore, the probability of the number of successes k over n observations is dependent on the rate at which the events take place and is known as **Frequentist probability**.

In contrast, **Bayesian probability** is probability of an event, based on prior knowledge of conditions that might be related to the event. It is presented in the form of an inference, which is the **prior probability** distribution and a **posterior probability** distribution.

Suppose we have a parameter ρ which is defined by a normal distribution and our objective is to estimate the parameter ρ. In this context, Bayesian probability can be defined by the following:

---

[1] A countably infinite set may take forever to count, but we can get to any particular element in the set in a finite amount of time.

- Likelihood—is the conditional density of the data given ρ, i.e., $\mathcal{L}(data, \rho)$. Suppose if ρ also has some inherent noise defined by a normal distribution with zero mean and variance of 1, i.e., $\mathcal{N}(\mu = 0, \sigma = 1)$, the likelihood of the data (denoted as Y), given ρ, can be written as $\mathcal{L}(Y, \rho) = \frac{1}{\sqrt{2\pi}} e^{-\frac{(Y-\rho)^2}{2}}$.
- Prior—is the distribution of ρ in the absence of any data. If it follows a normal distribution, it will have a mean μ and a variance σ and can be defined as $\mathcal{N}(\mu, \sigma)$.
- Posterior—is the conditional distribution of ρ, given the data, which is proportional to the likelihood and the prior.

To summarize the above, we have a distribution of ρ defined as $Y = \rho + \mathcal{N}(0, 1)$. The likelihood is $p(Y \mid \rho) = \frac{1}{\sqrt{2\pi}} e^{-\frac{(Y-\rho)^2}{2}}$ and the prior distribution is $p(\rho) = \frac{1}{\sqrt{2\pi}} e^{-\frac{(\rho-\mu)^2}{2\sigma^2}}$ (i.e., normally distributed).

The posterior probability distribution is therefore proportional to the product of the prior and the likelihood and is defined as $p(\rho \mid Y) \propto \frac{1}{\sqrt{2\pi}} e^{-\frac{(Y-\rho)^2}{2}} \frac{1}{\sqrt{2\pi}} e^{-\frac{(\rho-\mu)^2}{2\sigma^2}}$.

2.3.1 Marginal Probability

The probability of a subset of events irrespective of any other event over a set of events is the marginal probability of the event subset. For instance, the probability of a dice coming up with a particular number is the marginal probability of the number. Marginal probability can be represented by the following equations:

$$P(X = x) = \sum_{y} P(X = x, Y = y) \text{—for discrete variables}$$

$$(2.3.1)$$

$$p(x) = \int p(x, y) dy \text{—for continuous variables}$$

y represents all the possible values of the random variable Y. We are holding X constant $(X = x)$ while iterating over all the possible Y values and summing up the joint probabilities.

```
# CALCULATE MARGINAL PROBABILITY
# Create a sample outcome of rolling a six-sided die twice
S <- rolldie(times = 2, nsides = 6, makespace = TRUE)
# Find the marginal probability (Px = X1)
marginal(S, vars = c("X1"))
```

```
   X1       probs
1   1 0.1666667
2   2 0.1666667
3   3 0.1666667
4   4 0.1666667
5   5 0.1666667
6   6 0.1666667
```

2.3.2   Conditional Probability

The probability of the event X occurring when the secondary event Y has happened is the conditional probability of X given Y. Mathematically, the conditional probability that $X = x$ given $Y = y$ can be represented as $P(X = x \mid Y = y)$, which can be written as

$$P(X = x \mid Y = y) = \frac{P(X = x, Y = y)}{P(Y = y)} \tag{2.3.2}$$

```
# CALCULATE CONDITIONAL PROBABILITY
df <- data.frame('condition' = c('disease', 'no disease'),
                 'treatment' = c(5, 195),
                 'no treatment' = c(100, 500),
                 check.names=F)
```

Condition	Treatment	No treatment
Disease	5	100
No disease	195	500

```
# Find the conditional probability of a disease given a treatment
# P(disease | treatment) = p(disease & treatment)/p(treatment)
5/200
```

```
[1] 0.025
```

2.3.3   The Chain Rule

We can rearrange the formula of conditional probability to get a chain of conditional probabilities represented as $P(X, Y) = P(X \mid Y)P(Y)$.

We can extend the above for n variables

$$P(X_1, X_2, \cdots, X_n) = P(X_1 \mid X_2, \cdots, X_n) \times P(X_2 \mid X_3, \cdots, X_n)$$
$$\times \ P(X_{n-1} \mid X_n) \times P(X_n). \tag{2.3.3}$$

Equation 2.3.3 is known as the chain rule of conditional probabilities.

2.4 Bayes' Rule

It follows from Eq. 2.3.3 that $P(X, Y) = P(X \mid Y)P(Y)$. By symmetry, the same equation can also be written as $P(X, Y) = P(Y \mid X)P(X)$. The Bayes' rule can now be defined as

$$P(X \mid Y) = \frac{P(Y \mid X)P(X)}{P(Y)} \tag{2.4.1}$$

Bayes' rule can be thought of as updating our belief about a hypothesis X in the light of the evidence Y. The posterior belief $P(X \mid Y)$ is calculated by multiplying our prior belief $P(X)$ by the likelihood $P(Y \mid X)$. Given prior state knowledge, the Bayes' rules tell us how to update the belief based on the observations.

Fundamentally, the difference between frequentists and Bayesians revolves around the definition of probability. For frequentists, probabilities are related to the frequencies of the events. For Bayesians, probabilities are related to our own belief about an event and the likelihood of the data, given the event. Let us explore this with an example.

Frequentist Approach: A coin when flipped ends up "head" with probability P (the value of P is unknown) and "tail" with probability $(1 - P)$. Trying to estimate P, we flip the coin 14 times. It ends up "head" 10 times. We need to know if the next two tosses will get two "heads" in a row. We would say that the best (maximum likelihood) estimate for p is $= \frac{10}{14} \sim 0.714$. The probability of two heads is $0.714^2 \sim 0.51$; we therefore predict two "heads".

Bayesian Approach: In this approach, p is not a value but a distribution. The Bayesian approach would treat p as a random variable with its own distribution of possible values. What is the probability of a given value of p, given the data

$$P(p \mid data) = \frac{P(data \mid p)P(p)}{P(data)}$$

Let us assume that we have tossed the coin three times, each consisting of 14 tosses and we come up with the following results:

$$P(H = 7) = 0.5 \quad -7\ heads$$
$$P(H = 8) = 0.57 \quad -8\ heads$$
$$P(H = 9) = 0.64 \quad -9\ heads$$

The above is the **prior** distribution, which represents the knowledge we have, about how the data is generated prior to observing them.

The **likelihood** function $P(data|p)$ is the likelihood for the *data*, as it tells us how likely the data is, given the model specified by any value of p. The data consists of 10 "heads" and 4 "tails". Therefore,

$$P(data|p) = p^{10} \cdot (1 - p)^4$$

or,

$$P(data|p = 0.5) = 0.5^7 \cdot (1 - 0.5)^7 = 6.10e^{-05}$$
$$P(data|p = 0.57) = 0.57^8 \cdot (1 - 0.57)^6 = 7.04e^{-05}$$
$$P(data|p = 0.64) = 0.64^9 \cdot (1 - 0.64)^5 = 0.00011$$

Therefore, $P(data)$ (also known as *evidence*) can be calculated as

$$P(data) = \sum_p P(data|p) \cdot P(p)$$

$$P(data) = 6.1e^{-05} * 0.5 + 7.04e^{-05} * 0.57 + 0.00011 * 0.64 = 0.00014$$

The posterior probabilities are

$$P(p = 0.5|data) = \frac{P(data|p = 0.5) \cdot P(H = 7)}{P(data)} = 0.217$$

$$P(p = 0.57|data) = \frac{P(data|p = 0.57) \cdot P(H = 8)}{P(data)} = 0.287$$

$$P(p = 0.64|data) = \frac{P(data|p = 0.64) \cdot P(H = 9)}{P(data)} = 0.496$$

Considering the conditional independence between two tosses, $P(HH|p) = [P(H|p)]^2$, we can predict the probability of two heads as follows:

- if $p = 0.5$, $P(HH|p) = 0.217^2 = 0.047$
- if $p = 0.57$, $P(HH|p) = 0.287^2 = 0.082$
- if $p = 0.64$, $P(HH|p) = 0.496^2 = 0.246$

Since all the values are less than 0.5, we predict two "tails".
Summing it up in an application,

```
likelihood = function(p,heads){
  p^heads * (1 - p)^(14-heads)
}
likelihood = c(likelihood(0.5, 7), likelihood(0.57, 8), likelihood(0.64, 9))
prior = c(0.5, 0.57, 0.64)
evidence = sum(prior * likelihood)
posterior_prob = prior * likelihood / evidence
```

```
Likelihood values are   6.103516e-05 7.043842e-05 0.0001089262

Evidence =   0.0001403802

Posterior Probabilities are   0.2173923 0.2860082 0.4965995
```

2.5 Probability Distribution

A **probability distribution** (or probability measure) is a description of the outcome of a random experiment, i.e., it is a description of a random phenomenon in terms of the probabilities of its possible states. If the random variable takes any value between two specified limits, it is a continuous variable, or else a discrete variable and the probability distribution would depend on whether the variables are discrete or continuous.

2.5.1 Discrete Probability Distribution

A distribution of discrete variables is described using a **probability mass function** (PMF), denoted as P. It maps the state of a random variable to the probability of the random variable of assuming that state. If the probability that $X = x$ is 1, it indicates that $X = x$ is certain and a probability of 0 indicates that $x = x$ is impossible.

The PMF, P of a random variable X, needs to satisfy the **Kolmogorov axioms**:

- The domain of P must be the set of all possible states of X;
- $0 \leq P(x) \leq 1$ for all $x \in$ X; and
- $\sum_{x \in x} P(x) = 1$.

2.5.2 Continuous Probability Distribution

For continuous variables, we define the probability which the variable can take as **probability density function** (PDF), and the probability density function p needs to satisfy the **Kolmogorov axioms**:

- The domain of p must be the set of all possible states of X;
- $p(x) \geq 0$, for all $x \in$ X; and
- $\int p(X)dx = 1$.

A probability density function $p(x)$ gives the probability of existing inside an infinitesimal region δx, and is given by $p(x)\delta x$. The fact that $p(x) = p(X = x) = 0$ may seem paradoxical, but it can be thought of as an interval which has a positive length composed of points having zero length.

2.5.3 Cumulative Probability Distribution

The **cumulative distribution function** (CDF) is the probability that the random variable takes a value less than or equal to x, i.e., it is the probability of having a value less than x

$$f(x) = \int_{-\infty}^{x} f(t)dt \text{ for a continuous distribution}$$

$$F(x) = \sum_{t \leq x} f(t) \text{ for a discrete distribution}$$

(2.5.1)

2.5.4   Joint Probability Distribution

Joint probability is the distribution of many variables occurring at the same time. $P(X = x, Y = y)$ denotes the joint probability that $X = x$ and $Y = y$ occurs simultaneously.

2.6   Measures of Central Tendency

The **expected value** of a function $f(x)$ having a probability distribution $P(X)$ is the **mean** value of $f(x)$. The expectation or the expected value is computed as

$$\mathbf{E}[f(x)] = \sum_{x \in S} P(x)f(x) \text{ —for discrete variables}$$

$$\mathbf{E}[f(x)] = \int_{S} p(x)f(x)dx \text{ —for continuous variables}$$

(2.6.1)

Median is any x drawn from a probability distribution, having a value m such that half of the population has values of x less than m and the other half, from the population has values of x greater than m and satisfies the following equation:

$$\int_{-\infty}^{m} p(x)dx = \frac{1}{2} \qquad \text{for continuous distributions}$$

$$P(x \leq m) \geq \frac{1}{2} \text{ and } P(x \geq m) \geq \frac{1}{2} \qquad \text{for discrete distributions}$$

(2.6.2)

Mode of a discrete probability distribution is a value x which maximizes the probability mass function and that of a continuous probability distribution and, is a value x which maximizes the probability density function. It is the value that is most likely to be sampled from a distribution.

The above three measures are influenced by the **shape** of the distribution as well as by the presence of **outliers**.

2.7 Dispersion

Percentile is a measure indicating the value below which a given percentage of observations in a group of observations fall. The kth percentile of a set of observations is defined such that $k\%$ of the observations will lie below and $(100 - k)\%$ of the observations will lie above the defined percentile.

- The 25th percentile is the *lower quartile*;
- The 50th percentile is the *median*; and
- The 75th percentile is the *upper quartile*.

Sometimes, **quantiles** are more commonly used, which are the values taken from regular intervals of the quantile function of a random variable. The quantile q of a probability distribution is the inverse of its cumulative distribution function f. The quantile of order n for a distribution f can be written as $f(x) = P(X \leq x) \geq n$.

The **variance** and **standard deviation** of a vector $\mathbf{X} = [x_1, x_2, \cdots, x_n]$ are both measures of the spread of the distribution about the mean. It is a measure of how much the values of $f(\mathbf{X})$ vary as we sample different values of $\mathbf{X}$. The square root of the variance is the standard deviation:

$$Var(f(\mathbf{X})) = E([f(\mathbf{X}) - E[f(\mathbf{X})]])^2 \tag{2.7.1}$$

The variance of $\mathbf{X}$ is written as

$$Var(\mathbf{X}) = \sigma_{\mathbf{X}}^2$$
$$= \frac{1}{n-1} \mathbf{X}\mathbf{X}^\top \tag{2.7.2}$$

In Eq. 2.7.2, $\mathbf{X}\mathbf{X}^\top$ is a dot product, which gives us the length of the vector $\mathbf{X}$. If the length is large, it intuitively tells us that the variance is high and *vice versa*.

2.8 Covariance and Correlation

Covariance gives an indication as to how much two vectors are linearly related (i.e., how much, each one of the vectors are in each other), as well as the scale of these variables. Let us consider two vectors $\mathbf{X} = [x_1, x_2, \cdots, x_n]$ and $\mathbf{Y} = [y_1, y_2, \cdots, y_n]$

$$Cov(f(\mathbf{X}), f(\mathbf{Y})) = E[(f(\mathbf{X}) - E[f(\mathbf{X})])(f(\mathbf{Y}) - E[f(\mathbf{Y})])] \tag{2.8.1}$$

The covariance of $\mathbf{X}$ and $\mathbf{Y}$ can be written as

$$Cov(\mathbf{XY}) = \sigma_{\mathbf{XY}}^2$$
$$= \frac{1}{n-1}\mathbf{XY}^\top \tag{2.8.2}$$

Equation 2.8.2 is again a dot product of $\mathbf{A}$ and $\mathbf{B}$. If this value is 1, the two vectors are the same and, if it is 0, the two vectors are orthogonal (perpendicular) to each other, i.e., the two vectors have nothing to do with each other and are statistically independent. So covariance defines the measure of statistical dependence between the two vectors.

$$Cov(\mathbf{XY}) = \begin{pmatrix} \sigma_{x_1x_1}^2 & \sigma_{x_1y_1}^2 & \cdots & \sigma_{x_1x_n}^2 & \sigma_{x_1y_n}^2 \\ \sigma_{x_1y_1}^2 & \sigma_{y_1y_1}^2 & \cdots & \sigma_{x_ny_1}^2 & \sigma_{y_1y_n}^2 \\ \vdots & \vdots & \vdots & \vdots & \vdots \\ \sigma_{x_1x_n}^2 & \sigma_{x_ny_1}^2 & \cdots & \sigma_{x_nx_n}^2 & \sigma_{x_ny_n}^2 \\ \sigma_{x_1y_n}^2 & \sigma_{y_1y_n}^2 & \cdots & \sigma_{x_ny_n}^2 & \sigma_{y_ny_n}^2 \end{pmatrix}$$

$$\tag{2.8.3}$$

The diagonals of the matrix in Eq. 2.8.3 are the variance terms and the covariances of all the $\mathbf{X}$ and $\mathbf{Y}$ pairs are the off-diagonal terms (which, incidentally, are symmetric and is a *Hermitian* matrix).

Now, if the covariance terms are small in value, it implies that the variables are not dependent on each other but, if some (or all) of the covariance terms are high in value, it means that they are *redundant* variables, because they have a lot of dependency on each other.

The fact that redundant variables "may not" contribute toward determining the target variable is important in most machine learning algorithms, as they can become confounders in a model. So, ideally, the extreme requirement is that the non-diagonal terms should be either zero or close to zero.

Now, if the off-diagonal terms are either 0 or close to 0 and, if we reorient the diagonal terms from the largest value (i.e., $(i = 1, j = 1)$) to the smallest value $(i = n, j = n)$), we are in a position to identify the most important predictor variables, which contribute to determining the target variable. In other words, we can answer the question—**are all the predictor variables important OR redundant?**

At this stage, you may want to refer to Sect. 1.11 *on SVD*.

Correlation measures how much the two variables (vectors) are related to each other:

$$Cor(f(\mathbf{X}), f(\mathbf{Y})) = \frac{\sigma_{\mathbf{XY}}^2}{\sqrt{\sigma_{\mathbf{X}}^2 \sigma_{\mathbf{Y}}^2}} \tag{2.8.4}$$

2.9 Shape of a Distribution

The shape of a distribution is quantitatively measured by **Skewness** and **Kurtosis**. A distribution is said to be right-skewed (or positively skewed) if the right tail is stretched from the center. A left-skewed (or negatively skewed) distribution is stretched to the left side. A symmetric distribution is balanced about its center.

Some distributions have a flat shape with thin tails and are called *platykurtic*. Distributions with a steep peak and with heavy tails are called *leptokurtic*. Skewness is a measure of the absence of symmetry, while Kurtosis is the degree to which the distribution is peaked.

$$skew(x) = E[(\frac{x - \mu}{\sigma})^3] \qquad (2.9.1)$$

$$kurt(x) = E[(\frac{x - \mu}{\sigma})^4], \qquad (2.9.2)$$

where
$$\sigma^2 = var(x)$$
$$\mu = E(x)$$

2.10 Chebyshev's Inequality

Chebyshev's inequality states that **at least** $(1 - \frac{1}{k^2})$ of the data of a distribution will lie within k standard deviations away from the mean (k being a real number greater than 0). It provides a way to know what fraction of the data will fall within k standard deviations from the mean for any distribution. This is illustrated in Fig. 2.1.

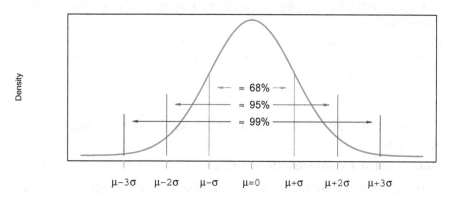

Fig. 2.1 Chebyshev's theorem, as applicable to a Gaussian distribution

2.11   Common Probability Distributions

We walk through two commonly used distributions within the discrete and continuous distribution spaces.

2.11.1   Discrete Distributions

Bernoulli Distribution

The Bernoulli distribution has two possible outcomes and is controlled by a parameter ϕ, which is the probability of the outcome registering a success (i.e., the probability is 1). The Bernoulli distribution can be defined as having the following properties:

$$P(x = 1) = \phi \qquad (2.11.1)$$
$$P(x = 0) = 1 - \phi \qquad (2.11.2)$$
$$P(x = x) = \phi^x (1 - \phi)^{1-x} \qquad (2.11.3)$$
$$E_x[x] = \phi \qquad (2.11.4)$$
$$Var_x(x) = \phi(1 - \phi) \qquad (2.11.5)$$

$$f(x) = P(x = x) = \binom{n}{x} \cdot p^x \cdot q^{n-x} = \frac{n!}{x!(n-x)!} \qquad (2.11.6)$$

x is the number of successes,
n is the number of experiments, and
p is the probability of success.

The probability of obtaining seven tails by flipping a coin eight times can be obtained as

```
# BERNOULLI DISTRIBUTION
# Probability of having seven tails by fliping a fair coin eight times
dbinom(x=7, size=8, prob=0.5)
```

```
[1] 0.03125
```

Approximately, 3% are the chances of obtaining seven tails by flipping a coin eight times.

Multinomial and Multinoulli Distributions

The Bernoulli distribution has only two outcomes from one trial. The binomial distribution is an extension of the bernoulli distribution having two outcomes for each of the multiple trials. The multinoulli distribution generalizes the bernoulli distribution and has more than two outcomes from a single trial. The multinomial distribution extends this even further by having multiple outcomes from multiple trials.

For continuous variables, there exist uncountable number of states, which are governed by a small number of parameters. These parameters which define a continuous distribution, necessarily, impose strict limits on such distributions.

Let us suppose we have a random vector $(x1, x2, x3)$ having a multinomial distribution. The probabilities associated with the occurrence of each variable x_1, x_2, x_3 are $p1 = 0.1$, $p2 = 0.4$, and $p3 = 0.5$. The number of times each variable occurs is $x_1 = 5, x_2 = 5, x_3 = 10$, i.e., 20 occurrences. The multinomial probability for these multiple outcomes can be found as follows:

```
# MULTINOMIAL DISTRIBUTION
dmultinom(x = c(5,5,10), size = 20, prob = c(0.1, 0.4, 0.5))
```

```
[1] 0.004655851
```

2.11.2 Continuous Distributions

Gaussian Distribution

If the number of events is large, the Gaussian distribution may be used to describe the events. The most commonly used Gaussian distribution is the **normal distribution**, where the density function is represented by the equation

$$f(x) = \mathcal{N}(x; \mu, \sigma) = \sqrt{\frac{1}{2\pi\sigma^2}} e^{-(\frac{1}{2\sigma^2}(x-\mu)^2)} \tag{2.11.7}$$

The parameter μ, which defines the central peak of the X-coordinate, is also the mean of the distribution, i.e., $E[X] = \mu$ and $\mu \in \mathbb{R}$. The distribution has a standard deviation represented by the symbol σ, where $\sigma \in (0, \infty)$. The variance is σ^2.

The **cumulative density function** for the Gaussian distribution is

$$F(x) = \int_{-\infty}^{x} \sqrt{\frac{1}{2\pi\sigma^2}} e^{-(\frac{1}{2\sigma^2}(x-\mu)^2)} \tag{2.11.8}$$

Figure 2.2 depicts the PDF and Fig. 2.3 depicts the CDF of the **standard normal distribution**, which has $\mu = 0$ and $\sigma = 1$.

If we do not have any prior knowledge about the form of a distribution, the normal distribution may be assumed as the default choice for two major reasons:

- The **Central Limit Theorem** proves that given sufficiently larges samples (sample sizes greater than 30) from a population, all of the samples are normally distributed. The mean of the sample will be closer to the mean of the population, as the sample size increases, irrespective of whether the sample is normally distributed

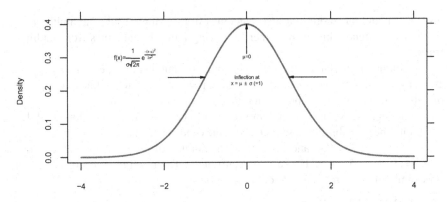

Fig. 2.2 PDF of Standard Normal

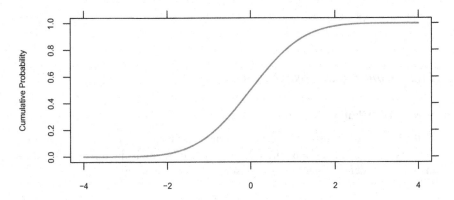

Fig. 2.3 CDF of Standard Normal

or not. The variance of the samples will approximate closely to the variance of the population divided by the sample size. The important take-away is that in practice, many distributions can be modeled successfully as approximations to the Gaussian distribution.

- **Entropy** is a mathematical formula used to measure information gain. The normal distribution has the maximum entropy among all continuous distributions having a fixed mean and variance. What this implies is that the normal distribution incorporates the minimum amount of prior knowledge into a model.

Logistic Distribution

The logistic distribution is used in a certain type of regression known as *logistic regression*. This distribution is symmetrical, unimodal (having one peak), and is similar in shape to the Gaussian distribution. The logistic distribution tends to have slightly fatter tails.

The CDF of the logistic distribution is

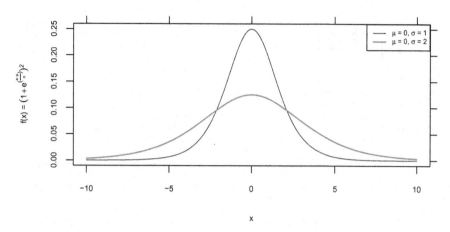

Fig. 2.4 PDF—Logistic Distribution

$$F(x) = \frac{e^x}{(1 + e^x)} \qquad (2.11.9)$$

Differentiating the above equation wrt x, we get the PDF

$$f(x) = \frac{e^x}{(1 + e^x)^2} \qquad (2.11.10)$$

The quantile of the distribution is

$$F^{-1}(x) = ln(\frac{p}{1 - p}) \qquad (2.11.11)$$

Figures 2.4 and 2.5 show the plots of the logistic distribution.

An interesting aspect of this distribution is that the ratio, $\frac{p}{1-p}$, is called the **odds** in favor of an event happening with probability p. The natural logarithm of the *odds ratio*, $ln(\frac{p}{1-p})$ is the logarithmic odds and is called the *logit*.

2.11.3 Summary of Probability Distributions

R has a range of probability distributions and for each of them, four functions are available—the pdf (which has a prefix **d**); the cdf (prefix **p**); quantiles of the distribution (**q**); and the random number generator (**r**). Each letter can be prefixed to the function names in Table 2.1.

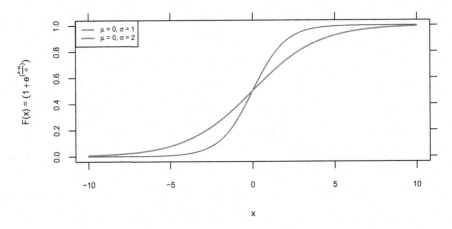

Fig. 2.5 CDF—Logistic Distribution

Table 2.1 Probability distributions and their respective parameters

R function	Distribution	Parameters
beta	beta	shape1, shape2
binom	binomial	sample size, probability
cauchy	Cauchy	location, scale
exp	exponential	rate
chisq	chi-squared	degrees of freedom
F	Fishers F	df1, df2
gamma	gamma	shape
geom	geometric	probability
lnorm	lognormal	mean, standard deviation
logis	logistic	location, scale
norm	normal	mean, standard deviation
pois	Poisson	mean
signrank	Wilcoxon signed rank statistic	sample size
t	Students t	degrees of freedom
Weibull	Weibull	shape

2.12 Tests for Fit

Tests for fit measure how well do the observed data correspond to the fitted (assumed) model. They test the following hypotheses:

H_0: The data fits the model

H_A: The data does not fit the model

There are many different tests for fit, namely Kolmogorov–Smirnov test, Anderson–Darling test, etc.; however, we shall discuss only the chi-square test.

2.12.1 Chi-Square Distribution

A standard normal deviate is a normal distribution with zero mean and unit standard deviation (i.e., $\mathcal{N}(0, 1)$. The chi-square distribution is a distribution of the sum of squared standard normal deviates. The degrees of freedom of the chi-square distribution is the number of standard normal deviates. The distribution of a squared single normal deviate is a chi-square distribution having a single degree of freedom (χ_1^2).

If we consider $Z_1, \cdots, Z_k$ as independent, standard normal variables, the sum of their squares is $\sum_i^k Z_i^2 \sim \chi_k^2$.

If $Z_1 \sim \mathcal{N}(0, 1)$, how do we find the pdf of $(Z_1)^2$? We have seen earlier that the pdf of x is

$$f(x) = \mathcal{N}(x; \mu, \sigma) = \sqrt{\frac{1}{2\pi\sigma^2}} e^{-(\frac{1}{2\sigma^2}(x-\mu)^2)}$$

If $g(x)$ is the pdf of $(Z_1)^2$ the pdf for the chi-square distribution can be derived as

$$
\begin{aligned}
g(x) &= \frac{d}{dx} p(x^2 \leq x) \\
&= \frac{d}{dx} p(-\sqrt{x} \leq x^2 \leq \sqrt{x}) \\
&= \frac{d}{dx} \frac{1}{\sqrt{2\pi}} \int_{-\sqrt{x}}^{\sqrt{x}} e^{-u^2/2} du \\
&= \frac{2}{2\pi} \frac{d}{dx} \int_0^{\sqrt{x}} e^{-u^2/2} du \\
&= \frac{2}{2\pi} e^{-\sqrt{x}^2/2} \frac{d}{dx} \sqrt{x} \\
&= \frac{2}{2\pi} e^{\frac{-x}{2}} \frac{1}{2\sqrt{x}} \\
&= \frac{e^{-x/2}}{2\pi\sqrt{x}} \\
&= \frac{1}{2\pi} x^{(\frac{1}{2}-1)} e^{-x/2}
\end{aligned}
\tag{2.12.1}
$$

The last term in Eq. (2.12.1) resembles another function known as the *Gamma function*, which defines the pdf of the chi-square distribution.

The degrees of freedom is the mean of the chi-square distribution. As the degrees of freedom increase, the chi-square distribution tends toward the normal distribution.

The chi-square test is used to test "goodness-of-fit" of data to a model. There are different types of "chi-square" test, as well as other tests that use the chi-square distribution. All of them estimate the probability of observing the results under the given hypotheses. If that probability is low, then one can confidently reject the hypothesis. Many test statistics are approximately distributed as chi-square.

A chi-square distribution having different degrees of freedom is shown in Fig. 2.6.

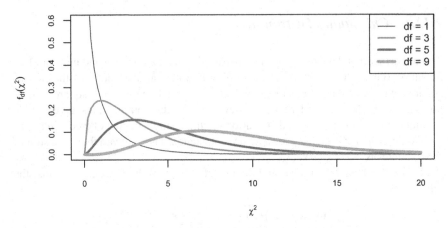

Fig. 2.6 Chi-square distributions with different degrees of freedom

2.12.2   Chi-Square Test

Of the many chi-squares tests, two important ones are as follows:

- Tests of deviations of differences between theoretically expected and observed frequencies *(one-way tables)*. This is also known as the **goodness-of-fit test** and determines if a sample data matches a population. It measures the "goodness-of-fit" between the observed and expected data.
- Test of relationship between categorical variables *(contingency tables)*. This test compares two categorical variables in a contingency table to see if they are related and is also called **test for independence**. In a more general sense, it is a test to see whether distributions of categorical variables differ from each another and determines whether there is a significant association between them.

Chi-square tests use the **chi-square test statistic** and the equation for this statistic is

$$\chi_c^2 = \sum \frac{(observed\ Value - expected\ Value)^2}{expected\ Value} \qquad (2.12.2)$$

Let us consider the following data on weekly customer visits in Table 2.2.

We need to find out if the observed and expected values come from the same distribution, given a significance level $\alpha = 0.05$.

First, let us define our hypotheses space:

Null Hypothesis H_0: There is no difference between the observed and expected customer visits.

Alternate Hypothesis H_A: There is a difference between the observed and expected customer visits.

The hypothesis is tested using Pearson's χ^2-test.

Table 2.2 Observed and expected customer visits data

Day	Observed no of visits	Expected probability (%)
Mon	30	10
Tue	14	10
Wed	34	15
Thur	45	20
Fri	57	30
Sat	20	15

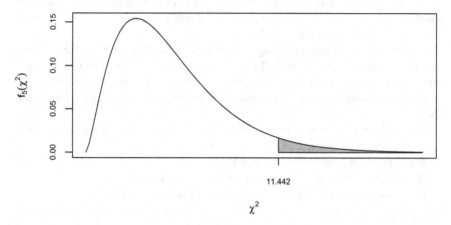

Fig. 2.7 Shaded area depicting the p-value of a chi-square distribution

```
# GOODNESS of FIT
chisq.test(x = c(30, 14, 34, 45, 57, 20),
           p = c(0.1, 0.1, 0.15, 0.2, 0.3, 0.15))
```

        Chi-squared test for given probabilities

data: c(30, 14, 34, 45, 57, 20)
X-squared = 11.442, df = 5, p value = 0.04329

p value = 0.04329 and χ^2 = 11.442

p value is the probability of obtaining a result equal to or more extreme (toward the direction of H_A) than what was actually observed, when the null hypothesis is true. This probability is the area under the curve at the point and beyond, given the null hypothesis.

The chi-square distribution showing the p value corresponding to the χ^2 value is shown in Fig. 2.7.

A small p value, in this case, implies that it is unlikely to find any difference between the observed and expected values due to chance, in the absence of any substantial difference between the observed and expected customer visits.

Table 2.3 Survey data

	Exercise: Frequently	Exercise: None	Exercise: Some
Heavy	7	1	3
Never	87	18	84
Occasional	12	3	4
Regular	9	1	7

Since 0.04329 is smaller the defined significance level, we reject H_0. We therefore conclude that there exists a significant difference between the observed and expected customer visits, i.e., it is not a good fit.

For the purpose of understanding the test for independence, we use the "survey" data table in the MASS library. In Table 2.3, the Smoker's column records students' smoking habit as either "Heavy", "Regular", "Occasional", and "Never", while the remaining columns record their exercise level as "Freq" (Frequently), "None", and "Some".

We would like to know if the smoking habit of students is independent of their exercise levels at a significance level, $\alpha = 0.05$ (5%).

The hypothesis space is defined as follows:

H_0: Students smoking habit and exercise level are independent.

H_a: Students smoking habit and exercise level are not independent.

```
# TEST for INDEPENDENCE
chisq.test(Survey.data, simulate.p.value = TRUE)

    Pearson's chi-squared test with simulated p value (based on 2000
    replicates)

data:  Survey.data
X-squared = 5.4885, df = NA, p value = 0.4868
```

As the p value is greater than 0.05 (the level of significance), we accept the null hypothesis and we can conclude that the smoking habit of the students is independent of the exercise level they indulge.

2.13 Ratio Distributions

A ratio distribution is the ratio of two random variables having two different known distributions.

2.13.1 Student's t-Distribution

The t-distribution is the ratio of a normal random variable and an independent chi-distributed random variable (i.e., the square root of a chi-squared distribution).

If **U** and **V** are two random variables, where **U** is a standard normal distribution and **V** is a chi-squared distribution with m degrees of freedom, then the student's t-distribution having m degrees of freedom can be written as

$$t = \frac{U}{\sqrt{\frac{V}{m}}} \sim t_m \tag{2.13.1}$$

The t-distribution is used to estimate population parameters when the sample size is small and/or when the population variance σ^2 is unknown. t-distributions describe the samples drawn from a full population (where the full population is described by a normal distribution). The t-distribution for different sample sizes are different—the larger the sample, the more it resembles a normal distribution.

The student t-distribution with different degrees of freedom is shown in Fig. 2.8.

t-Statistic

The t-statistic in a t test is a test statistic and is used to compare the actual sample mean and the population mean. A significant difference indicates that the hypothesized value for μ should be rejected. The t test uses the t-statistic, t-distribution, and degrees of freedom to find the p value. The p value determines whether the population means differ.

The most common hypothesis test involves testing the null hypothesis:

$H_0 : \hat{\mu} - \mu = 0$, i.e., there is no difference between sample and population mean.

$H_a : \hat{\mu} - \mu \neq 0$, i.e., there exists a difference between the sample and population means.

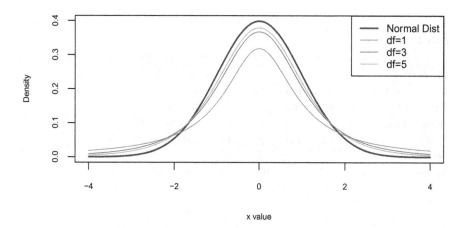

Fig. 2.8 Plot of t-distributions, with different degrees of freedom

The hypothesis test attempts to decide the following:

- Is the difference between $\hat{\mu}$ and μ simply due to chance (sampling error)?
- Is the discrepancy between $\hat{\mu}$ and μ more than as would be expected by chance, i.e., it tests whether the sample mean is significantly different from the population mean.

The critical step for the above hypothesis test is to calculate exactly how much difference between $\hat{\mu}$ and μ is reasonable to expect. And, this depends on the **standard error** SE($\hat{\mu}$), which tells us the average amount by which the estimate $\hat{\mu}$ differs from the actual value of μ, and is written as follows:

$$SE(\hat{\mu}) = s/\sqrt{n} \tag{2.13.2}$$

s is the sample standard deviation and n is the sample size

Equation 2.13.2 also tells us that the deviation, $SE(\hat{\mu})$, shrinks with larger values of n.

The t-statistic is thus defined as

$$t = \frac{(\hat{\mu} - \mu)}{SE(\mu)} \tag{2.13.3}$$

The above equation measures the number of standard deviations, $\hat{\mu}$ is from μ. The t-statistic thus defines how much difference between $\hat{\mu}$ and μ is reasonable to expect—if the ratio is large, the difference would be significantly greater than what could be attributed to chance and accordingly we reject H_0. But, if the ratio is small, the difference is not significant and we accept H_0.

For the purpose of our analysis, we use the mtcars data set (from the *stats* library). This data set was extracted from the 1974 Motor Trend US magazine, and comprises 11 different aspects of automobile design and performance for 32 automobile models (1973 to 1974). Table 2.4 shows a brief description of the variables in the data set:

Table 2.4 mtcars data

	mpg	cyl	disp	hp	drat	wt	qsec	vs	am	gear	carb
Mazda RX4	21.0	6	160	110	3.90	2.620	16.46	0	1	4	4
Mazda RX4 Wag	21.0	6	160	110	3.90	2.875	17.02	0	1	4	4
Datsun 710	22.8	4	108	93	3.85	2.320	18.61	1	1	4	1
Hornet 4 Drive	21.4	6	258	110	3.08	3.215	19.44	1	0	3	1
Hornet Sportabout	18.7	8	360	175	3.15	3.440	17.02	0	0	3	2
Valiant	18.1	6	225	105	2.76	3.460	20.22	1	0	3	1

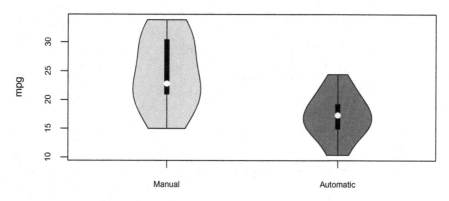

Fig. 2.9 Violin Plot of Transmission vs MPG

Table 2.5 T Test Results

t.statistic	df	p.value	automatic.mean	manual.mean
−3.767	18.332	0.001	17.147	24.392

It is worthwhile to visualize in Fig. 2.9 how MPG (miles per gallon) scores, for "automatic" and "manual" transmission, respectively.

It appears from the plot that automatic cars have lower miles per gallon than manual cars. To find out, which of the two, automatic or manual transmission, is better for MPG, we proceed as follows:

H_0: Cars with automatic transmission use more fuel than cars with manual transmission.

H_a: Cars with automatic transmission **do not** use more fuel than cars with a manual transmission.

The two-sample t test is used to compare the means of the two samples (if they have different means) and the results are shown in Table 2.5.

```
# TESTING SIGNIFICANCE for TWO MEANS
test <- t.test(mpg ~ am, data = mtcars)
```

The p value (i.e., the probability of the difference in means, between the two groups) is very low (much lower than 0.05), and therefore we reject H_0, i.e., cars with automatic transmission **do not** use more fuel than cars with a manual transmission The t test shows that the apparent pattern in Fig. 2.9 happened by random chance, i.e., the samples that were picked were a group of automatic cars with high fuel efficiency and a group of manual cars with low fuel efficiency.

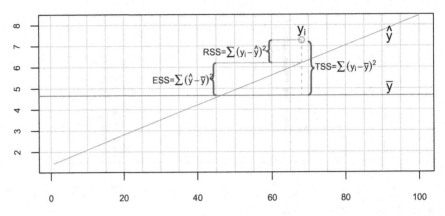

Fig. 2.10 Explained and unexplained variances of a regression model

2.13.2   F-Distribution

The F-distribution arises while dealing with ratios of variances. The F-distribution can be used among others for testing the equality of two population variances and testing the validity of a multiple regression model. The F-distribution has two important properties:

- It is defined only for positive values.
- It is positively skewed and thus not symmetric about its mean.

F-Statistic

An F-Statistic is a value obtained during a regression analysis to find out if the means between two populations are significantly different. It is similar to a t-statistic; a t-statistic tells us if a single variable is statistically significant and an F-statistic tells us if a group of variables are jointly significant.

The F-Statistic is defined as the quotient of the following ratio:

$$F = \frac{Effect \; (Explained \; Variance)}{Error \; (Unexplained \; Variance)}$$

The explained and unexplained variance of a regression model are shown in Fig. 2.10.

Total Sum of Squares (TSS) measures the variation of y_i values around their mean $\bar{y}$. Residual Sum of Squares (RSS) is the variation attributable to factors other than the relationship between x and y. Explained Sum of Squares (ESS) is the explained variation attributable to the relationship between x and y. The total variation is made up of two parts and is represented as

$$\sum (y - \bar{y})^2 = \sum (y - \hat{y})2 + \sum (\hat{y} - \bar{y})^2 \qquad (2.13.4)$$

As shown in Fig. 2.10, the explained/unexplained variance can be written as

$$TSS - RSS = Explained\ Variance = \sum_{i=1}^{n} (\hat{y}_i - \bar{y})^2 \qquad (2.13.5)$$

$$RSS = Unexplained\ Variance = \sum_{i=1}^{n} (y_i - \hat{y}_i)^2 \qquad (2.13.6)$$

The F-Test

In the process of estimating the parameters $\beta_0, \beta_1, ..., \beta_n$, we are interested to find if at least one or a subset of the predictors $X_1, X_2, ..., X_n$ are useful in predicting the dependent variable, Y. The steps involved are as follows:

1. Hypotheses statement:
   $H_0 : \beta_1 = \beta_2 = ... = \beta_n = 0$
   $H_a : For\ at\ least\ one\ of\ j,\ \beta_j \neq 0$
2. The F-test-statistic is computed assuming H_0 is true:

$$F = \frac{Explained\ Variance}{Unexplained\ Variance}$$
$$= \frac{(TSS - RSS)/p}{RSS/(m - p - 1)} \qquad (2.13.7)$$

3. Determine the p value of the F-statistic.
4. Reject the null hypothesis if the p value for the F-statistic is below the level of significance α (usually, 0.05).

The above implies that when there is no relationship between the response and the predictors (i.e., parameters $\beta_1, ..., \beta_n$ are all zero), F-statistic is very close to or

Table 2.6 Data on blood pressure, age, and weight

BP	Age	Wt
132	52	173
143	59	184
153	67	194
162	73	211
154	64	196
168	74	220
137	54	188
149	61	188
159	65	207
128	46	167
166	72	217

Table 2.7 Summary of linear regression model

	Estimate	Std. error	t value	Pr(>|t|)
(Intercept)	30.99	11.94	2.595	0.03186
Age	0.8614	0.2482	3.47	0.00844
Wt	0.3349	0.1307	2.563	0.03351

equal to 1. On the other hand, if there exists some relationship between the response and the predictors (i.e., parameters $\beta_1, \ldots, \beta_n$ are **not** all zero), we would expect the F-statistic to be greater than 1.

We use a multiple regression model on the data set shown in Table 2.6 to predict BP from the predictors "Age" and "Wt". The summary of the regression model is shown in Table 2.7.

The regression equation is **BP** $= 31 + 0.86$**Age** $+ 0.33$**Wt**

The model F-statistic = 168.8 corresponding to a very small p value. Thus, the probability of accepting the null hypothesis is extremely low, and therefore we can assume there is a statistically significant relationship between the variables.

This concludes our discussion on probability and distributions. We are now ready to discuss the concepts of machine learning.

Chapter 3
Introduction to Machine Learning

All models are wrong, the practical question is how wrong do they have to be to not be useful

-George Box, 1987

We start with an introduction to scientific enquiry and its evolution to e-Science and machine learning.

A learning algorithm is a set of instructions which is required to be understood by a computer so that it can learn from data. We discuss this concept as defined by Mitchell (1997).

To learn from data, the algorithm uses a "training" data set and evaluates its performance on an unseen data set known as the "test" data set. Cross-validation is another technique to evaluate an algorithm. The errors generated by the algorithm on the training and test data sets give us an idea as to how the algorithm is behaving.

The errors can be classified into categories and we will study the categories of errors in detail. The errors also tell us if the algorithm is performing at its optimal capacity which leads us to discuss what is underfitting and overfitting.

We will then look into some of the methods we can deploy to address underfitting and overfitting, i.e., by regularization, hyparameter tuning, etc. Regularization is an exercise in optimization and we will discuss one of the commonly used optimization techniques namely gradient descent.

Based on the above discussions, we will summarize our learnings and discuss the common ingredients which we need to focus to build an appropriate learning algorithm.

Finally, we touch upon some of the key challenges facing learning algorithms today.

© Springer Nature Singapore Pte Ltd. 2017
A. Ghatak, *Machine Learning with R*, DOI 10.1007/978-981-10-6808-9_3

3.1 Scientific Enquiry

As per The National Science Education Standards[1] scientific inquiry is defined as "the diverse ways in which scientists study the natural world and propose explanations based on the evidence derived from their work. Scientific inquiry also refers to the activities through which students develop knowledge and understanding of scientific ideas, as well as an understanding of how scientists study the natural world."

Any scientific enquiry most commonly contains the following steps:

- Observe the phenomenon being studied and document the observations.
- Explain the observations by forming a hypothesis. This is also called inductive reasoning.
- The hypothesis is then tested under varying conditions to understand the implications and outcomes if the hypothesis is to be true, resulting in a testable hypothesis.
- The hypothesis is then verified by experiments or other analytical means to provide evidence that the hypothesis is verifiable. Once verified, further research is initiated upon the hypothesis, till it stands the test of time.

When a hypothesis has survived a sufficient number of tests, it may be promoted to a "Theory".

All through the history of science, the process of scientific enquiry has been mostly empirical and theoretical in nature. However, in the last 50 years or so, with the advent of technology, simulation techniques, algorithmic power, data storage capacities, and computational speed, there has been a transition to computational science and e-science.

3.1.1 Empirical Science

Empirical science is a study based on verifiable evidence rather than theory. It therefore relies on information gained by experience, observation, or experiment. The hypothesis is then tested based on the experiment or observation and constitutes the central theme of this scientific method.

Empirical data is produced by experiment and observation and the empirical cycle consists of the following stages:

- Observe the phenomenon by collecting empirical facts and organize and document the evidences.
- Explain the evidences by inductive reasoning to form an hypotheses
- The hypothesis is studied further to understand its constraints and boundary conditions.
- This hypothesis is subjected to further experiments and the outcomes are evaluated for consistency.

---

[1] http://www.nsta.org/about/positions/inquiry.aspx.

3.1.2 Theoretical Science

Theoretical science is involved with a deeper interpretation of the experimental results, making predictions, and making new theories. New theories may suggest new experiments by reinforcing the empirical methods. Theoretical research aims at acquiring new knowledge about the phenomenon and improve upon its general understanding. An understanding of the nature of the smallest components of matter could be a result of theoretical science.

3.1.3 Computational Science

With the advent of computers, networks, storage devices, software, and algorithms, computational science evolved to solve problems, by doing simulations, to create new knowledge. Computational science, as the name suggests is "computational" as opposed to "experimental" or "theoretical" and relies on computers and computational techniques involving mathematical models to study scientific problems.

3.1.4 e-Science

Today, the advent of massive amounts of data, along with the availability of high performance computers, cloud storage, sophisticated algorithms, and software, has brought about a paradigm shift in how scientific and engineering investigations are carried out. e-Science promotes data-intensive research across all disciplines. We have thus moved from "Querying the World" (Empirical and Theoretical enquiry), to "Downloading the World and Querying the Data".

3.2 Machine Learning

Machine learning, as defined by Mitchell (1997) is, "A computer program is said to learn from experience **E** with respect to some class of tasks **T** and performance measure **P**, if its performance at tasks in T, as measured by P, improves with experience E."

Machine learning, therefore, is the set of techniques concerned with getting a program to perform a task better with respect to some metric as the program gains more experience.

3.2.1 A Learning Task

Machine learning allows us to tackle tasks that are either too complex or computationally intensive making it difficult to work around a solution manually. From a scientific point of view, developing our understanding of machine learning allows us to develop our own understanding of the underlying principles of intelligence. A learning task is therefore the ability to perform a task and gather experience while performing the task. Some of the common machine learning tasks include the following:

- Classification—In this type of task, the algorithm is tasked with specifying which of the k classes does an input belong to. If the algorithm is defined by a generic function $y = f(x)$, the classification task is to take an input defined by a vector **X**, so that the algorithm assigns a category class k as the output of the function f, identified by y. A numeric output from the function f could be a probability distribution, assigning a probability to the predicted classes k. An example of a classification task is identifying images based on pixel values.
- Regression—In this type of task, the algorithm is tasked to predict a numeric value given an input. The regression task also uses a generic function $y = f(x)$ defined by the algorithm and using an input vector **X** to predict a numeric output. An example of a regression task is to predict house prices based on available data.
- Estimation of the probability "density" or "mass" function—While estimating a probability distribution, a machine learning algorithm learns a function $f(X = x) = p$. For such a task, the algorithm learns the structure of the data, i.e., where the data is clustered closely and where they are not. Computations can then be performed on the distribution to solve other tasks.

3.2.2 The Performance Measure

In order to evaluate the learning of our algorithm, we need to evaluate and measure its performance. The measurement attribute P is specific to the task T being carried out by the algorithm. For tasks such as classification, we measure the classification error or the accuracy of the algorithm. For regression tasks, we can measure the mean error, which is the average of the differences between the actual output and the predicted output. For probability estimation functions, we measure the mean value of the logarithm of the probability which the algorithm assigns to the data.

But in most cases, we are interested in how well the algorithm performs on unseen data as this is a more accurate measure of the efficiency of the algorithm when it is deployed in the real world. The performance is therefore measured on an unseen data set, called the test set, which is different from the data set on which the algorithm trains itself, known as the training set in a machine learning system.

3.2.3 The Experience

The type of experience a learning algorithm acquires during a learning process can be broadly categorized as unsupervised learning or supervised learning. In unsupervised learning, the algorithm gathers experience from a data set which contains only the features, without any dependent variable. In the process of experiencing the structure of data, it tries to derive "interesting" summaries. Examples of unsupervised learning include clustering, which divides the data set into clusters of similar data points. On the other hand in supervised learning, the algorithm gathers experience from a data set which not only contain features but also a target variable, which is a function of the features. Examples of supervised learning include predicting the price of a house based on a host of features or classifying a response into a specific class given the features, which are related to the response.

However, there is another type of learning called **reinforcement** learning. Here, the model not only experiences a data set but also interacts with an environment, to get a feedback about its experience.

A machine learning algorithm can therefore be defined as an algorithm, which is capable of improving the **performance** of a computer program by gathering **experience**, from the specific **task** it performs.

3.3 Train and Test Data

Data sets are ideally generated from a probability distribution. While generating the data, we normally assume that the observations in the data set are independent from each other and also that they are identically distributed. This assumption is also known as independent and identically distributed (i.i.d.). The training and test data sets for our algorithms necessarily need to come from the same probability distribution and are i.i.d.

Having partitioned our data set into training and test sets, we train the learning algorithm using the training set so as to reduce the training error. We then apply our "trained" model to the test set, which is the unseen data. The test error is always greater than or equal to the training error. Therefore, we aim to reduce the training error as well as reduce the difference between the training error and test error.

3.3.1 Training Error, Generalization (True) Error, and Test Error

The fundamental goal of machine learning is to learn beyond the examples provided in the training set. This is because it is physically impossible to train a model with all the data in the population. No matter how much data we have to train a model, it is extremely unlikely that the same observations will be repeated, when we test the model on a test set. Learning beyond the data which is "seen" by the learning algorithm is called generalizaion.

The error obtained on the training set after the algorithm was trained on the training data is the training error of the model. The training error is often used as a surrogate for the test error because it provides us a error baseline for our trained model. The training error of a learning algorithm can be represented as the average loss defined as

$$\text{Training Error} = \frac{1}{m} \sum_{i=1}^{m} L(y_i, f_{\hat{w}}(x_i)) \tag{3.3.1}$$

where L is the Loss function specific to the learning algorithm
m is the number of samples
$f_{\hat{w}}(x_i)$ is the estimated model predicting the response
y_i is the true value of the response

For a linear regression model, the training error is defined by the root mean square error (RMSE)

$$Train_{RMSE} = \sqrt{\frac{1}{m_{train}} \sum_{(i \in \text{ train data})}^{m_{train}} (y_i - f_{\hat{w}}(x_i))^2} \tag{3.3.2}$$

Training error is often overly optimistic because the coefficients $\hat{w}$ are fitted to the training data. What this implies is that a small training error is not a good indicator of an appropriate model.

The **generalization (True) error** is the estimate of the actual loss and is the average over all possible (x, y) pairs weighted by how likely each of the data point is. This typically depends on the distribution of all the **structural parameters** (the coefficients of a regression model); and since we do not know the distribution of all the parameters, we cannot compute the generalization error.

The **test error** is an approximation of the true error and is what we can actually compute. This is arrived at by fitting the model to an unseen portion of the data. If the size of the test data is small, we would get a bad approximation of the true error. In such cases we can incorporate **cross-validation**.

Figure 3.1 depicts a simulation of polynomial regression models, with complexity varying from degree 1 to 30 on 100 training sets (randomly sampled), each of size 50. With each of these different training sets, we train 100 different models.

The models are then evaluated on the training set to get the train error and on the unseen data to get the test error.

The plotted errors show how the train and test errors vary as the model complexity increases.

In Fig. 3.1, the training errors decrease monotonically[2] as the learning algorithm gets more complex.

---

[2](of a function or quantity) varying in such a way that it either never decreases or never increases.

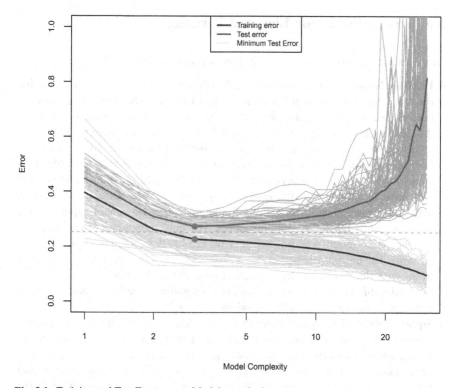

Fig. 3.1 Training and Test Error versus Model complexity

The test error initially starts decreasing, reaches a nadir and from there starts going up again. This change is marked by the orange circle *(sweet spot)*, corresponding to model complexity with polynomial degree 5. This is where the capacity of the algorithm is appropriate and provides a good compromise between bias and variance (discussed in the next section). The phenomenon of increasing test error for degrees of freedom larger than 5 is called overfitting, which is discussed in Sect. 3.7.

3.4   Irreducible Error, Bias, and Variance

Every learning algorithm is beset with three sources of error and they are

- **Intrinsic Noise**—In any prediction (or classification) model, we cannot determine the true and exact relation between the predictor and the dependent variables because we simply cannot realistically determine them. Consider, for example, the price of a house depends upon lot of factors which are measurable, i.e., the area, location, condition, etc., among many. However, there are many factors which may be either impossible to measure or may not be accurately measured, like, how somebody feels when the person about a house, personal relationship the owner may have with the buyer, etc., among many. Noise can also arise due to spurious data and measurement error. This information which we cannot capture is the noise, which is inherently present in data. The noise function has a mean and a variance (i.e., variation of house prices we are likely to see, based on the noise present). The unfortunate part is that we cannot control this error as it has nothing to do with the model or any estimation procedure. Therefore it is also known as **irreducible error**, because we cannot do anything to reduce this error and is represented by the bar in the left-hand plot of Fig. 3.2.
- **Squared Bias**—This quantity measures how closely the model's average prediction over all possible training sets, matches the target. Intuitively, it is how well the estimated model fits the true relationship between the predictor and the target. To understand this a little better, let us ask the question—if we consider different data sets of size m, what do I expect my fits to be? The answer is that there would exist a continuum of different possible fits to different data sets. And for these different fits, we will have an mean fit, averaged over all the model fits based on how likely they were to have appeared. Therefore the squared bias is the difference between the average fit and the true function.

$$Squared\ Bias(f_{\hat{w}}(x)) = f_{w_{true}}(x) - f_{\bar{w}}(x) \qquad (3.4.1)$$

$f_{\hat{w}}(x)$ is the estimated model
$f_{w_{true}}(x)$ is the true model
$f_{\bar{w}}(x)$ is the average of of all models based on how likely they were
In the center plot of Fig. 3.2, we consider a continuum of very simple fits called train functions, for different data sets and we average out these train functions to get a mean train function. The true function is represented by the blue regression line and the bias is represented as the shaded region, which is the difference between the true function and the average fit. Intuitively, bias can be interpreted as-"Is our model flexible enough on average, to capture the true relationship." It is also easy to interpret that oversimplified, low complexity models will have a high bias.
- **Variance**—This quantity measures how much the model's prediction fluctuates with different training sets of the given size. It is the tendency to learn random things irrespective of the real signal. To understand variance, let us ask this question—how different can our specific fits from specific data sets be different from the

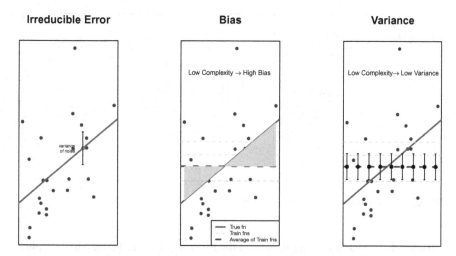

Fig. 3.2 The left-hand plot depicts the noise in the data, which has a mean and a variance. The center plot depicts the difference between the mean of all simple models and the true model, which depict a high bias. In the right-hand side, plot shows that a simple model has a low variance

expected fit? To understand, let us refer to the right-hand plot in Fig. 3.2, where we consider a continuum of simple fits from different data sets. Since we have considered a very simple function to fit different data sets, the variance of the average of the training functions are (more or less) equal. So in essence, if the specific fits had varied widely we would have erratic predictions, i.e., the model would be very sensitive to the data set under consideration; and that will be the source of error in the predictions.

Now, let us fit two complex polynomial models trained with two different data sets which are sampled from the same population. In Fig. 3.3 the dark-orange line is the true function. The blue and green lines are different fits of two, degree-25 polynomial models. It is apparent that the models have high variance, leading us to define **Variance** as **the difference of a specific fit from the expected average fit from all data sets**

$$Variance(f_{\hat{w}}(x)) = E_{train}[(f_{\hat{w}(train)}(x) - f_{\bar{w}}(x))^2] \qquad (3.4.2)$$

where
$f_{\hat{w}}(x)$ is the estimated model
E_{train} signifies the estimate over all training sets of size N
$f_{\hat{w}(train)}(x)$ is the fit on a specific training set
$f_{\bar{w}}(x)$ is what we expect to learn from overall training sets (average of all fits)
   Note: Be careful to distinguish between $\hat{w}$ and $\bar{w}$.
   If we consider a continuum of highly complex models with specific data sets, the average of all these models will not be a close representation of any one of the fits

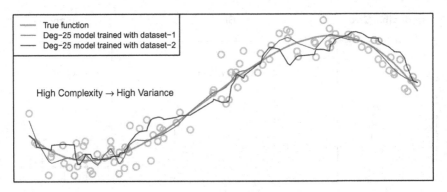

Fig. 3.3 Variance between two complex models

considered. The variation within each of the fits would be very large, which implies that *High Complexity models have High Variance*.

3.5   Bias–Variance Trade-off

As discussed in the previous section

- As model complexity increases, bias decreases
- As model complexity increases variance increases

We can also now say that-

- Bias Error—is the difference between the average prediction of our model and the correct value which we are trying to predict.
- Variance Error—is how much the predictions for a given point vary between different realizations of the model.

The bias–variance trade-off can be represented by the mean squared error as

$$MSE = Bias^2 + Variance + Irreducible\ Error \qquad (3.5.1)$$

All machine learning algorithms are intrinsically intertwined with bias and variance (alongwith the noise), and the goal is to find the *sweet spot*. The sweet spot *(the dark-orange circle in* Fig. 3.1) represents the appropriate level of complexity at which increase in bias results in reduction of variance. Any model complexity short of the sweet spot will result in an underfitted model and if we are overstepping the sweet spot, we are overfitting the model.

This implies that we need to find the bias and variance of our model to find the sweet spot. The challenge is that we cannot compute bias and variance as both are defined with respect to the true function and getting the fits from all the possible data sets which, we do not know.

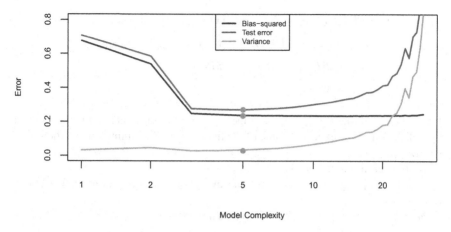

Fig. 3.4 Bias–variance trade-off

The good part is that even if we cannot compute them exactly, we can still optimize the trade-off between bias and variance.

In Fig. 3.4, a polynomial regression model (with degree 1 to 30) is trained with 100 different data sets, each having a sample size of 50. Each of these trained models are fitted to predict the unseen (test) data having a sample size of 1000. The average bias and variance respectively are calculated from the fitted models and plotted. As expected, the bias decreases monotonically and the variance increases. The test-MSE, initially decreases, but as the model becomes more complex (signifying overfitting, discussed in the next section), the error starts increasing. An overfitted model fits the noise present in the data and not the true relationships between the variables. It turns out that the polynomial model with degree 5 complexity has the lowest test-MSE and is identified by the 'sweet-spot', denoted by the orange circle.

3.6 Deriving the Expected Prediction Error

The derivation has two steps

- Decomposing the prediction error into Irreducible Error and MSE
- Decomposing MSE into Bias Error and Variance Error.

The loss function $L(y, f_{\hat{w}}(x))$ for a regression model is the squared error difference between the actual and predicted values, which is $(y - f_{\hat{w}_{train}}(x))^2$

We will denote the loss function as the expected train error and for the sake of convenience we will represent $f_{w_{true}}(x)$ as f, and $f_{\hat{w}_{train}}(x)$ as $\hat{f}$.

Also note that $(y - f)^2$ is the irreducible error ϵ^2 and ϵ has zero mean implying $E[\epsilon] = 0$ The loss function can now be written as

$$L(y, f_{\hat{w}}(x)) = E_{train}[(y - f_{w_{true}}(x) + f_{w_{true}}(x) - f_{\hat{w}_{train}}(x))^2]$$
$$= E_{train}[(y - f)^2] + 2E_{train}[(y - f)(f - \hat{f})] + E_{train}[(f - \hat{f})^2]$$
$$= \epsilon^2 + 2[E[\epsilon] \times E[f - \hat{f}] + MSE(\hat{f})$$
$$= \epsilon^2 + MSE(\hat{f})$$

(3.6.1)

It may be noted that $f_{\bar{w}}(x)$ is the average fit overall training sets and is represented by $\bar{f}$. This is also the expected value of the fit on a specific training set and therefore, $\bar{f} = E_{train}[\hat{f}]$.

By the definition of Bias, $[Bias(\hat{f})]^2 = (f - \bar{f})^2$.

$E_{train}[\bar{f} - \hat{f}] = \bar{f} - E_{train}[\hat{f}] = 0$ and by the definition of variance, $Var(\hat{f}) = E[(\hat{f} - \bar{f})^2]$

Now let us decompose $MSE(\hat{f})$ into bias and variance

$$MSE(\hat{f}) = E_{train}[(f - f)^2]$$
$$= E_{train}[((f - \bar{f}) + (\bar{f} - \hat{f}))^2]$$
$$= E_{train}[(f - \bar{f})^2 + 2E_{train}[(f - \bar{f})(\bar{f} - \hat{f})] + E_{train}[(\bar{f} - \hat{f})^2] \quad (3.6.2)$$
$$= [Bias(\hat{f})]^2 + 2(f - \bar{f})E_{train}[\bar{f} - \hat{f}] + E[(\hat{f} - \bar{f})^2]$$
$$= [Bias(\hat{f})]^2 + 0 + Var(\hat{f})$$

The expected prediction error can now be written as

$$L(y, f_{\hat{w}}(x)) = \epsilon^2 + MSE(\hat{f})$$
$$= \epsilon^2 + [Bias(\hat{f})]^2 + Var(\hat{f})$$

(3.6.3)

3.7 Underfitting and Overfitting

This brings us to consider the two most important challenges in machine learning—**underfitting** and **overfitting**. Underfitting occurs when the model does not fit the data very well resulting in its inability to capture the trend in the data. Overfitting occurs when the model describes the noise in the data rather than capturing the trend in the data.

Both these factors are inherently connected to the **capacity** of the model. We therefore exercise control over whether a model will overfit or underfit by altering its capacity. Models having low capacity may struggle to fit the training set and those with high capacity will overfit the data.

The hypothesis space of a learning algorithm is the set of functions the algorithm may select, as a possible solution. These set of functions may range from the most simple to the most complex. The algorithm is allowed to search through this hypothesis space and arrive at the true model capacity which is most appropriate for the task. It can be understood that an algorithm which is too simple will be unable to accomplish complex tasks and those with very high complexity may be an "overkill".

The model capacity is again dependent on two other factors—the model's **structural parameters** and its **tuning parameters**. The structural parameters are the estimates of the model's coefficients and parameter tuning is a process by which we optimize the parameters that impact the model and enable it to perform at its "best". To illustrate this, we can consider the *kNN* clustering algorithm, where we have to specify the number of centroids, $k's$ to be used. We do this by tuning the clustering algorithm and there are ways this can be done so that we minimize the errors.

To illustrate the capacities of predictive learning algorithms, we fit three polynomial regression models, in Fig. 3.5. The training data was generated synthetically by evaluating a degree-5 polynomial and adding some noise to the y values. We compare a linear predictor, a degree-5 predictor and a degree-25 predictor, all attempting to fit a model where the true underlying function is a degree-4 polynomial.

The simple linear function is completely unable to capture the underlying data and therefore it underfits. The degree-25 predictor oscillates erratically in the process of memorizing the properties of the training set. The degree-5 predictor, however, is the closest to the true function.

3.8 Regularization

Overfitting is associated with very large estimated (structural) parameters. Overfitting also results when the number of features is very high compared to the number of observations. To illustrate this, we consider Fig. 3.5 and calculate the absolute sum of the model coefficients (ℓ_1) for every 5th degree polynomial model.

```
Sum of model(deg-1)  coefficients =8.125628
Sum of model(deg-5)  coefficients =14.411696
Sum of model(deg-10) coefficients =20.569774
Sum of model(deg-15) coefficients =27.025744
Sum of model(deg-20) coefficients =32.022248
Sum of model(deg-25) coefficients =35.763115
```

Sum of the absolute values of the coefficients of each of the regression models, increase as the model capacity goes up. The measure of magnitude of the coefficients can be represented as

$$\ell_1 \ norm = |w_0| + |w_1| + \ldots + |w_n| = \sum_{j=0}^{n} |w_j| = \|w\|_1^1 \tag{3.8.1}$$

$$\ell_2 \ norm = w_0^2 + w_1^2 + \ldots + w_n^2 = \sum_{j=0}^{n} w_j^2 = \|w\|_2^2 \tag{3.8.2}$$

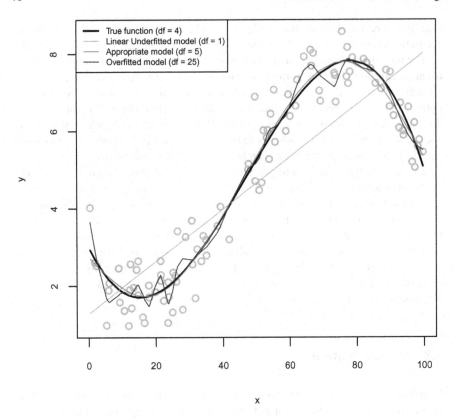

Fig. 3.5 Fitted models showing Underfitting and Overfitting. The linear function is unable to capture the underlying data and it is underfitting. The degree-25 model oscillates erratically and it overfits. The degree-5 predictor, however, is the closest to the true function

The objective behind choosing an algorithm is to reduce the total cost, represented by the loss function $L(y, f_{\hat{w}}(x))$. The loss function itself is dependent on

- How well the model fits the data
- Model capacity or the magnitude of the coefficients

i.e., Total cost = Measure of fit + measure of magnitude of coefficients

The measure of fit to training data in a regression model is the residual sum of squares (RSS) = $\sum_{i=1}^{n}(y_i - \hat{f}(x))^2$ and the measure of magnitude of coefficients is represented by the ℓ_1 / ℓ_2 norms. If we consider the ℓ_2 norm as representing the model's capacity, we can write

$$Total\ Cost = RSS(w) + \|w\|_2^2 \tag{3.8.3}$$

Our objective is to select the model's structural parameters w such that we minimize the total cost by using a weight decay, **regularization** parameter λ and selecting $\hat{w}$ so as to minimize the Cost-

$$Cost(w) = RSS(w) + \lambda||w||_2^2 \qquad (3.8.4)$$

When $\lambda = 0$, we impose no preference on the weights, and since the model does not have any regularization it results in an ordinary least squares model (for linear regression) and maximum likelihood model (for logistic regression).

Large value of λ forces the weights to become smaller and in the extreme case, when $\lambda = \infty$, we have no solution.

We thus define **regularization** as a modification we make to the learning algorithm which will reduce its generalization error (and not its training error). In other words, regularization discourages complex interpretations of the underlying data even if they fit well to the training data.

From the bias–variance trade-off viewpoint

- Large λ: High Bias, Low Variance (Low complexity)
- Small λ: Low Bias, High Variance (High complexity)

We will go through regularization in detail in the subsequent sections dedicated to ridge and lasso regularization techniques.

3.9 Hyperparameters

In machine learning, we define hyparameters (in contrast to its structural parameters) as those which cannot directly learn from the data. These parameters, as stated earlier, are inherent to the model and are used to control the behavior of the model. Some of the hyperparameters in a learning model are

- The number of centroids in a clustering algorithm
- The learning rate of an algorithm
- The number of leaves or depth of a tree in tree-based algorithms
- The strength of weight decay in regularization

By allowing the learning algorithm to iterate over a range of values, the "best" values of the hyperparameters may be obtained, which decreases the loss function on unseen data.

We will learn about hyperparameters in later chapters as we dig deeper in under-standing the concepts of individual machine learning algorithms.

3.10 Cross-Validation

For large data sets, the original sample of data may be partitioned into a training set on which to train the model, a validation set on which to validate our models and a test set to evaluate our trained model.

However, when we do not have large samples of data, cross-validation is particularly useful. Cross-validation (CV) allows us to select a model and estimate the error in the model. When we select a model using CV, we do that by selecting one model from a range of other models, trained on a particular data set and/or by selecting the hyperparameters of a particular model.

The CV process involves partitioning the data into k-folds consisting of k number of equal sized subsamples of the original data set. From the k subsamples, the first $k - 1$ subsamples are used to train the model and the remaining one subsample is used to validate the model. The process is repeated k times and an average error is arrived at across all the k trials.

The question arises as to how do we choose the right value of k? To answer this, we need to recollect that a lower value of k increases bias and a higher value of k increases variance. However, a general thumb rule is to use $k = 10$.

CV allows us to approximate the model error as close as possible to the generalization error. CV also allows us to observe the variance in prediction from fold to fold. If the variance between the predicted values is high, it could tell us that the model is overfitting.

After performing CV with different models and different hyperparameters, we chose the one model that has the best performance with respect to its error and its variance. We then need to rebuild the model from the training data set and evaluate on the test data set. If the model does not work well on the test data set, we need to reevaluate our list of models and the tuning parameters.

Leave one out cross-validation (LOOCV) uses a single observation from the original sample as the validation data, and the remaining observations are used as the model training data. In essence, we are training the model with one observation less and validating the model on the left out observation. The k value here is the number of observations present in the data. LOOCV may be used when the size of the data is very small as otherwise it can be computationally expensive because the training process is repeated by the number of observations present in the data set.

3.11 Maximum Likelihood Estimation

Rather than estimating an entire distribution, sometimes it is sufficient to find a single "best-case" value for a parameter. We call this a **point estimate**. We will briefly discuss a widely used point estimate, the maximum likelihood (ML) estimate.

Earlier in Sect. 3.7, we had seen that a model function f_w is defined by its structural parameters w, called weights. But where did these weights (estimators) come from?

We would like to have some principle from which we can derive "good" weights (for different f_w) and then analyze it's bias and variance.

Maximum likelihood estimation (MLE) is a method of estimating these structural parameters of a model given the data (observation), by finding those parameter values, which maximize the likelihood of the data (observations). Intuitively, this maximizes the "agreement" of the selected model with the observed data.

Let us consider a sample set $x_1, x_2, \ldots, x_n$ of n independent and identically distributed observations, (i.e., n data sets), coming from a unknown data distribution $p_{data}(x)$. Let p_{model} $(\mathbf{x}; \mathbf{w})$ be a parametric family of data distributions indexed by $\mathbf{w}$. In other words, $p_{model}(\mathbf{x}; \mathbf{w})$ maps the arrangement in $\mathbf{x}$ to the true probability $p_{data}(\mathbf{x})$.

If we consider the observed values $x_1, x_2, \ldots, x_n$ to be fixed and w as the variable, the **likelihood** function can be written as

$$\log \mathcal{L}(w; x_1, \ldots, x_n) = \sum_{i=1}^{n} \log p_{model}(x_i \mid w)$$

$$= \prod_{i=1}^{n} p_{model}(x_i \mid w)$$

(3.11.1)

For convenience, we take the natural logarithm of the likelihood function and write the same equation as

$$\log \mathcal{L}(w; x_1, \ldots, x_n) = \sum_{i=1}^{n} \log p_{model}(x_i \mid w) \qquad (3.11.2)$$

The method of maximum likelihood tries to find a value of $\mathbf{w}$ that maximizes $\sum_{i=1}^{n} \log f(x_i \mid w)$ and this method of estimation defines a **maximum likelihood estimator (MLE)** as

$$\{\hat{w}_{\text{mle}}\} = \{\arg \max_{w \in \Theta} \hat{\ell}(w; x_1, \ldots, x_n)\}$$

$$= \{\arg \max_{w \in \Theta}\} \sum_{i=1}^{m} log[p_{model}(x_i; w)]$$

(3.11.3)

MLE, therefore, is a technique to find the most likely function that explains the observed data.

To understand this better let us do the math and code it in R (Fig. 3.6).

We create a set of data points defined by the parameters β and σ.

```
sigma = 0.1
beta = 0.3
x <- runif(100, min = 1, max = 10)
y <- 0 + 0.3*x + rnorm(100, mean = 0, sd = sigma)
```

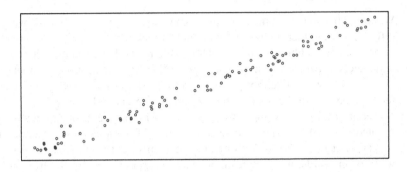

Fig. 3.6 A normally distributed set of data points to illustrate the maximum likelihood estimation

We assume that the data belongs to a Gaussian distribution and the probability distribution function is represented as

$$\frac{1}{\sqrt{2\pi\sigma^2}} e^{-(\frac{(y_i - \beta x_i)^2}{2\sigma^2})}$$

We would like to seek the parameters β and σ by maximizing the probability of the data. The likelihood function can be written as

$$\mathcal{L} = \prod_{i=1}^{n} \frac{1}{\sqrt{2\pi\sigma^2}} e^{-(\frac{(y_i - \beta x_i)^2}{2\sigma^2})}$$

$$\log \mathcal{L} = -\frac{n}{2}\log(2\pi) - \frac{n}{2}\log(\sigma^2) - \frac{1}{2\sigma^2}\sum_{i=1}^{n}(y_i - \beta x_i)^2$$

The above equation can be coded as below. The "param" argument is the parameter values—β and σ.

```
neg_log_lik <- function(param, y, X) {
    m <- nrow(X)
    n <- ncol(X)
    beta <- param[1:n]
    sigma <- param[n + 1]
    e <- y - X %*% beta
    log_like <- -0.5 * m * log(2 * pi) - 0.5 * m * log(sigma^2) -
        ((t(e) %*% e)/(2 * sigma^2))
    return(-log_like)
}
```

We can find the parameters $(\beta_0, \beta_1, \sigma)$ that specify the maximum log-likelihood by an optimization algorithm below. The β values from the optimization output and the ordinary least squares (OLS) output compare well with the initial values.

```
mle <- optim(fn = neg_log_lik,
             par = c(1,1,1),
             hessian = TRUE,
             y = y,
             X = cbind(1, x),
             method = "BFGS")
mle$par
```

```
[1] 0.000758898 0.298665195 0.104088433
```

```
lm(y ~ x)$coef
```

```
(Intercept)                x
0.0007598116 0.2986651257
```

3.12 Gradient Descent

Most learning algorithms use one very important optimization procedure called the **gradient descent**. This was discussed in Sect. 1.8, here we will try to understand it from a fundamental point of view.

In regression we try to find the line/plane, which minimizes the sum of the Euclidean distances to the data points as shown in Fig. 3.7.

We obtain the regression plane which minimizes the distance between the data points and their orthogonal projections onto the plane. In other words, we try to reduce the cost (as defined in Sect. 1.7). Mathematically, this means, we are seeking to find a regression weight $\mathbf{w}$, which minimizes the objective or cost function $f(w)$-

$$f(w) = \|y - Hw\|^2 \tag{3.12.1}$$

Gradient descent repeatedly performs two steps to generate a sequence of parameter estimates $w^{(t=1)}, w^{(t=2)}, \ldots, w^{(t=n)}$

- At iteration t = t, calculate $\frac{\partial f(w^{t=t})}{\partial w}$, which is the gradient of $f(w)$ at t = t and
- Takes a step in the opposite direction with a step increment η times the gradient, such that

$$w^{(t=t+1)} \leftarrow w^{(t=t)} - \eta \frac{\partial f(w^{(t=t)})}{\partial w}$$

In practice, we stop when the Euclidean norm, $\|\frac{\partial f(w^{(t=t)})}{\partial w}\|$ is less than a defined *tolerance* value. The gradient of $f(w^{(t=t)})$ is $-2H^T(y - Hw)$- (Refer *Eqn* 1.7.2).

Gradient descent tries to minimize the function $f(w)$ by solving a sequence of simple quadratic approximations to $f(w)$. It makes use of Taylor's theorem, which states

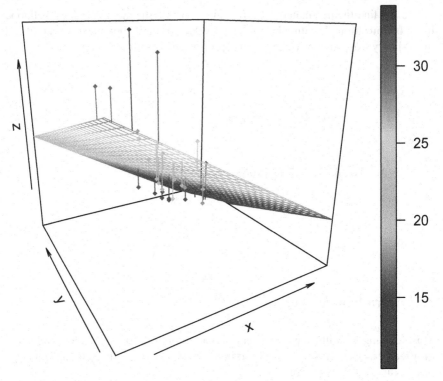

Fig. 3.7 We try to find a regression plane such that the sum of the Euclidean distances from the points to the plane are minimum

that if a function is differentiable at a point x, than there exists a linear approximation at the point x, defined by a function g_1 such that-

$$f(w) = f(x) + f(x)(w - x) + g_1(w)(w - x) \qquad (3.12.2)$$

3.13   Building a Machine Learning Algorithm

We have discussed the constructs that go in to make a machine learning algorithm. Let us concisely go through the recipe for building machine learning algorithms.

As you may appreciate now, most learning algorithms start with a data set which is i.i.d., from which the model is constructed. The model needs to be evaluated for overfitting/underfitting. This is directly related to the capacity of the model.

The loss function of the model is a combination of its fit and its capacity. We therefore need to regularize our model to find an optimal balance between the fit and the model capacity by an optimization process. If the model is linear it has a closed form solution[3] and we can use appropriate optimization algorithms to optimize the loss function; however, if the model is nonlinear the loss function may not be optimized in closed form and would require an iterative numerical optimization procedure like gradient descent or coordinate descent. The model capacity defines the structural parameters of the model.

The hyperparameters of the model are inherent to the model itself which controls its behavior. We have to search out the best parameter values of the model by a process known as model tuning. This is achieved by CV.

Finally, after arriving at the "best" algorithm, we evaluate the model on the unseen data and compare the results with other algorithms.

This recipe is applicable to both supervised and unsupervised learning algorithms.

3.13.1 Challenges in Learning Algorithms

Learning algorithms are well suited for a wide variety of problems when the data set is of a finite size; but emerging areas like AI (recognizing voice, images), Genetics (dealing with gigantic genetic data), Robotics, and IoT, involve dealing with very high-dimensional data. Arriving at generalizations in such high-dimensional spaces is often difficult but not insurmountable.

3.13.2 Curse of Dimensionality and Feature Engineering

One of the biggest challenges in machine learning is the **curse of dimensionality** and it refers to the fact that most learners which work very well in low dimensions become hard to control with high-dimensional data which in turn makes it exponentially difficult to generalize.

What happens is that if there are irrelevant features in the input data, the noise from these features can completely overrun the signal from the relevant features. This phenomenon is known as the curse of dimensionality.[4]

Suppose, that in order to make a good prediction, our learning algorithm needs to distinguish (produce a substantially different answer) between 10 different values of each of $n = 2$ variables. Then it may need to distinguish between $10^2 = 100$ different configurations of the two-dimensional input data. With n dimensions and v values to be distinguished, v^n different configurations need to be distinguished.

A small data set having many features will have a large number of distinct configurations, leading us to seriously undersample the data space.

---

[3] An equation is said to have a closed form solution if it solves a given problem in terms of functions and mathematical operations from a given data set.

[4] William of Ockham's principle states that, "entities should not be multiplied unnecessarily", circa 14th century.

Sometimes, it is also possible that the input data may not be in a form that is tractable to learning. In such cases, however, it may be possible to construct features from the raw data using the domain knowledge of an subject matter expert. The process of constructing features from data using domain knowledge is called **feature engineering**. A simple example of feature engineering is considering a data on house prices having a feature "number of bedrooms", which ranges from 1 to 3. If we want to inflate the importance of higher number of bedrooms as a feature, it would be a good idea to consider the squared number of bedrooms, where the values would become 1, 4, and 9.

Feature engineering is often one of the most interesting aspects of machine learning where intuition, domain knowledge, and "art" is as important as the algorithm and where most of the time and effort is spent.

Dimensionality reduction and feature engineering are not discussed in detail but touched upon where relevant in this book.

3.14   Conclusion

In the first three chapters, we discussed the required basic concepts in linear algebra, probability and distributions, and machine learning. We are now ready to get to the bottom of some of the basic machine learning algorithms.

Chapter 4
Regression

*An approximate answer to the right problem is worth a good
deal more than an exact answer to an approximate problem.*

−John Tukey

4.1 Linear Regression

Linear regression with one variable x is also known as **univariate linear regression**
or **simple linear regression**. Simple linear regression is used to predict a single
output from a single input. This is an example of **supervised learning**, which means
that the data is labeled, i.e., the output values are known in the training data. Let us
fit a line through the data using simple linear regression as shown in Fig. 4.1.

4.1.1 Hypothesis Function

Linear regression with many variables x is known as **multivariate linear regression**
or **multiple linear regression**. The hypothesis function for linear regression can then
be written as

$$h_w(x) = w_0 + w_1 x_1 + w_2 x_2 + \cdots + w_n x_n + \epsilon$$

$$= \sum_{j=0}^{n} w_j x_j + \epsilon \tag{4.1.1}$$

© Springer Nature Singapore Pte Ltd. 2017
A. Ghatak, *Machine Learning with R*, DOI 10.1007/978-981-10-6808-9_4

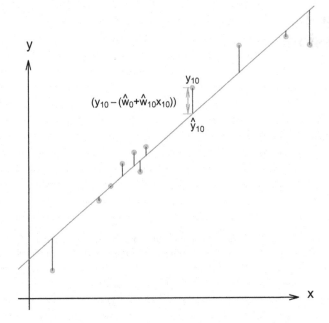

Fig. 4.1 Ordinary least squares fit for simple linear regression. The green line is the regression line and the blue lines are the difference between the actual values and the predicted values, i.e., the error

4.1.2 Cost Function

Now, there may exist many such values of w_0, w_1, ..., w_n for which we would have many such regression lines. Our objective is to find the regression line which minimizes the cost function, which in the case of regression is the residual sum of squares (RSS). The cost function for a generalized regression equation can be written as

$$RSS(w) = \sum_{i=1}^{m}(y^{(i)} - (\sum_{j=0}^{n} w_j x_j^{(i)}))^2$$

$$= \frac{1}{2m}\sum_{i=1}^{m}(y^{(i)} - h_w(x^{(i)})^2$$

$$= (y - Hw)^T(y - Hw) \qquad -(\text{refer Eq. 1.6.2}) \qquad (4.1.2)$$

The $\frac{1}{2}$ is there for convenience, which becomes useful when we take the first derivative of the function.

$x^{(i)}$, $y^{(i)}$ are the ith row values of x and y in the data set, respectively, and m is the number of training examples, and n is the number of input variables

It may be recalled that

- output y is a scalar
- inputs $\mathbf{x} = \mathbf{x}[1], \mathbf{x}[2], ..., \mathbf{x}[n]$ is a n-dimensional vector
- the jth input, $\mathbf{x}[j]$ is a scalar
- the jth feature, $h_j(\mathbf{x})$ is a scalar
- the input of the ith data point, $\mathbf{x\_i}$, is a vector
- the jth input of the ith data point, $\mathbf{x}_i[j]$, is a scalar

4.2 Linear Regression as Ordinary Least Squares

In Fig. 4.1, the fit is calculated by minimizing the sum of squared errors.

If $\hat{y}_i = \hat{w}_0 + \hat{w}_1 x_i$, then $e_i = y_i - \hat{y}_i$ is the error for the ith observation.

For all observations, we can write

$$
\begin{aligned}
RSS &= e_1^2 + e_2^2 + \cdots + e_m^2 \\
&= (y_1 - \hat{w}_0 - \hat{w}_1 x_1)^2 + (y_2 - \hat{w}_0 - \hat{w}_1 x_2)^2 + \cdots + (y_n - \hat{w}_0 - \hat{w}_1 x_m)^2 \\
&= \sum_{i=1}^{m} (y_i - \hat{w}_0 - \hat{w}_1 x_i)^2
\end{aligned}
$$

(4.2.1)

We need to minimize RSS and we do that by differentiating with respect to w_0 and w_1, respectively.

$$
\begin{aligned}
\frac{\partial RSS}{\partial w_0} &= \frac{\partial}{\partial w_0} \sum_{i=1}^{m} (y_i - \hat{w}_0 - \hat{w}_1 x_i)^2 \\
&= -2 \sum_{i=1}^{m} (y_1 - w_0 - w_1 x_i)
\end{aligned}
$$

(4.2.2)

and

$$
\begin{aligned}
\frac{\partial RSS}{\partial w_1} &= \frac{\partial}{\partial w_0} \sum_{i=1}^{m} (y_i - \hat{w}_0 - \hat{w}_1 x_i)^2 \\
&= -2 \sum_{i=1}^{m} x_i (y_1 - w_0 - w_1 x_i)
\end{aligned}
$$

(4.2.3)

Equating Eq. 4.2.2 to zero gives us

$$
\begin{aligned}
w_0 &= \frac{\sum_{i=1}^{m} y_i}{m} - w_1 \frac{\sum_{i=1}^{m} x_i}{m} \\
&= \bar{y} - w_1 \bar{x}
\end{aligned}
$$

(4.2.4)

Equating Eq. 4.2.3 to zero gives us

$$0 = \sum_{i=1}^{m} y_i x_i - \sum_{i=1}^{m} w_0 x_i - \sum_{i=1}^{m} w_1 x_i^2$$

substituting the value of w_0 from above

$$w_1 \sum_{i=1}^{m} x_i^2 = \sum_{i=1}^{m} y_i x_i - \left[\frac{\sum_{i=1}^{m} y_i}{m} - w_1 \frac{\sum_{i=1}^{m} x_i}{m}\right] \sum_{i=1}^{m} x_i \qquad (4.2.5)$$

$$w_1 \sum_{i=1}^{m} x_i^2 = \sum_{i=1}^{m} y_i x_i - \frac{\sum_{i=1}^{m} y_i \sum_{i=1}^{m} x_i}{m} - w_1 \frac{(\sum_{i=1}^{m} x_i)^2}{m}$$

$$w_1 = \frac{\sum_{i=1}^{m} y_i x_i - \frac{\sum_{i=1}^{m} y_i \sum_{i=1}^{m} x_i}{m}}{\sum_{i=1}^{m} x_i^2 - \frac{(\sum_{i=1}^{m} x_i)^2}{m}}$$

In matrix form, Eqs. 4.2.4 and 4.2.5 can be combined to arrive at the ordinary least squares (OLS) regression equation

$$\mathbf{w} = (\mathbf{X}^\top \mathbf{X})^{-1} \mathbf{X}^\top \mathbf{Y} \qquad (4.2.6)$$

Let us consider fitting a model using some example data and fit $Y = w_0 + w_1 * x_1$. We will calculate the OLS coefficients using Eq. 4.2.6, $(\mathbf{X}^\top \mathbf{X})^{-1} \mathbf{X}^\top \mathbf{Y}$ (Table 4.1).

```
# Let's set up our data with the constant column of 1's
set.seed(61)
x <- runif(100, 0, 10)
X <- cbind(1, x)

y <- runif(100, 5, 100)
eps <- rnorm(100, 0, 0.5)
# add some noise to the output
y <- (y + eps)

## t(X) transposes the matrix X
## solve(X) calculates the inverse of matrix X
## use %*% for matrix multiplication

OLS_coef <- solve(t(X) %*% X) %*% t(X) %*% y
lm_coef <- lm(y~X)$coef
```

Table 4.1 Coefficients calculated using OLS equation and lm function in R

	Intercept (w_0)	w_1
OLS_coef	49.26502	0.0224736
lm_coef	49.26502	0.0224736

4.3 Linear Regression as Maximum Likelihood

As stated in Sect. 3.11, linear regression can be justified as a maximum likelihood procedure. The estimation of weights as we had done earlier was to choose a $\mathbf{w}$ which would minimize the MSE.

We now revisit linear regression from the point of view of maximum likelihood estimation. We now think of the model as producing a conditional distribution $p(y \mid x)$. To derive the linear regression algorithm, we define

$$p(y \mid x) = \mathcal{N}(y \mid \hat{y}(\mathbf{x}, \mathbf{w}), \sigma^2) \tag{4.3.1}$$

The function $\hat{y}(\mathbf{x}, \mathbf{w})$ gives the prediction of the mean of the Gaussian.
We can write the likelihood of Eq. 4.2.1 as the product of the probabilities

$$
\begin{aligned}
\mathcal{L}(p(y \mid x)) &= \prod_{i=1}^{m} \sqrt{(2\pi\sigma^2)} \, exp(-\frac{1}{2}\frac{(y_i - \mathbf{w}x_i)^2}{\sigma^2}) \\
&= (2\pi\sigma^2)^{m/2} exp(-\frac{1}{2\sigma^2} \sum_{i=1}^{m}(y_i - \mathbf{w}x_i)^2)
\end{aligned}
\tag{4.3.2}
$$

The log-likelihood from Eq. 4.3.2 follows:

$$\ell\ell(p(y \mid x)) = log((2\pi\sigma^2)^{m/2} exp(-\frac{1}{2\sigma^2}\sum_{i=1}^{m}(y_i - \mathbf{w}x_i)^2))$$

$$\sum_{i=1}^{m} log\, p(y^{(i)} \mid x^{(i)}; \mathbf{w}) = -mlog\sigma - \frac{m}{2}log(2\pi) - \sum_{i=1}^{m}\frac{\|\hat{y}^{(i)} - y^{(i)}\|^2}{2\sigma^2} \tag{4.3.3}$$

As

$$MSE_{train} = \frac{1}{m}\sum_{i=1}^{m}\|\hat{y}^{(i)} - y^{(i)}\|^2 \tag{4.3.4}$$

we can see that maximizing the log-likelihood with respect to $\mathbf{w}$ yields the same estimate of the parameters as does minimizing the MSE.

The gradient descent tries to find the parameters $\mathbf{w}$ so as to find the lowest MSE, which we explore in the next section.

4.4 Gradient Descent

4.4.1 Gradient of RSS

Elaborating from Sect. 4.1.2, the gradient descent algorithm tries to find the parameters (*weights*), which would result in the minimum cost. The steps involved are:

$$
\frac{\partial}{\partial w}(RSS(w)) = \frac{\partial}{\partial w}(\frac{1}{2m}\sum_{i=1}^{m}(y^{(i)} - h_w(x^{(i)}))^2)
$$

$$
= -\frac{1}{m}\sum_{i=1}^{n}(y^{(i)} - h_w(x^{(i)})x^{(i)} \tag{4.4.1}
$$

$$
= -2H^T(y - Hw) \qquad \text{-refer Eq. 1.7.1}
$$

4.4.2 Closed Form Solution

$$
\frac{\partial}{\partial w}RSS(w) = -2H^T(y - Hw) = 0
$$

Solving for w yields the parameters as derived by the method of ordinary least squares.

$$
\hat{w} = (H^T H)^{-1}(H^T)y \tag{4.4.2}
$$

4.4.3 Step-by-Step Batch Gradient Descent

In this procedure, we update the weights with every input

$$
while \; \|\frac{\partial}{\partial w}RSS(w^{(t)})\| > \nu
$$

for features in j = 0, 1, .., n

$$
\frac{\partial}{\partial w}RSS(w_j^{(t)}) = -\frac{1}{m}\sum_{i=1}^{m}(y^{(i)} - h_w(x_j^{(i)}))(x_j^{(t)})
$$

$$
w_j^{(t+1)} \leftarrow w_j^{(t)} - \eta\frac{\partial}{\partial w}RSS(w_j^{(t)})
$$

$$
w_j^{(t+1)} \leftarrow w_j^{(t)} + 2\eta H^T(y - Hw^{(t)})
$$

η is the step size

The norm of the gradient of the cost is what we try to minimize, by a defined *tolerance* value and is defined as

$$\left\| \frac{\partial}{\partial w} RSS(w^{(t)}) \right\| = \sqrt{\frac{\partial}{\partial w} RSS(w_0^{(t)})^2 + \frac{\partial}{\partial w} RSS(w_1^{(t)})^2 + \cdots + \frac{\partial}{\partial w} RSS(w_m^{(t)})^2}$$

$$(4.4.3)$$

4.4.4 Writing the Batch Gradient Descent Application

The batch gradient descent algorithm as described above sums up the gradient terms over all the *m* cases in the data before modifying the parameters. Now let us get down to writing an application for executing batch gradient descent, step by step.

The following four functions will define our batch gradient descent application-

The *data_matrix* function accepts the selected features and adds the constant column of "ones" and scales the features before returning as a matrix. Scaling the data ensures faster convergence during gradient descent.

```
data_matrix <- function(data, features, output){
  scaled_feature_matrix <- data.frame(scale(data[features]), row.names=NULL)
  length <- nrow(data)
  scaled_features <- as.matrix(cbind('Intercept' = rep(1, length),
                                     scaled_feature_matrix[, features]
                                    )
                              )
  output <- as.matrix(scale(data[output]))
  return(list(scaled_features, output))
}
```

The *predict_output* function accepts the feature data and a list of "weights" corresponding to each feature and returns the predicted values.

```
predict_output = function(feature_matrix, weights) {
  predictions = (as.matrix(feature_matrix)) %*% weights
  return(predictions)
}
```

The *featureDerivative* function calculates the gradient of the RSS at each feature.

```
featureDerivative = function(errors, features) {
  derivative = -1/nrow(features) * (t(features) %*% errors)
  return(derivative)
}
```

This function performs a step-by-step gradient descent and converges if the square root of the squared sums of each of the partial gradients (ℓ_2 *norm*) is less than the defined tolerance. It returns the computed weights for each feature and the number of iterations it took to converge.

Table 4.2 First five rows of selected features from the house data

Price	Bedrooms	sqft_living
221900	3	1180
538000	3	2570
180000	2	770
604000	4	1960
510000	3	1680
1225000	4	5420

```
regression_gradient_descent = function(feature_matrix, output,
    initial_weights, step_size, tolerance) {
    converged = FALSE
    weights = initial_weights
    i = 0
    while (!converged) {
        predictions = predict_output(feature_matrix, weights)
        errors = predictions - output
        gradient = featureDerivative(errors, feature_matrix)
        gradient_norm = sqrt(sum(gradient^2))
        weights = weights + step_size * gradient
        if (gradient_norm < tolerance) {
            converged = TRUE
        }
        i = i + 1
    }
    return(list(weights = weights, Iters = i))
}
```

We consider a data set consisting of housing prices in King County, Portland, Oregon (KC house data), which includes homes sold between May 2014 and May 2015 and is available at kaggle.[1] The data set has 21, 613 observations and 21 features however, for simplicity, we select the dependent variable *price*, and predictor variables *sqft_living*, *bedrooms* (Table 4.2).

```
kc_house_data <- read.csv(paste(file_path, "kc_house_data.csv",
    sep = ""))
house_data <- kc_house_data[, c("price", "bedrooms", "sqft_living")]
```

Let us partition the data set into training and test data sets

```
set.seed(22)
inTrain <- createDataPartition(house_data$price, p = 0.5, list = F)

house_train_data = house_data[inTrain,]
house_test_data  = house_data[-inTrain,]
```

---

[1] https://www.kaggle.com/harlfoxem/housesalesprediction, downloaded on May 11, 2017, 8:17 am IST.

Table 4.3 Calculated weights from our gradient descent model

	Price
Intercept	0.000
sqft_living	−0.149
Bedrooms	0.789

Define the features and the response.

```
my_features <- c("bedrooms", "sqft_living")
my_output <- "price"
```

Construct the feature matrix, the response matrix and set the initial weights, step size, and the tolerance.

```
feature_matrix = data_matrix(house_train_data,
                             my_features,
                             my_output)[[1]]

output_matrix = data_matrix(house_train_data,
                            my_features,
                            my_output)[[2]]

initial_weights = c(0, 0, 0)
step_size = 0.01
tolerance = 1e-5
```

Finally, our own gradient descent algorithm returns the feature weights (Table 4.3).

```
weights = regression_gradient_descent(feature_matrix,
                                      output_matrix,
                                      initial_weights,
                                      step_size,
                                      tolerance)
```

```
[1] "Number of iterations to converge = 2484"
```

We can cross-check the values with OLS regression in R

```
scaled_house_data <- data.frame(scale(house_train_data))
lm(price ~ ., data = scaled_house_data)$coef
```

To make our work easier, R has a "gdescent" function—gdescent(f, grad_f, X, y, alpha, iter, tol, ...) in the *gettingtothebottom* package. It allows us to define the objective function f, the gradient of the objective function grad_f, feature matrix X, the response vector y, the step size alpha, the number of iterations iter, and the tolerance (in our case, this is the norm of the gradient vector) tol for determining convergence. We will compare our results with this function in R (Table 4.4).

Table 4.4 Summary of multiple linear regression in R

	Estimate	Std. error	t value	Pr (>|t|)
(Intercept)	0.000	0.007	0.00	1
Bedrooms	−0.149	0.008	−17.79	0
sqft_living	0.789	0.008	94.16	0

```
library(gettingtothebottom)
X <- as.matrix(feature_matrix[, -1])
y <- as.vector(output_matrix)

# initialise the weights
b <- c(0, 0, 0)

# define the objective function
f <- function(X, y, b) {
    (1/2) * norm(y - X %*% b, "F")^2
}

# Calculate gradient of the objective function
grad_f <- function(X, y, b) {
    t(X) %*% (X %*% b - y)
}
```

```
gradient_descent <- gdescent(f,
                             grad_f,
                             X, y,
                             alpha = 10e-5,
                             iter = 10e7,
                             tol = 1e-5)
```

```
Minimum function value:
 2671.742

Intercept:
 -2.073897e-17

Coefficient(s):
 -0.1489809 0.7885384
```

It turns out that we get the same results.

Convergence depends on the values of the step size and the tolerance. A higher value of step size may lead to non-convergence, and a lower tolerance value might take a long time to converge. A general thumb rule is to start with a higher step size and a low convergence criterion, and keep changing the values.

In the **Batch Gradient Descent** algorithm described above, the algorithm sums up the gradient terms over all the m cases in the data before modifying the parameters. For a large size data set say, $m = 1e20$, this would take a long time to converge. In such cases, stochastic gradient descent is a very good option.

4.4.5   Writing the Stochastic Gradient Descent Application

In stochastic gradient descent, the algorithm selects a single observation at random (instead of sweeping through all the cases, in batch gradient descent), from the data set and starts modifying the parameters right away. This process is repeated and the weights modified, till it has worked through the entire data set. It then repeats the above procedure for the number of iterations defined.

```
sgd<-function(x, y, betas, iters, lambda)
{
  beta<-as.matrix(cbind(rep(betas[1], iters),
                        rep(betas[2], iters),
                        rep(betas[3],iters))
                 )

  for (i in 2:iters)
  {
    m <- nrow(x)
    sample_num <- sample.int(m, 1)
    row_x <- x[sample_num,]
    row_y <- y[sample_num]

    beta[i, 1] <- beta[i-1, 1] - (lambda*(beta[i-1, 1] +
                                    beta[i-1, 2]*row_x[[1]] +
                                    beta[i-1, 3]*row_x[[2]] -
                                    row_y)
                                 )
    beta[i, 2] <- beta[i-1, 2] - (lambda*(beta[i-1, 1] +
                                    beta[i-1, 2]*row_x[[1]] +
                                    beta[i-1,3]*row_x[[2]] -
                                    row_y)*row_x[[1]]
                                 )
    beta[i, 3] <- beta[i-1,3] - lambda*(beta[i-1, 1] +
                                    beta[i-1, 2]*row_x[[1]] +
                                    beta[i-1,3]*row_x[[2]] -
                                    row_y)*row_x[[2]]
  }
  return(beta);
}
```

Let us apply the above function to our feature_matrix and compare the results with the standard multiple regression function in R (Table 4.5).

```
betas = c(0, 0, 0)
iters = 3000
lambda = 0.0001
weights = sgd(feature_matrix[, -1],
              output_matrix,
              betas,
              iters = iters,
              lambda = lambda)
```

It may be observed that the parameter outputs from a stochastic gradient descent are not exactly the same as the regression equation output but it is very close. In fact,

Table 4.5 Coefficients obtained from our SGD model and linear regression model in R

	Intercept	sqft_living	Bedrooms
SGD	0.0028	0.0704	0.1802
lm	0.0000	−0.1490	0.7885

the stochastic gradient generally hovers around the local minima without actually converging. For most practical purposes, this suffices when we are using large data sets.

We now have a fair understanding of linear regression. However, an important aspect of linear regression is the validity of certain assumptions, which need to hold true. We will go through these assumptions in the next section.

4.5 Linear Regression Assumptions

For the regression algorithms to be actually usable, the model should conform to the assumptions of linear regression, which are

1. Linear Relationship: The response and the predictors have a linear relationship. To test this relationship, we plot the residuals versus the predicted (or *fitted*) values. If there exists any particular pattern in the plot, this would indicate presence of nonlinearity. Consider the plot in Fig. 4.2.

There is a pronounced nonlinearity in the data, which can be seen and the true regression model is of the form

$$y = w_0 + w_1 \times x + w_2 \times x^2 + w_3 \times x^3 + w_4 \times x^4 + w_5 \times x^5 \qquad (4.5.1)$$

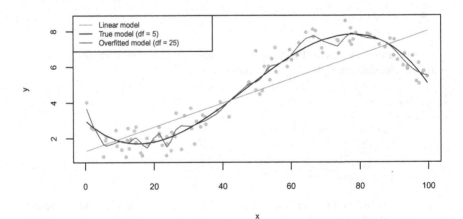

Fig. 4.2 Model fitting to a nonlinear data set

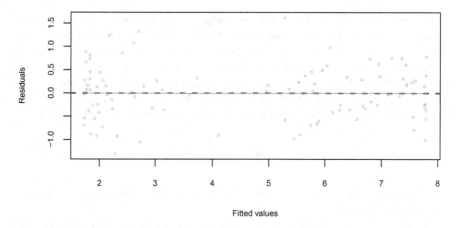

Fig. 4.3 Residual versus fitted values

However, this does not mean that the relationship is not linear. Evidence of this can be found in Fig. 4.3, where the plot between fitted values and the residuals (i.e., the "noise" or random disturbance in the relationship between the independent variables and the dependent variable) of the polynomial regression model does not show any pattern and the red line shows a smooth fit to the residuals.

2. Residuals have zero mean:

```
mean(fit$residuals)
```

```
[1] -1.404042e-19
```

3. No autocorrelation of residuals: This implies that the residuals $\epsilon_1, \epsilon_2, \cdots, \epsilon_n$ are uncorrelated. Correlation between the error terms frequently occurs with *time series* data. The 'dwtest' function in the *lmtest* package, tests the null hypothesis-autocorrelation of the residuals is 0.

```
(lmtest::dwtest(fit))$p.value
```

```
[1] 0.3654994
```

The p-value is >0.05, and therefore we accept the null hypothesis that autocorrelation is 0.

4. Homoscedasticity of residuals:

The assumption of homoscedasticity implying "equal variance" describes a situation in which the error term is the same across all values of the independent variables. Heteroscedasticity (which is the violation of homoscedasticity) is present when the size of the error term differs across values of an independent variable.

Existence of homoscedasticity can be visually detected in Fig. 4.3—the red line is more or less straight and the residuals do not seem to increase as the fitted values increase. The inference here is that there exists equal variance in the residuals.

5. Absence of collinearity within the independent variables: Collinearity refers to the situation when two or more independent variables are closely related to one another. This assumption is important as the presence of collinearity can make it difficult to separate out the individual effects of these variables on the response. The variance inflation factor (VIF) is a metric computed for all predictor variables. If the VIF of a variable is high, it means the information in that variable is already explained by other predictor variable(s). Lower the VIF (<2) the better. VIF is calculated as

$$VIF = \frac{1}{(1 - R^2)} \tag{4.5.2}$$

R^2 is the proportion of the variance explained by the regression model. This is explained in Sect. 4.6.

There is a "vif" function in the *car* package, which can be used to detect multi-collinearity. We will use the longley data set to evaluate the variance inflation

```
fit <- lm(Employed~ GNP + Year, data = longley)
car::vif(fit)
```

```
     GNP      Year
106.0368 106.0368
```

```
fit <- lm(Employed~ GNP + Unemployed, data=longley)
car::vif(fit)
```

```
      GNP Unemployed
 1.575129   1.575129
```

It appears that the variables "GNP" and "Year" are highly correlated and the variables "GNP" and "Unemployed" are not collinear. To understand the hazards of multicollinearity, refer to Fig. 4.4.

In Fig. 4.4, the right-hand panel plots the RSS values using β_{GNP} and β_{Year}. Due to the presence of collinearity between the variables there exist many pairs of β_{GNP} and β_{Year}, with a similar value of the RSS. However, in the left-hand panel, the β_{GNP} and $\beta_{Unemployed}$ have distinct values for a similar value of the RSS. What this implies is that in the presence of correlation, β_{GNP} and β_{Year} tend to increase/decrease together, making it difficult to separate out the individual effects of each variable to the response variable.

Highly correlated variables from the correlation matrix can also be found using the findCorrelation function in the *caret* package

```
highlyCorrelated <- findCorrelation(cor(longley), cutoff=0.7)
colnames(longley)[highlyCorrelated]
```

```
[1]"Year"     "GNP.deflator" "GNP"     "Population"
```

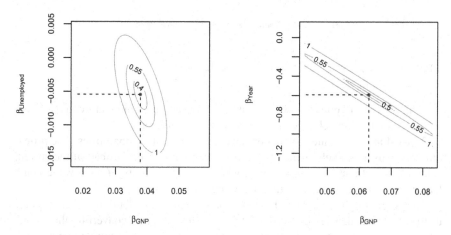

Fig. 4.4 Contour plots for RSS of correlated and uncorrelated variables

4.6 Summary of Regression Outputs

Having come thus far, let us now summarize some of the outputs of a linear regression model. We consider the housing data for our regression model. Let us do a regression of "price" with "sqft_living" and "bedrooms".

The null and alternate hypothesis for a regression equation is

- Null Hypothesis, H_0: All the coefficients are 0, i.e., there is no relationship between the predictor(s) and the response.
- Alternate Hypothesis, H_a: All the coefficients are $\neq 0$, i.e., there is some relationship between the predictors and the response.

1. t value—measures how many standard deviations away is the estimated coefficient from the original value of 0 (considering H_0 to be true). This can be obtained by dividing the estimated coefficient by the standard error—(*estimated coefficient* − 0)/*standard error*, as the baseline assumption is 0 (Table 4.6).

```
model <- lm(price ~ sqft_living + bedrooms, data = kc_house_data)
```

Table 4.6 Summary of regression coefficients

	Estimate	Std. error	t value	Pr (>|t|)
(Intercept)	79469.3591	6604.7640	12.0321	0
sqft_living	313.9487	2.3374	134.3137	0
Bedrooms	−57066.7589	2308.2231	−24.7232	0

```
t_value <- model$coef / coef(summary(model))[, "Std. Error"]
t_value
```

```
(Intercept) sqft_living      bedrooms
   12.03213    134.31369     -24.72324
```

A high t value implies that we should keep the corresponding feature in our linear model as it has a high chance of being a nonzero coefficient.

2. p-value—is a value which, converts the t value into probabilities. The probabilities tell us how likely is the coefficient to be equal to zero instead of the current value of the estimate. In other words, what is the probability of the t value being larger or smaller than the ones that our model estimated?

The probability is calculated based on the student's t distribution, which requires us to specify the degrees of freedom. We can calculate it by converting the t value into absolute values and then calculate the upper tail of the distribution to obtain the probability of being larger and multiply it by 2 (1.96 to be precise), to include the probability of being smaller.

```
# Find degree of freedom

dof <- nrow(kc_house_data) - length(model$coef + 1)
# 1 is added to include the Intercept term
dof
```

```
[1] 21610
```

The function "pt" in R calculates the quantile of the t-distribution.

```
pt(abs(coef(summary(model))[, "t value"]), df = dof, lower.tail = FALSE) * 2
```

```
  (Intercept)      sqft_living         bedrooms
3.076594e-33   0.000000e+00    4.244531e-133
```

A variable with a high p-value implies that after including all variables into the model, this particular feature does not provide any new information to the output.

3. R-Squared—measures the proportion of the output variance that is explained by the model and is represented by the following equation

$$R^2 = 1 - \frac{RSS}{TSS}$$
$$= 1 - \frac{\sum_{i=1}^{n}(y_i - \hat{y}_i)^2}{\sum_{i=1}^{n}(y_i - \bar{y})^2}$$

(4.6.1)

```
Rsquared <- function(y, yhat)
{
    rss <- sum( (y - yhat)^2 )
    tss <- sum( ( y - mean(y) )^2 )
    return( 1 - rss / tss )
}
```

The R^2 value of the model in R is

```
summary(model)$r.squared
```

```
[1] 0.5068033
```

```
Rsquared(kc_house_data$price, model$fitted.values)
```

```
[1] 0.5068033
```

A value close to 1 implies that the model explains most of the variance in the target variable. A low value implies that other important features need to be included in the model.

4. Adjusted R Square—also measures the amount of explained variance but adjusts the R-square based on the complexity of the model. In the model, if we add more variables, the R^2 value of the model will go up, even if they do not contribute towards explaining the response (i.e., redundant variables). The adjusted R-square attempts to discern this "overfitting".

```
k  <- length(model$coef) # Intercept term is not included
adjustedRSquared <- function(y, yhat, k)
{
    n  <- length(y)
    r2 <- Rsquared(y, yhat)
    return( 1 - (1 - r2) * (n - 1) / (n - k - 1) )
}
```

The adjusted R^2 value of the model in R is

```
summary(model)$adj.r.squared
```

```
[1] 0.5067576
```

```
adjustedRSquared( kc_house_data$price, model$fitted.values, k )
```

```
[1] 0.5067348
```

5. AIC and BIC

AIC (Akaike information criterion) and BIC (Bayesian information criterion) are measures of goodness of fit. They penalize complex models, i.e., a model with fewer parameters is preferred than the one with more parameters. In general, BIC penalizes models more for free parameters than does AIC. Both criteria depend on the maximized value of the likelihood function $\mathcal{L}$ of the estimated model. If we have two models, the model with the lower AIC and BIC score is a better choice.

4.7 Ridge Regression

Earlier in Sect. 3.8, we had seen that adding higher degree polynomials to a regression equation led to overfitting. Overfitting occurs when the model fits the training data all too well and does not generalize to unseen data.

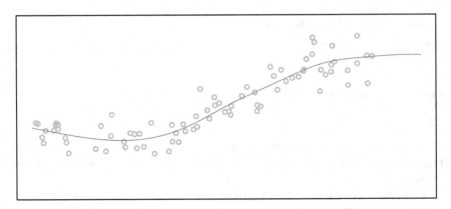

Fig. 4.5 Hard to overfit due to many observations

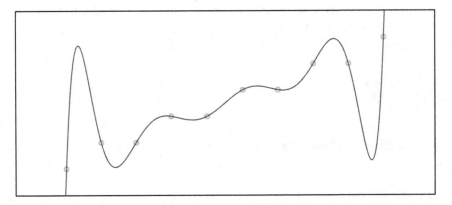

Fig. 4.6 Easy to overfit due to very few observations

Overfitting can also happen if there are too many predictor variables in the regression equation or, if there are too few observations refer Figs. 4.5 and 4.6.

Overfitting is also associated with very large estimated parameters (weights) $\hat{w}$. We therefore want to seek a balance between

- How well our model fits the data (measure of fit)
- Magnitude of the coefficients

The total cost of the model is therefore a combination of the measure of fit and the measure of the magnitude of the coefficients. The measure of fit is represented by the *RSS* and a small *RSS* is indicative of a good fit. The measure of magnitude of the coefficients is either the sum of the absolute value of the coefficients ℓ_1 norm or, the sum of the squared values of the coefficients ℓ_2 norm. They are represented as follows:

$$\|w_0\| + \|w_1\| + \cdots + \|w_n\| = \sum_{j=0}^{n} \|w_j\| = \|w\|_1 \ (\ell_1 \ Norm)$$

$$w_0^2 + w_1^2 + \cdots + w_n^2 = \sum_{j=0}^{n} w_j^2 = \|w_j = \|w\|_2^2 \ (\ell_2 \ Norm)$$

In ridge regression, we will consider the ℓ_2-norm as the measure of the magnitude of the coefficients. The total cost is therefore

$$Total \ Cost = RSS(w) + \|w\|_2^2 \tag{4.7.1}$$

Our objective in ridge regression is to find $\hat{w}$ so as to minimize the total cost in Eq. 4.7.1. The balance between the fit and the magnitude is achieved by introducing a tuning parameter λ so that

$$Total \ Cost = RSS(w) + \lambda\|w\|_2^2 \tag{4.7.2}$$

If $\lambda = 0 \rightarrow$ reduces to minimizing $RSS(w) \rightarrow \hat{w}^{Least \ Squares(LS)}$
If $\lambda = \infty \rightarrow$, total cost is ∞ when ($\hat{w} \neq 0$) and total cost is 0 when ($\hat{w} = 0$).
If λ is in between $\rightarrow 0 \leq \|\hat{w}\|_2^2 \leq \|\hat{w}^{(LS)}\|_2^2$

4.7.1 Computing the Gradient of Ridge Regression

Closed Form Solution

$$RSS(w) = (y - Hw)^\top (y - Hw)$$

The total cost in the case of ridge regression is

$$\begin{aligned} Total \ Cost &= (y - Hw)^\top (y - Hw) + \lambda\|w\|_2^2 \\ &= (y - Hw)^\top (y - Hw) + \lambda w^\top w \end{aligned} \tag{4.7.3}$$

The gradient of Eq. 4.7.3 is

$$\begin{aligned} \Delta[RSS(w) + \lambda\|w\|_2^2] &= \Delta(y - Hw)^\top (y - Hw) + \lambda\|w\|_2^2 \\ \Delta Cost(w) &= -2H^\top(y - Hw) + \lambda(2w) \\ &= -2H^\top(y - Hw) + 2\lambda I w \end{aligned} \tag{4.7.4}$$

Equating Eq. 4.7.4 to 0, we get

$$\Delta Cost(w) = 0$$

$$-2H^\top(y - Hw) + 2\lambda Iw = 0$$

$$-H^\top y + H^\top H\hat{w} + \lambda I\hat{w} = 0 \qquad (4.7.5)$$

$$(H^\top H + \lambda I)\hat{w} = H^\top y$$

$$\hat{w}_{ridge} = (H^\top H + \lambda I)^{-1}H^\top y$$

If $\lambda = 0 :\rightarrow (\hat{w}_{ridge} = H^\top H)^{-1}H^\top y = \hat{w}^{LS}$

If $\lambda = \infty :\rightarrow \hat{w}_{ridge} = 0$

The fact that we are taking care of model complexity is called **regularization** (refer Sect. 3.8). The model complexity is taken care of by the tuning parameter λ, which penalizes the model (by way of cost), if the model complexity increases.

Gradient Descent

The element-wise ridge regression gradient descent algorithm can be written as

$$w_j^{(t+1)} \leftarrow w_j^{(t)} + \Delta Cost(w)$$

$$w_j^{(t+1)} \leftarrow w_j^{(t)} - 2H^\top(y - Hw) + 2\lambda w$$

$$w_j^{(t+1)} \leftarrow w_j^{(t)} - \eta[-2\sum_{i=1}^{n} h_j(x_i)(y_i - \hat{y}_i(w^{(t)})) + 2\lambda w_j^{(t)}] \qquad (4.7.6)$$

$$w_j^{(t+1)} \leftarrow w_j^{(t)}(1 - 2\eta\lambda) + 2\eta\sum_{i=1}^{n} h_j(x_i)(y_i - \hat{y}_i(w^{(t)}))$$

In Eq. 4.7.6, η is the step size and the term $(1 - 2\eta\lambda)$ is always less than or equal to 1, while $\eta > 0, \lambda > 0$. The term $2\eta\sum_{i=1}^{n} h_j(x_i)(y_i - \hat{y}_i(w^{(t)}))$, is the update term from *RSS*.

Figure 4.7 shows that $w_j^{(t)}$ reduces by a scale of $(1 - 2\eta\lambda)$, at the intermediate step and then increases by the update term $2\eta\sum_{i=1}^{n} h_j(x_i)(y_i - \hat{y}_i(w^{(t)}))$ at $w_j^{(t+1)}$.

To summarize,

- For Least Squares Regression: $w_j^{(t+1)} \leftarrow w_j^{(t)} - \eta * (Update\ term)$
- For Ridge Regression: $w_j^{(t+1)} \leftarrow (1 - 2\eta\lambda)w_j^{(t)} - \eta * (Update\ term)$

We can always fit the training set better with a complex model and a weight decay setting of $\lambda = 0$, than we could with a less complex model and a positive weight decay. This brings us to the question of how do we choose the tuning parameter λ? To find λ, we use k fold cross-validation (Sect. 3.10).

The process includes fitting $\hat{w}_\lambda$ to the training set, test the performance of the model with $\hat{w}_\lambda$ on the validation set to select λ^*, and finally assesses the generalization error of the model with $\hat{w}_{\lambda^*}$. The average error is computed as follows:

$$Average\ Error\ CV(\lambda) = \frac{1}{k}\sum_{k=1}^{k} error_k(\lambda) \qquad (4.7.7)$$

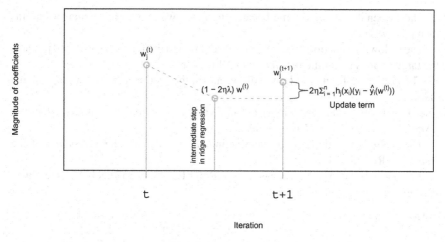

Fig. 4.7 Regularization of weights in ridge regression

4.7.2 Writing the Ridge Regression Gradient Descent Application

We will now write our own ridge regression application from scratch and we will use the kc_house_data used earlier.

Let us first use the "lm" function in R and extract the coefficients, regressing price with sqft_living and bedrooms, from the house_train_data.

```
lm(price ~ sqft_living + bedrooms, data=house_train_data)$coef
```

```
(Intercept) sqft_living     bedrooms
 97050.0942    305.2103  -57429.9302
```

The first function in our ridge regression gradient descent application is to make the data matrix.

```
data_matrix <- function(data, features, output){
  scaled_feature_matrix <- data.frame(scale(data[features]), row.names=NULL)
  length <- nrow(data)
  scaled_features <- as.matrix(cbind('Intercept' = rep(1, length),
                                   scaled_feature_matrix[, features]))

  output <- as.matrix(scale(data[output]))
  return(list(scaled_features, output))
}
```

The *predict_output* function predicts the targeted values.

```
predict_output<-function(feature_matrix, weights){
  predictions=(feature_matrix) %*% (weights)
  return(predictions)
}
```

The ℓ_2 penalty gets its name because it causes weights to have small ℓ_2 norms than otherwise.

The following function takes the initial weights and the feature matrix and predicts the target values using the *predict_output* function.

The *errors* are found out by the difference in the predicted values and the actual values.

The derivative or the *gradient* is calculated using the feature matrix and *errors* $(\Delta cost(w) = 2\boldsymbol{H}^{\top}(y - \boldsymbol{H}w) + 2\lambda w)$.

The weights are updated by subtracting the product of the *gradient* and the *step_size* (Refer Eq. 4.7.6).

The norm of the gradients is calculated (Refer Eq. 4.4.3) to check if it is less than the *tolerance* in a "while" loop.

```
ridge_regression_gradient_descent = function(feature_matrix, output,
    initial_weights, step_size, l2_penalty, tolerance) {

    converged = FALSE
    weights = matrix(initial_weights)

    j = 0
    while (!converged) {
        predictions = predict_output(feature_matrix, weights)
        errors = predictions - output

        # Loop over each feature weight
        for (i in 1:length(weights)) {
            if (i == 1) {
                gradient = 2 * (feature_matrix[, i] %*% errors)
                gradient_norm = sqrt(sum(gradient^2))
                weights[1, 1] = weights[1, 1] - (step_size * gradient)
            } else {
                gradient = 2 * (feature_matrix[, i] %*% errors) +
                  2 * (l2_penalty * weights[i, 1])
                gradient_norm = sqrt(sum(gradient^2))
                if (gradient_norm < tolerance) {
                  converged = TRUE
                }
                weights[i, 1] = weights[i, 1] - (step_size * gradient)
            }
        }
        j = j + 1
    }
    print(paste0("Gradient descent converged at iteration:", j -
        1))
    return(weights)
}
```

We will assign two different values to the tuning parameter λ- 0 and ∞, and explore how the parameters (weights) get penalized. We will consider a model with two features, i.e., *sqft_living* and *bedrooms*.

```
features <- c("sqft_living", "bedrooms")
target <- "price"
train_data <- house_train_data[, c(features, target)]
```

```
feature_matrix = data_matrix(train_data,
                             features,
                             target)[[1]]

output_matrix = data_matrix(train_data,
                            features,
                            target)[[2]]

initial_weights = c(0, 0, 0)
step_size = 1e-6
tolerance = 1e-8
```

```
weights_with_0_penalty = ridge_regression_gradient_descent(feature_matrix,
                                                           output_matrix,
                                                           initial_weights,
                                                           step_size,
                                                           l2_penalty = 0,
                                                           tolerance)
```

[1] "Gradient descent converged at iteration: 3002"

```
print(weights_with_0_penalty)
```

```
              [,1]
[1,]  -5.560047e-17
[2,]   7.885384e-01
[3,]  -1.489809e-01
```

The coefficients with $\lambda = 0$ are the same as OLS regression. Let us check if we get the same results using the "lm" function in R.

```
train_data_features <- data.frame(scale(house_train_data[, features]))
train_data_output <- data.frame(scale(house_train_data[, target]))
train_data <- cbind(train_data_features, train_data_output)
colnames(train_data) <- c("sqft_living", "bedrooms", "price")
(OLS_coef <- lm(price ~ sqft_living + bedrooms, data = train_data)$coef)
```

```
(Intercept)    sqft_living         bedrooms
2.600634e-17   7.885384e-01   -1.489809e-01
```

Indeed we do!

R has a "glmnet" function in the *glmnet* package. The features and the output belong to the class *matrix*. The argument "alpha" is 0 for ridge regression and 1 for lasso regression. The tolerance as defined in our algorithm is the "thresh", which defaults to 1e-07. There are many other hyparameters which can be explored by typing *help(glmnet)*.

Let us test our results with the "glmnet" function in R (Table 4.7).

```
library(glmnet)
ridge_model_lambda_0 <- glmnet(x = feature_matrix,
                               y = output_matrix,
                               alpha = 0,
                               lambda = 0,
```

Table 4.7 Comparison of coefficients of ridge regression with lambda = 0 for, our application, OLS regression model and glmnet

	Application	OLS	glmnet
(Intercept)	0.00000	0.00000	0.00000
sqft_living	0.78854	0.78854	0.78853
Bedrooms	−0.14898	−0.14898	−0.14898

Table 4.8 Comparison of coefficients of ridge regression with lambda = 1e+5 for our application and glmnet

	Application	glmnet
Intercept	0.00000	0e+00
sqft_living	0.06679	$1e-05$
Bedrooms	0.02696	0e+00

```
                                   thresh=1e-8)

glm_ridge_0_coef <- coef(ridge_model_lambda_0)[, 1]
```

Indeed our application compares well!

Now let us try out our application with $\lambda = 1e + 05$

```
initial_weights = c(0, 0, 0)
step_size = 1e-6
tolerance = 1e-8
weights_with_high_penalty = ridge_regression_gradient_descent(feature_matrix,
                                                              output_matrix,
                                                              initial_weights,
                                                              step_size,
                                                              l2_penalty = 1e+05,
                                                              tolerance)
```

This model has a very low bias.

Let us test our results with the *glmnet* function in R (Table 4.8).

```
ridge_model_lambda_1e5 <- glmnet(x = feature_matrix,
                                 y = output_matrix,
                                 alpha = 0,
                                 lambda = 1e+5,
                                 thresh=1e-8)

glm_ridge_1e5_coef <- coef(ridge_model_lambda_1e5)[, 1]
```

Indeed, we get the same results, i.e., all coefficients are very close to 0!

Let us visualize the ridge regression equations for the two λ values in Fig. 4.8. The ridge regression model with gradient descent iterates to a null model with 0 intercept (high bias) when, $\lambda = \infty$ and an LS regression model when $\lambda = 0$.

Our next objective is to find the best value of λ; and we will use cross-validation, as discussed in Sect. 3.10.

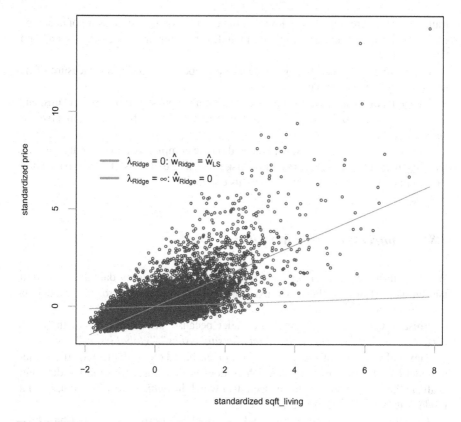

Fig. 4.8 Ridge regression with $\lambda = 0$ and $\lambda = 1e+05$

4.8 Assessing Performance

We have been referring to the cost of a model in various sections. In essence, the cost of a model is the measure of the errors of the model, i.e., how close can the model predict *vis-a-vis* the actual value. That is, if a model makes zero prediction errors, the cost attributed to the model is zero and therefore, its measure of accuracy is 100%.

We have seen earlier that the cost for a regression model is measured by the loss function defined as

$$
\begin{aligned}
Loss(y, f_{\hat{w}}(x)) &= (y - f_{\hat{w}}(x))^2 \text{ -Squared Error} \\
Loss(y, f_{\hat{w}}(x)) &= |y - f_{\hat{w}}(x)| \text{ -Absolute Error}
\end{aligned}
\tag{4.8.1}
$$

The measure of accuracy of the model can be judged by the cost of the model on the training data and the unseen data. We have seen in Sect. 3.7, while training a model, the model tries to fit the training data. Therefore as model complexity increases the training error decreases. A very low training error is not a good measure of accuracy of the model unless the training data includes the "universe", i.e., the "seen" and "unseen" data.

Therefore the model's performance can only be assessed by the measure of its accuracy with "unseen" data.

The **generalization error** is the error of a model from the "universe" of "unseen" data. The **true error** is the error from the available subset, from the "universe" of "unseen" data.

The model errors discussed here depend on the complexity and other algorithmic features in the model. But there could exist errors in the data itself. The next section tries to find out how we can overcome this challenge.

4.8.1 Sources of Error Revisited

We have discussed how errors can arise from a model training data and that from unseen data. However, there also exist three other sources of error in a model, as discussed in Sect. 3.4—noise, bias, and variance.

Noise always creeps into the data under because, we cannot record the same perfectly say, *"human emotions"*, *"relationship issues"* *"global issues"*, etc.

Bias and variance also creep into our models based on available data. If we train a model based on the training data which does not have any *noise* in the data and evaluate the same model on the unseen data which has *noise*, we will end up with a model with very low accuracy.

Therefore, as discussed in Sect. 3.4, the prediction error in a model has three components—noise, bias, and variance, which can be written as

$$
\begin{aligned}
\text{Prediction Error} &= \sigma^2 + MSE[f_{\hat{w}}(x)] \\
&= \sigma^2 + [bias(f_{\hat{w}}(x))]^2 + var(f_{\hat{w}}(x))
\end{aligned}
\tag{4.8.2}
$$

The appropriate model is selected by choosing the tuning parameter λ, which controls the model complexity. This is done using cross-validation. Having chosen the appropriate model, we assess the generalization error.

Let us consider the house_train_data and house_test_data which we partitioned from the kc_house data set. The training and test data sets have $10,807$ and $10,806$ observations respectively.

```
train_features = as.matrix(data.frame(scale(house_train_data[,
    features])))
train_output = as.matrix(data.frame(scale(house_train_data[,
    target])))

test_features = as.matrix(data.frame(scale(house_test_data[,
    features])))
test_output = as.matrix(data.frame(scale(house_test_data[, target])))
```

We train a ridge regression model with $\lambda = 0$ using our training data, i.e., replicate the OLS regression and use our model to predict the unseen test data using $\lambda = 10$.

```
ridge_model_train <- glmnet(x = train_features,
                            y = train_output,
                            alpha=0,
                            lambda = 0)

ridge_predict = predict(ridge_model_train,
                        newx = test_features,
                        s = 10,
                        exact = TRUE)

MSE_lambda_10 = mean((ridge_predict - test_output)^2)
```

```
[1] "MSE_lambda_10 = 0.903155"
```

The mean squared error for this model is 0.903155.

R has a built-in cross-validation function, cv.glmnet(). By default, the function performs 10-fold cross-validation, but this can be changed using the argument "nfolds".

We perform a 10-fold cross-validation on the training data and find the value of λ for which the cross-validation error is the least.

```
cv_ridge = cv.glmnet(x = train_features,
                     y = train_output,
                     alpha=0)

ideal_lambda=min(cv_ridge$lambda)
```

```
[1] "ideal_lambda = 0.076901"
```

```
ridge_predict = predict(ridge_model_train,
                        s=ideal_lambda,
                        newx = test_features,
                        exact = TRUE)

MSE_ideal_lambda = mean((ridge_predict - test_output)^2)
```

```
[1] "MSE with ideal_lambda = 0.495869"
```

The mean squared error using $\lambda = 0.076901$ is 0.495869, i.e., the MSE has dropped by 45%.

Let us find out the coefficients of this model

```
ridge_train = glmnet(x = train_features, y = train_output, alpha = 0)
ridge_ideal_lambda_coef <- predict(ridge_train, type = "coefficients",
    s = ideal_lambda)
ridge_ideal_lambda_coef[, 1]
```

```
 (Intercept)    sqft_living        bedrooms
-1.397232e-16  6.998124e-01  -8.978171e-02
```

Let us visualize this ridge regression equation with the predictor *sqft_living*. Figure 4.9 plots the regularized ridge regression equation.

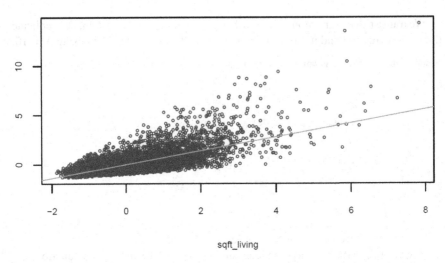

sqft_living

Fig. 4.9 Ridge regression equation with $\lambda = 0.076901$ obtained with cross-validation

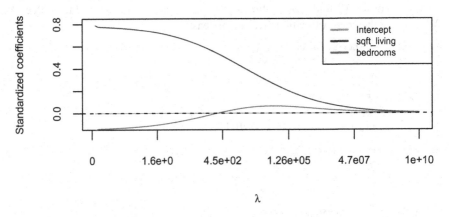

Fig. 4.10 Standardized Ridge regression coefficients with changing λ. The coefficients do not abruptly drop to 0 as $\lambda \to \infty$

Let us visualize how the standardized coefficients change with different values of λ. In Fig. 4.10, it may be seen that the coefficients change gradually from when $\lambda = 0$, till $\lambda \to \infty$. It never reduces to 0 abruptly.

4.8.2 Bias–Variance Trade-Off in Ridge Regression

A large λ will result in high bias (simple model) and consequently low variance ($\hat{w} = 0$, for $\lambda = \infty$).

A small λ will result in low bias and consequently high variance.

4.9 Lasso Regression

If we have a "wide" array of features (say 1e+10), ridge regularization can pose computational problems as all features are selected.

The lasso algorithm discards less important/redundant features by translating their coefficients to zero. This allows us interpretability of the features as well as reducing computation time. Lasso (ℓ_1 regularized regression) uses the ℓ_1 norm as the penalty, instead of the ℓ_2 norm in ridge regression.

Before we get into the lasso objective function let us revisit the ridge regression algorithm. Ridge regression chooses the parameters β with the minimum RSS, subject to the constraint that the ℓ_2 norm of the parameters $\beta_1^2 + \beta_2^2 + \cdots + \beta_n^2 \leq t$, the ridge constraint.

Figure 4.11 plots the RSS contours and the parameter constraints for ridge and lasso regression.

The RSS contours are the ellipses, centered at the least squares estimate (point in color red). The constraint is plotted for different values of the β parameters.

In the case of ridge regression, $\beta_1^2 + \beta_2^2 \leq t$, the ridge constraint. The constraint takes the form of a circle for two parameters and it becomes a sphere with higher number of parameters. The first point where the RSS contour hits the circle is the point describing the ridge parameters β_1 and β_2. The β values turn out to be nonzeros in most cases. If t is small, the parameters will be small and if it is large, it will tend towards a least squares solution.

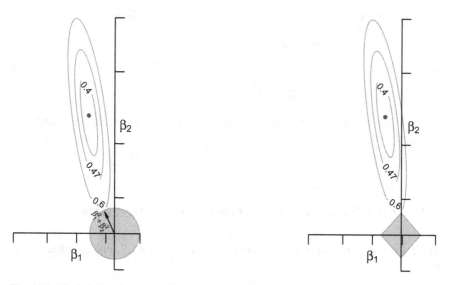

Fig. 4.11 The left plot shows the ridge regression RSS contours and the constraint on the ridge coefficients $\beta_1^2 + \beta_2^2 \leq t$ (ridge constraint). The right plot shows the lasso regression RSS contours and the constraint on the lasso coefficients $|\beta_1| + |\beta_2| \leq t$ (lasso constraint)

In the case of lasso regression,the β parameters are chosen such that, $|\beta_1| + |\beta_2| \le t$, the lasso constraint, for a minimum RSS.

As shown in the right-hand plot of Fig. 4.11 for lasso regression with two parameters, the constraint has a diamond shape with four corners; for more than two features, the contour becomes a rhomboid, with many corners. If the RSS contour touches a corner, it forces one of the β's to become zero.

We can rewrite the total cost in Eq. 4.7.3, for lasso regression as

$$Total\ Cost = RSS(w) + \lambda \|w\|_1 \tag{4.9.1}$$

If $\lambda = 0 \rightarrow \hat{w}^{lasso} = \hat{w}^{Least\ Squares}$

If $\lambda = \infty \rightarrow \hat{w}^{lasso} = 0$

If λ is in between $\rightarrow 0 \le \hat{w}^{lasso} \le \hat{w}^{Least\ Squares}$

Lasso chooses the parameters β with the minimum RSS, subject to the constraint that the ℓ_1 norm of the parameters $(|\beta_1| + |\beta_2| + \cdots + |\beta_n|) \le tolerance$.

We have seen in Fig. 1.5, that the optimal solution for the lasso minimization problem occurs at the origin and therefore we cannot calculate the gradient.

The solution is therefore an convex optimization algorithm called the *Coordinate descent*. This algorithm tries to minimize

$$f(w) = f(w_0, w_1, \cdots, w_n)$$
$$\underset{min}{find\ f\ (w)} \tag{4.9.2}$$

The coordinate descent algorithm can be described as follows:

Initialize $\hat{w}$

while not converged, pick a coordinate j $\qquad\qquad$ (4.9.3)

$\hat{w}_j \leftarrow \underset{min}{f\ (\hat{w}_0, \hat{w}_1, \cdots, w, \hat{w}_{j+1}, \cdots, \hat{w}_n)}$

If we choose the next coordinate at random, it becomes a *stochastic coordinate descent*.

In coordinate descent, we do not have to choose a step size.

4.9.1 Coordinate Descent for Least Squares Regression

The following is the algorithm for coordinate descent for LS, one coordinate at a time

$$RSS(w) = \sum_{i=1}^{n}(y_i - \sum_{j=0}^{n} w_j h_j(x_i))^2$$

fix all coordinates w_{-j} and take partial derivative of w_j

$$\frac{\partial}{\partial w_j}RSS(w_j) = -2\sum_{i=1}^{n} h_j(x_i)(y_i - \sum_{j=0}^{n} w_j h_j(x_i))^2$$

$$= -2\sum_{i=1}^{n} h_j(x_i)(y_i - \sum_{k \neq j} w_k h_k(x_i) - w_j h_j(x_i))$$

$$= -2\sum_{i=1}^{m} h_j(x_i)(y_i - \sum_{k \neq j} w_k h_k(x_i)) + 2w_j \sum_{i=1}^{n} h_j(x_i)^2 \qquad (4.9.4)$$

Ref:

(i) by definition of normalized features, $\sum_{i=1}^{n} h_j(x_i)^2 = 1$

(ii) we shall denote $(\sum_{i=1}^{n} h_j(x_i)(y_i - \sum_{k \neq j} w_k h_k(x_i)) = \rho_j$

$$= -2\rho + 2w_j$$

set partial derivative =0 and solve, giving us

$$w_j = \rho_j$$

4.9.2 Coordinate Descent for Lasso

The following is the algorithm for coordinate descent for the lasso objective, one coordinate at a time

Initialize $\hat{w}$

while not converged

for j in $0, 1, 2, \cdots, n$

compute: $\rho_j = \sum_{i=1}^{n} h_j(x_i)(y_i - \hat{y}_i(\hat{w}_j))$ $\qquad (4.9.5)$

set: $w_j = \begin{cases} \rho_j + \frac{\lambda}{2} & \text{if } \rho_j < -\frac{\lambda}{2} \\ 0 & \text{if } \rho_j in[-\frac{\lambda}{2}, \frac{\lambda}{2}] \\ \rho_j - \frac{\lambda}{2} & \text{if } \rho_j > \frac{\lambda}{2} \end{cases}$

4.9.3   Writing the Lasso Coordinate Descent Application

We are now ready to write the lasso regression algorithm.

The function *get_features* subsets the data based on the selected features.

```
get_features <- function(data, features){
  selected_features <- matrix(nrow = nrow(data), ncol = length(features))
  for (i in 1: length(features)){
    selected_features[,i] <- as.numeric(data[[features[[i]]]])
  }
  selected_features
}
```

The function *add_constant_term* appends a column of 1's to the feature matrix.

```
add_constant_term <- function(data_features){
  length <- nrow(data_features)
  combined <- cbind(rep(1, length), data_features)
  combined
}
```

The function *construct_matrix* accepts—the feature names and the output from a data.frame. It then selects the feature values and the output values, by calling the *get_features* function and returns them as a list.

```
construct_features_matrix <- function(features, outputs, data) {
  features <- as.list(features)
  data_features <- get_features(data, features)
  output_data <- get_features(data, outputs)
  features_data <- add_constant_term(data_features)
  list(features_data, output_data)
}
```

The function *normalize_features* calculates the norm for each feature and normalizes the feature_matrix.

```
normalize_features <- function(feature_Matrix) {
  norms <- as.numeric(vector(length = ncol(feature_Matrix)))
  normalized_features <- matrix(nrow = nrow(feature_Matrix),
      ncol = ncol(feature_Matrix))
  for (i in 1:ncol(feature_Matrix)) {
    v <- feature_Matrix[, i]
    norms[i] <- sqrt(sum(v^2))
    normalized_features[, i] <- feature_Matrix[, i]/norms[i]
  }
  list(normalized_features, norms)
}
```

The *predict_output* function predicts the output values.

```
predict_output <- function(feature_matrix, weights){
  predictions<-feature_matrix[[1]]%*%weights
  predictions
}
```

In Eq. 4.9.4, we had seen that $\rho_j = \sum_{i=1}^{n} h_j(x_i)(y_i - \sum_{k \neq j} w_k h_k(x_i))$. For the sake of understanding the subsequent code where we calculate ρ, let us consider a data set with 3 features and we want to find ρ_2. This can be written as

$$
\begin{aligned}
\rho_2 &= h_2(x_2)[(y_1 + y_2 + y_3) - (\hat{w}_1 h_1(x_1) + \hat{w}_3 h_3(x_3))] \\
&= h_2(x_2)[(y_1 + y_2 + y_3) - (\hat{y}_1 + \hat{y}_3)] \\
&= h_2(x_2)[(y_1 - \hat{y}_1) + (y_2 - \hat{y}_2) + (y_3 - \hat{y}_3)) + \hat{y}_2] \\
&= h_2(x_2)[(target - predicted) + \hat{w}_2 h_2(x_2)]
\end{aligned}
\tag{4.9.6}
$$

```
get_ro <- function(feature_matrix, output, weights, i) {
    prediction = predict_output(feature_matrix, weights)
    feature_i = feature_matrix[[1]][, i]
    ro_i = sum(feature_i * (output - prediction + weights[i] * feature_i))
    return(ro_i)
}
```

We now implement the coordinate descent function, which will minimize the cost function over a single feature i. The function returns a new weight for feature i.

```
lasso_coordinate_descent_step <- function(i, data_matrix, weights,
    l1_penalty) {
    normalized_features <- normalize_features(feature_Matrix = data_matrix[[1]])

    rho <- get_ro(normalized_features, data_matrix[[2]], weights,
        i)

    if (i == 1) {
        new_weight_i <- rho
    } else if (rho < -l1_penalty/2) {
        new_weight_i <- rho + l1_penalty/2
    } else if (rho > l1_penalty/2) {
        new_weight_i <- rho - l1_penalty/2
    } else {
        new_weight_i <- 0
    }
    return(new_weight_i)
}
```

Now that we have a function that optimizes the cost function over a single coordinate, let us implement cyclical coordinate descent where we optimize coordinates 1 *to n* in order and repeat.

```
lasso_cyclical_coordinate_descent <- function(data_matrix, initial_weights,
    l1_penalty, tolerance) {
    normalized_features <- normalize_features(feature_Matrix = data_matrix[[1]])
    norms <- normalized_features[[2]]

    converged <- FALSE
    weights <- initial_weights
    new_weights <- vector(length = length(weights))
    while (!converged) {
        old_weights <- weights
        for (i in 1:length(weights)) {
```

```
        weights[i] <- lasso_coordinate_descent_step(i = i,
            data_matrix = data_matrix, weights = weights,
            l1_penalty = l1_penalty)
    }
    delta <- vector()
    for (i in 1:length(weights)) {
        delta[i] <- old_weights[i] - weights[i]
    }
    if (max(abs(delta)) < tolerance) {
        converged <- TRUE
    }
  }
  weights/norms
}
```

4.9.4 Implementing Coordinate Descent

We will use the complete KC house data set, consisting of 21, 613 observations and partition it as train and test data consisting of 19, 451 and 2162 observations, respectively.

We will use two features namely, "sqft_living" and "bedrooms" and execute our lasso_cyclical_coordinate_descent function with ℓ_1 penalty = 0, which is the same as LS regression.

```
features = c("sqft_living", "bedrooms")
target = "price"
data_matrix <- construct_features_matrix(features = features, outputs = target,
    data = house_train_data)
weights <- lasso_cyclical_coordinate_descent(data_matrix = data_matrix,
    initial_weights = c(0, 0, 0), l1_penalty = 0, tolerance = 1e-07)
weights
```

```
[1]   97050.0942    305.2103  -57429.9302
```

Let us compare our results with the glm and lm function in R.

```
x = model.matrix(price ~ sqft_living + bedrooms, data = house_train_data)[,
    -1]
y = house_train_data$price
lasso_model = glmnet(x, y, alpha = 1, lambda = 0, thresh = 1e-07)
predict(lasso_model, type = "coefficients", s = 0, exact = T)[1:3]
```

```
[1]   97052.1826    305.1896  -57417.7511
```

```
lm(price ~ sqft_living + bedrooms, data = house_train_data)$coef
```

```
(Intercept) sqft_living      bedrooms
 97050.0942     305.2103  -57429.9302
```

Indeed our lasso algorithm compares very well and gives the same results!

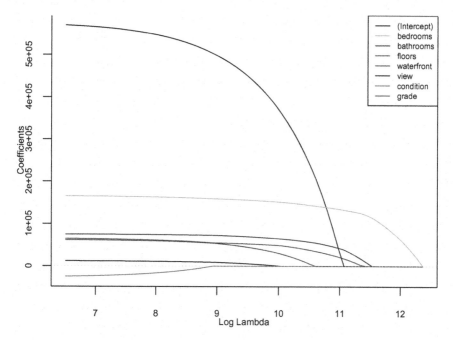

Fig. 4.12 Lasso regression coefficients with changing λ. The coefficients abruptly drop to 0 as $\lambda \to \infty$

In lasso, when $\lambda = 0$, the lasso solution is the least squares fit, and when λ becomes sufficiently large, lasso gives the null model in which all coefficient estimates equal zero.

In Fig. 4.12, we have plotted 7 lasso coefficients as λ is varied from 0 to 1e+10. It may be observed that between the two extremes of the LS fit and the null model, depending on the value of λ, lasso creates models with any number of variables and most of them are rejected as the value of λ increase.

4.9.5 Bias Variance Trade-Off in Lasso Regression

A large λ will result in high bias (simple model) and consequently low variance ($\hat{w} = 0$, for $\lambda = \infty$).

A small λ will result in low bias and consequently high variance.

We have discussed regression in detail; we shall now move onto the next area of supervised learning—Classification.

Chapter 5
Classification

There are no routine statistical questions, only questionable
statistical routines.

—D.R. Cox

In machine learning, the task of classification means to use the available input data to learn a function which can assign a category to a data point.

5.1 Linear Classifiers

In machine learning classifiers identify class membership of a new observation. A linear classifier is a two-class classifier that decides class membership by comparing a linear combination of the features to a score.

Let us understand linear classifiers for document classification.

In two dimensions, a linear classifier is a line having the functional form $w_1 x_1 + w_2 x_2 = c$. The classification rule of a linear classifier is to assign a document to a particular class if $w_1 x_1 + w_2 x_2 < c$ or $w_1 x_1 + w_2 x_2 \geq c$.

The algorithm of a linear classifier can be written as

$$Score = \sum_{i=1}^{n} w_i x_i$$
$$if \ Score < c \qquad (5.1.1)$$
$$return \ +1$$
$$else \ -1$$

© Springer Nature Singapore Pte Ltd. 2017
A. Ghatak, *Machine Learning with R*, DOI 10.1007/978-981-10-6808-9_5

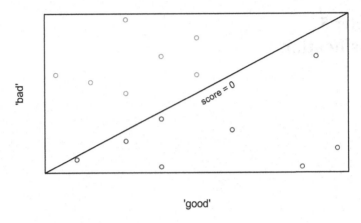

Fig. 5.1 A linear decision boundary

Let us consider a set of documents, where each document has word occurrences
good and *bad*

Let one of the samples from the set of documents be

Bad data, I guess is not *good* news.

If $x_1 =$ good, $x_2 =$ bad and the corresponding weights are $w_1 = +1$ and $w_2 = -1$, respectively.

The score for the above document is $1 * 1 + (-1) * 1 = 0$. However, there may
be other documents having a score less than or greater than 0. We can then represent
the *good bad* words along with the score in Fig. 5.1.

This brings us to what is known as the decision boundary. In Fig. 5.1, the **linear
decision boundary** between two inputs is the line where the score is 0.

If there are three inputs, the decision boundary is a plane and for more than three
inputs, it is a hyperplane.

There also exist **nonlinear decision boundaries**, as shown in Fig. 5.2

5.1.1 Linear Classifier Model

A linear classifier model can be defined as one which can be trained to predict the
sign of the *Score*, given the inputs. In most cases, a *positive sign* is represented as a
factor 1 and and *negative sign*, as factor 0. In other words, a linear classifier model
can be represented as

$\hat{y}_i = sign(Score(x_i))$,

where, $Score(x_i) = w_0 + w_1 x_i[1] + \cdots + w_n x_i[n] = w^\top x_i$

For a n-dimensional hyperplane, the model can be represented as

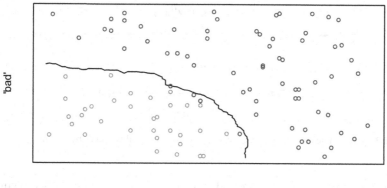

Fig. 5.2 A non-linear decision boundary

$$Score(x_i) = w_0 + w_1 x_i + \cdots + w_n x_i$$

$$= \sum_{j=0}^{n} w_j h_j(x_i) \tag{5.1.2}$$

$$= w^\top h(x_i)$$

5.1.2 Interpreting the Score

The Score $w^\top h(x_i)$ can be interpreted as the predicted class and it is related to the probability $p(y = +1 \mid x, \hat{w})$. Therefore, if we can link the predicted class to a probabilistic scale, we are in a position to predict probabilities from the Scores.

The Score values range from $-\infty$ to $+\infty$ and the probability values lie between 0 and 1. The question is, how do we **link** a range of values from $-\infty$ to $+\infty$ to 0 and 1. Let us try to understand this intuitively.

In Fig. 5.3, the Score line is squeezed onto the probability line by a **sigmoid link function, g** defined as

$$\hat{P}(y = +1 \mid x_i, w) = g(w^\top h(x_i)) \tag{5.1.3}$$

5.2 Logistic Regression

Logistic regression was invented in the late 1930s by statisticians, Ronald Fisher and Frank Yates. Logistic regression is a *categorical* tool, used to predict categories

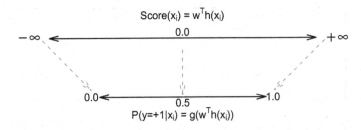

Fig. 5.3 Score values of a linear classifier are linked to probability values by a sigmoid function

(fraud/not-fraud, yes/no, etc.), instead of numeric scores in regression. The predictor variable is defined as a "category" in R, and can be represented as *("Yes"/"No")*, *(0/1)*, etc.

The logistic function (also known as *sigmoid*), is a **link** function defined as

$$
\begin{aligned}
p(y = +1 \mid x_i, w) &= g(w^\top h(x_i)) \\
&= sigmoid(Score(x_i)) \\
&= sigmoid(w^\top h(x_i)) \\
&= \frac{1}{1 + e^{-Score(x_i)}} \\
&= \frac{1}{1 + e^{-w^\top h(x_i)}} \\
&= \frac{1}{1 + e^{-(w_0 h_0(x_i) + \cdots + w_n h_n(x_i))}}
\end{aligned}
\tag{5.2.1}
$$

Some algebraic manipulation of Eq. 5.2.1, will give us

$$
ln(\frac{p}{1-p}) = w_0 h_0(x_i) + w_1 h_1(x_i) + \cdots + w_n h_n(x_i)
\tag{5.2.2}
$$

Equation 5.2.2 is also called the *logit* or the log-odds of the probability.

Let us try to understand how the Score maps to a range between 0 and 1.
If the Score varies from $-\infty$ to $+\infty$ in Eq. 5.2.1, the respective sigmoid function transformations are as listed below:

Score	sigmoid(Score)
$-\infty$	$\frac{1}{1+e^{\infty}} = 0$
-2	$\frac{1}{1+e^{2}} = 0.12$
0	$\frac{1}{1+e^{0}} = 0.5$
$+2$	$\frac{1}{1+e^{-2}} = 0.88$
$+\infty$	$\frac{1}{1+e^{-\infty}} = 1$

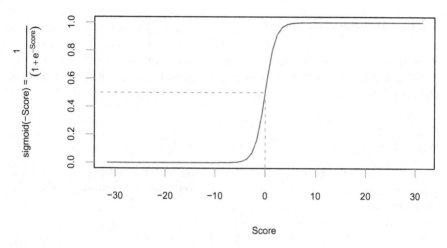

Fig. 5.4 The sigmoid link function

We can see that the *Score* function, converts the Scores $(-\infty\ to\ +\infty)$ to a probability function having values between 0 to 1. If we plot the sigmoid function, we will get the curve shown in Fig. 5.4

The logistic regression model assigns probabilities using a function of the form

$$p(y = +1 \mid x_i, w) = \frac{1}{1 + e^{-(w^\top h(x))}} \tag{5.2.3}$$

where $w^\top h(x)$ is the dot product of the weights and the feature vector.

Logistic regression is a linear optimizer, which tries to find probabilities p that maximizes the sum of the natural logarithm (ln) of the probabilities

$$ln(\ell(w)) = \max_{max} \left(\sum ln(p(y = +1 \mid x, w)) + \sum ln(p(y = -1 \mid x, w)) \right) \tag{5.2.4}$$

It may be noted that, maximization of the sum of probabilities for either class, works against each other, i.e., if the threshold for $p(y = +1 \mid, x_i, w) > 0.5$, than $p(y = -1 \mid, x_i, w) < 0.5$.

We can alter the threshold of the probability, depending on our requirement, i.e., if the detection of a disease is more important (which is usually the case), we can increase the threshold of the probability to a value higher than say, 0.5. This is discussed in detail at Sect. 5.4.

5.2.1 Likelihood Function

Suppose that $x_1, \ldots, x_n$ are random samples from a distribution $f(x \mid w)$, than $f(x \mid w)$ is the *probability distribution function* (if x is a continuous distribution). For every observed sample $x_1, \ldots, x_n$, we define the likelihood function as

$$
\begin{aligned}
\ell(w) &= f(x_1, \ldots, x_n \mid w) \\
&= f(x_1 \mid w) \cdots f(x_n \mid w)
\end{aligned}
\tag{5.2.5}
$$

The likelihood function $\ell(w)$ depends on the parameter w and $f(x_1, \ldots, x_n \mid w)$, which is a *joint probability distribution* (for a continuous distribution), and can be represented as

$$
\begin{aligned}
\ell(w ; x_1, \ldots, x_n) &= p(x_1, x_2, \ldots, x_n \mid w) \\
&= p(x_1 \mid w) p(x_2 \mid w) \cdots p(x_n \mid w)
\end{aligned}
\tag{5.2.6}
$$

Earlier in Sect. 3.11, we had seen that the ideal weights are the maximum likelihood estimation (MLE) of the weights w given the data. In logistic regression, the **quality metric** is the **likelihood function**. This measures the **quality of the fit** of the logistic regression model with its coefficients w. We, therefore, try to maximize the likelihood function to improve the quality of fit of the regression model.

For convenience, we take the natural logarithm (ln) of the likelihood, because this transforms the likelihood function from a product of the probabilities to a sum of the probabilities and is represented as

$$
\ell\ell(w ; x_1, \ldots, x_n) = ln(p(y_i \mid x_1, x_2, \ldots, x_n, w))
$$
$$
\ell\ell(w) = ln \prod_{i=1}^{n} p(y_i \mid x_i, w)
\tag{5.2.7}
$$

5.2.2 Model Selection with Log-Likelihood

Let us try to understand intuitively, how the parameters are estimated with the log-likelihood function with the following hypothetical data points.

Data Pt	x[1]	x[2]	y	Probability of the data
x_1, y_1	1	1	+1	$P(y = +1 \mid x_1, w)$
x_2, y_2	0	3	−1	$P(y = +1 \mid x_2, w)$
x_3, y_3	2	3	−1	$P(y = -1 \mid x_3, w)$

$$\ell(w) = \prod_{i=1}^{n} P(y_i \mid x_i, w)$$
$$= P(y = +1 \mid x_1, w) * P(y = +1 \mid x_2, w) * P(y = -1 \mid x_3, w)$$
$$= P(y = +1 \mid x[1] = 1, x[2] = 1, w) * P(y = +1 \mid x[1] = 0, x[2] = 3, w) \quad (5.2.8)$$
$$* \ P(y = -1 \mid x[1] = 2, x[2] = 3, w)$$
$$\ell\ell(w) = ln(P(y = +1 \mid x[1] = 1, x[2] = 1, w)) + ln(P(y = +1 \mid x[1] = 0, x[2] = 3, w))$$
$$ln\ (P(y = -1 \mid x[1] = 2, x[2] = 3, w))$$

In Eq. 5.2.8, we choose w, which maximizes the log likelihood. Therefore, the maximum likelihood estimate is

$$\hat{w}_{\mathrm{mle}} = \{\arg \max_{w \in W}\}ln \prod_{i=1}^{n} p(y_i \mid x_i, w) \quad (5.2.9)$$

Figure 5.5 shows the best model is the one with the highest likelihood. To find the weights, corresponding to the maximum value of $\ell\ell(w)$, we optimize the log-likelihood function, using gradient ascent.

5.2.3 Gradient Ascent to Find the Best Linear Classifier

In multiple regression, we were interested in finding the parameters resulting in the lowest cost. In a linear classifier like logistic regression, we are interested in finding the parameters which maximize the log-likelihood function. Instead of gradient descent in regression, we will now be using gradient ascent.

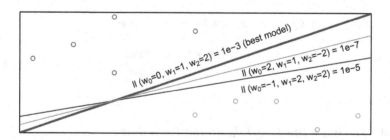

Fig. 5.5 Model linear boundary having the maximum likelihood is the best model

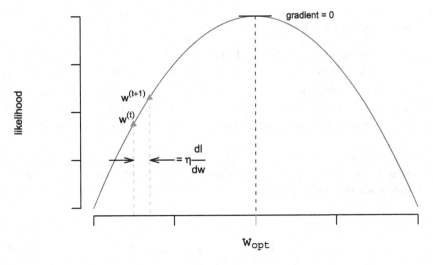

Fig. 5.6 'Hill climbing' for MLE

In Fig. 5.6, we are trying to find the maximum value of the likelihood via a hill-climb process, where the algorithm can be represented as

$$w^{(t+1)} \leftarrow w^{(t)} + \eta \frac{dl}{dw}|_{w^{(t)}} \qquad (5.2.10)$$

For n parameters,

$$\Delta \ell(w) = \begin{bmatrix} \frac{\partial \ell}{\partial w_0} \\ \frac{\partial \ell}{\partial w_1} \\ \vdots \\ \frac{\partial \ell}{\partial w_n} \end{bmatrix}$$

The gradient ascent algorithm can now be summarized as

$$\begin{array}{l} \text{while not converged} \\ w^{(t+1)} \leftarrow w^{(t)} + \eta \Delta \ell(w^{(t)}) \end{array} \qquad (5.2.11)$$

5.2.4 Deriving the Log-Likelihood Function

Earlier in Eq. 5.2.3, we had seen that the probability of $y = +1$ is represented as

$$p(y = +1 \mid x_i, w) = \frac{1}{1 + e^{-w^\top h(x_i)}}$$

$$= \frac{1}{1 + \frac{1}{e^{w^\top h(x_i)}}} \qquad (5.2.12)$$

$$= \frac{e^{w^\top h(x_i)}}{1 + e^{w^\top h(x_i)}}$$

The probability that the model predicts $y = -1$ is represented as

$$1 - p(y = +1 \mid x_i, w) = 1 - \frac{1}{1 + e^{-w^\top h(x_i)}}$$

$$= \frac{e^{-w^\top h(x_i)}}{1 + e^{-w^\top h(x_i)}} \qquad (5.2.13)$$

$$= \frac{1}{1 + e^{w^\top h(x_i)}}$$

If we have estimated the weights w, the predicted outcome of a new observation is $\hat{p}(x)$, such that

$$\hat{f}(x) = \begin{cases} 1 & if \ \hat{p}(x) > 0.5 \\ 0 & if \ \hat{p}(x) \leq 0.5 \end{cases} \qquad (5.2.14)$$

The logit or log-odds is defined as

$$ln(Odds) = ln \frac{p(y = +1 \mid x_i, w)}{1 - p(y = +1 \mid x_i, w)}$$

$$= ln(\frac{1}{e^{-w^\top h(x_i)}}) \qquad (5.2.15)$$

$$= -ln(e^{-w^\top h(x_i)})$$

$$= w^\top h(x_i)$$

We will be using the above equations while deriving the log-likelihood.

In Eq. 5.2.7, we saw that the likelihood is a product of the probabilities, i.e., $\ell(w \mid x_1, \ldots, x_n) = p(x_1 \mid w) \cdots p(x_n \mid w)$. Therefore for each observation, we have a vector of features x_i, and an observed class, y_i. It follows that the likelihood is then

$$\ell(w) = \prod_{i=1}^{n} p(x_i)^{y_i} (1 - p(x_i)^{(1-y_i)}) \qquad (5.2.16)$$

The log-likelihood turns the products of the probabilities into sums

$$ln(\ell(w)) = \sum_{i=1}^{n} y_i ln[p(y_i = +1 \mid x_i, w)] + (1 - y_i)ln[1 - p(y_i = +1 \mid x_i, w)]$$

$$\ell\ell(w) = \sum_{i=1}^{n} y_i [ln(p(y_i = +1 \mid x_i, w) - y_i ln(1 - p(y_i = +1 \mid x_i, w)]$$

$$+ ln(1 - p(y_i = +1 \mid x_i, w)$$

$$= \sum_{i=1}^{n} y_i ln[\frac{p(y = +1 \mid x_i, w)}{1 - p(y = +1 \mid x_i, w)}] + ln(1 - p(y_i = +1 \mid x_i, w) \qquad (5.2.17)$$

Ref:

(i) $ln(1 - p(y_i = +1 \mid x_i, w) = ln[\dfrac{1}{1 + e^{w^{T}h(x_i)}}] = -ln(1 + e^{w^{T}h(x_i)})$

$$\ell\ell(w) = \sum_{i=1}^{n} y_i w^{T} h(x_i) - \sum_{i=1}^{n} ln(1 + e^{w^{T}h(x_i)})$$

5.2.5   Deriving the Gradient of Log-Likelihood

In Eq. 5.2.17, the log-likelihood for the ith observation was $y_i w^{T} h(x_i) - ln(1 + e^{w^{T}h(x_i)})$. Therefore,

$$\frac{\partial \ell\ell}{\partial w_j} = \frac{\partial}{\partial w_j}(y_i w^{T} h(x_i)) - \frac{\partial}{\partial w_j} ln(1 + e^{w^{T}h(x_i)})$$

Ref:

(i) $\dfrac{\partial}{\partial w_j} w^{T} h_j(x_i) = h_j(x_i)$

(ii) $\dfrac{\partial}{\partial w_j} ln(1 + e^{w^{Th_j(x_i)}}) = h_j(x_i)\dfrac{e^{w^{T}h(x_i)}}{1 + e^{w^{T}h(x_i)}}$

$$\frac{\partial \ell\ell}{\partial w_j} = y_i h_j(x_i) - h_j(x_i)\frac{e^{w^{T}h(x_i)}}{1 + e^{w^{T}h(x_i)}}$$

$(5.2.18)$

The gradient for all observations is

$$\frac{\partial \ell\ell}{\partial w_j} = \sum_{i=1}^{n} y_i h_j(x_i) - \sum_{i=1}^{n} h_j(x_i)\frac{e^{w^{T}h(x_i)}}{1 + e^{w^{T}h(x_i)}}$$

$$= \sum_{i=1}^{n} h_j(x_i)(y_i - p(y_i = +1 \mid x_i, w))$$

$(5.2.19)$

Equation 5.2.19 is intuitively the matrix multiplication of the feature matrix and the prediction errors.

Let us interpret the derivative with respect to some extreme cases to get a better understanding of what is happening. Let $\Delta_i = (y_i - p(y_i = +1 \mid x_i, w))$ and,

$$\text{suppose } h_j(x_i) = 1:$$

	$P(y = +1 \mid \mathbf{x_i}, \mathbf{w}) \approx 1$	$P(y = +1 \mid \mathbf{x_i}, \mathbf{w}) \approx 0$
$\mathbf{y_i = +1}$	$\Delta_i = (1 - 1) \approx 0$	$\Delta_i = (1 - 0) \approx 1$
$\mathbf{y_1 = 0}$	$\Delta_i = (0 - 1) \approx -1$	$\Delta_i = (0 - 0) \approx 0$

When $\Delta_i \approx 0$, it implies that the weights do not change, and that happens when the actual value and the predicted value are approximately the same.

When $\Delta_i \approx 1$, it implies that when the actual value $y_i = +1$, the predicted probability is ≈ 0; therefore the value of w_j needs to increase, which in turn increases the $Score(x_i)$ which in turn, tends to increase the value of $P(y = +1 \mid x_i, w)$ from ≈ 0.

When $\Delta_i \approx 0$, it has the opposite effect.

5.2.6 Gradient Ascent for Logistic Regression

Based on the above, we are now in a position to write the algorithm for gradient ascent for the logistic function.

$$\text{init } w^{(1)} = 0$$
$$\text{while } \|\Delta \ell(w^{(t)})\| > \epsilon$$
$$\text{for } j = 0, 1, \ldots, n$$
$$\frac{\partial \ell(w)}{\partial(w_j)} = \sum_{i=1}^{n} h_j(x_i)[y_i - p(y = 1 \mid x_i, w^{(t)})] \qquad (5.2.20)$$
$$w_j^{(t+1)} \leftarrow w_j^{(t)} + \eta[\frac{\partial \ell(w)}{\partial(w_j)}]$$

5.2.7 Writing the Logistic Regression Application

We will now write our own logistic regression application from scratch.

For the sake of our application, we will consider a data set of reviews written by customers about fine food restaurants, available at kaggle.[1] The dataset consists

---

[1]https://www.kaggle.com/snap/amazon-fine-food-reviews, downloaded on Jun 07, 2017, 2:48 pm IST.

of 568,454 observations and, we consider the features *"Text"* (written reviews) and *"Score"* (the score rated by the reviewers).

```
review <- read.csv(file_path)
review <- review[, c("Score", "Text")]
```

Remove all punctuations from the written reviews in *"Text"* column and store it in another column, *"Text_cleaned"*.

```
review["Text_cleaned"] <- apply(review["Text"], 2, function(y)
    gsub("[[:punct:]]", "", y))
```

The "Score" column is rated from 1 to 5. We will consider all Score values greater than or equal to 4 to be a positive sentiment and assign a value of 1 and the others a value of 0.

```
review$Sentiment <- ifelse(review$Score >= 4, 1, 0)
```

```
sentiment_neg <- review[review$Sentiment == 0, ]
sentiment_pos <- review[review$Sentiment == 1, ]
```

```
dim(sentiment_neg)
```

```
[1] 12958      4
```

```
dim(sentiment_pos)
```

```
[1] 43042      4
```

The number of positive and negative sentiments differ hugely. The data is imbalanced, therefore we undersample.

```
sentiment_neg$sentiment  <- 0
sentiment_pos$sentiment  <- 1
sentiment_pos <- sentiment_pos[1:nrow(sentiment_neg), ]
```

```
review <- select(rbind(sentiment_pos, sentiment_neg), -Sentiment, -Score, -Text)
```

A list of 23 positive and negative words has been compiled and stored in a *json* file. We will extract the contents of the file and store it in a vector, *pos_neg_words*.

```
pos_neg_words <- fromJSON(file=json_file_path)
pos_neg_words
```

```
 [1] "bad"          "never"          "small"      "stale"
 [5] "not"          "terrible"       "good"       "great"
 [9] "healthy"      "delicious"      "favorite"   "love"
[13] "glad"         "recommended"    "variety"    "better"
[17] "best"         "like"           "free"       "easy"
[21] "pleased"      "disappointed"   "unique"
```

For each word in *pos_neg_words*, we compute a count for the number of times the particular pos_neg_word occurs in the '*Text_cleaned*' column. We store this count in separate columns, one for each *pos_neg_word*. In text mining, this is also called a *term document matrix*.

```
for (word in pos_neg_words) {
    for (i in 1:nrow(review)) {
        review[i, word] <- str_count(review$Text_cleaned[i],
            paste0("\\b", word, "\\b"))
    }
}

review <- subset(review, select = -c(Text_cleaned))
```

```
colSums(review['great'])
```

```
great
5126
```

The word "great" appears 5126 times in all of 25,916 reviews.
We partition our data set into training data and testing data.

```
set.seed(22)
inTrain <- createDataPartition(review$sentiment, p = 0.5, list = F)
review_train_data = review[inTrain, ]
review_test_data  = review[-inTrain, ]
```

We now start with our logistic regression application.

The following function imports the data, adds the constant column and creates a feature matrix and a label matrix, which is the "sentiment" values reported by the reviewers.

```
get_data <- function(dataframe, features, label){
    dataframe['intercept'] = 1
    features = c('intercept', features)
    features_frame = dataframe[features]
    feature_matrix = as.matrix(features_frame)
    label_array = dataframe[label]
    return(list(feature_matrix, label_array))
}
```

This function predicts the probability of the *sentiment* using the link function $p(y = +1|x_i, w) = \frac{1}{1+e^{-w^\top h(x_i)}}$ as defined in Eq. 5.2.1

```
predict_probability <- function(feature_matrix, weights) {
    scores = as.matrix(feature_matrix) %*% (weights)
    probability = 1/(1 + exp(-scores))
    return(probability)
}
```

For details of the following function, please refer Eq. 5.2.17

```
compute_log_likelihood <- function(feature_matrix, sentiment,
    coefficients) {
    scores = as.matrix(feature_matrix) %*% (coefficients)
    logexp = log(1 + exp(scores))
    ll = sum((sentiment) * scores - logexp)
    return(ll)
}
```

As discussed in Eq. 5.2.19, the gradient is the matrix multiplication of the features and the prediction errors.

```
feature_derivative <- function(errors, feature){
    derivative = (feature)  %*% as.matrix(errors)
    return(derivative)
 }
```

And, finally our logistic regression function:

```
logistic_regression <- function(feature_matrix, sentiment,
    initial_coefficients, step_size, tolerance) {

    coefficients = matrix(initial_coefficients)
    converged = FALSE
    k = 0

    log_like_1 = compute_log_likelihood(feature_matrix,
        sentiment, coefficients)

    while (!converged) {
        predictions = predict_probability(feature_matrix,
            coefficients)
        errors = sentiment - predictions

        for (i in 1:length(coefficients)) {
            gradient = sum(feature_derivative(errors, feature_matrix[,
                i]))
            coefficients[i] = coefficients[i] + step_size *
                gradient
        }

        log_like_2 = compute_log_likelihood(feature_matrix,
            sentiment, coefficients)

        if (abs(log_like_2 - log_like_1) < tolerance) {
            converged = TRUE
        }
        log_like_1 = log_like_2
        k = k + 1
    }
    print(paste0("Gradient ascent converged at iteration:",
        k - 1))
    return(coefficients)
}
```

Create our feature and output matrix.

```
feature_matrix <- get_data(review_train_data, pos_neg_words,
                    'sentiment')[[1]]
sentiment <- get_data(review_train_data, pos_neg_words,
                    'sentiment')[[2]]
```

Find the estimated coefficients of our logistic regression model with initial coefficients set to 0, step size of 1e-4, and a tolerance of 1e-8. We use our "compute_log_likelihood" function to calculate the log-likelihood.

```
model_MLE_coef = logistic_regression(feature_matrix,
                                      sentiment,
                                      initial_coefficients =
                                          rep(0, ncol(feature_matrix)),
                                      step_size=1e-4,
                                      tolerance = 1e-8)
```

[1] "Gradient ascent converged at iteration: 5453"

[1] "Log Likelihood of our model is: -7592.67863768205"

Logistic regression in R uses the "glm" function. The log-likelihood is calculated using the "logLik" function.

```
glm.fit = glm(sentiment ~ ., data = review_train_data, family = binomial)
coef <- coef(glm.fit)
print(paste0("Log Likelihood of glm model is: ", logLik(glm.fit)))
```

[1] "Log Likelihood of glm model is: -7592.67863396885"

The log-likelihood of the models are the same. We will compare the coefficients of the models in the next section, but before that let us compare the accuracy of our application versus the glm function.

```
appln_probs <- predict_probability(feature_matrix, model_MLE_coef)
pos_neg_sentiments <- ifelse(appln_probs > 0.5, 1, 0)
prediction_correct <- length(which(sentiment == pos_neg_sentiments))
accuracy <- prediction_correct/length(pos_neg_sentiments)
```

[1] "Accuracy of our model = 0.6922"

```
glm.probs <- predict(glm.fit, newdata = review_train_data, type = "response")
glm.pred <- rep(0, 12958)
glm.pred[glm.probs > 0.5] <- 1
```

[1] "Accuracy of glm model = 0.6922"

It looks like our model gives a better training accuracy however, if you recall from earlier sections, this may not guarantee an equal degree of accuracy on unseen data. We will discuss this further in Sect. 5.4.1

5.2.8 A Comparison Using the BFGS Optimization Method

As discussed in Sect. 1.14 on optimization methods, it may be reiterated that in our application, we have used the **Newton–Raphson** method of optimization for the log-likelihood function.

Likewise, the *glm* function in R uses the IRWLS (Iteratively Re-Weighted Least Squares) algorithm.

We will now optimize the log-likelihood function in our application by modifying our *compute_log_likelihhod* function and using the **BFGS** optimization algorithm, instead of the Newton–Raphson method.

The *optim* function in R allows us to optimize the criterion function employing the BFGS algorithm.

The criterion function, namely *log_likelihood* is a slight modification from our *compute_log_likelihhod* defined earlier. This function as defined below, returns a negative value, as we are trying to minimize the function; in contrast to our application using the Newton–Raphson method, where we were trying to minimize the absolute differences of the log-likelihood between two iterations.

```
log_likelihood <- function(feature_matrix, sentiment, coefficients) {
    scores = as.matrix(feature_matrix) %*% (coefficients)
    logexp = log(1 + exp(scores))
    ll = -sum((sentiment) * scores - logexp)
    return(ll)
}
```

```
beta_zero = rep(0, ncol(feature_matrix))
bfgs_optim_alg = optim(beta_zero,
                       log_likelihood,
                       feature_matrix = feature_matrix,
                       sentiment = sentiment,
                       method = 'BFGS',
                       hessian = TRUE)
coefs <- cbind(coef(glm.fit), bfgs_optim_alg$par, model_MLE_coef)
print(coefs)
```

	glm_coefs	bfgs_coefs	model_MLE_coefs
(Intercept)	-0.01689346	-0.01689444	-0.01689377
bad	-1.01298318	-1.01297609	-1.01298243
never	-0.24593687	-0.24593577	-0.24593625
small	-0.04470091	-0.04470172	-0.04469817
stale	-1.33362181	-1.33367670	-1.33363273
not	-0.56877378	-0.56877226	-0.56877225
terrible	-1.98458412	-1.98458707	-1.98409944
good	0.26620336	0.26620195	0.26620224
great	0.76659152	0.76659226	0.76658873
healthy	0.35738338	0.35738432	0.35738708
delicious	1.51004405	1.51004655	1.51004495
favorite	0.92272878	0.92272412	0.92272858
love	0.48603456	0.48603606	0.48603447
glad	1.02798906	1.02796167	1.02798407
recommended	0.52667661	0.52666692	0.52667143
variety	0.28655564	0.28655072	0.28655392
better	-0.21108284	-0.21108410	-0.21108108
best	1.09683870	1.09684318	1.09684169

```
like             -0.17989694 -0.17989688      -0.17989710
free              0.27767977  0.27768116       0.27767961
easy              0.96390746  0.96391032       0.96390211
pleased           1.28420656  1.28421616       1.28419678
disappointed     -1.62805763 -1.62805096      -1.62805526
unique            0.76481669  0.76477283       0.76425151
```

Indeed the computed outputs from the three different optimization techniques are very similar. Isn't this amazing!

I hope you have appreciated the wonder of machine learning as much as I do everyday!

5.2.9 Regularization

Overfitting in logistic regression is a bigger issue. Maximum likelihood expectation for parameter estimation results in choosing the most certain model. If the data is linearly separable, the training algorithm will try to find the parameters for the most ideal decision boundary, which in turn can inflate the values of the coefficients.

Let us try to understand overfitting in logistic regression intuitively.

If one of our coefficients turns out to have a very low value say, -21.62, given all other estimates are 0, the probability estimate for the review to be positive is

$p(x = +1 \mid x, w) = \frac{1}{1+exp(-21.68)} = 1.00000000038 \approx 1$

Likewise, a coefficient with a value of $+21.68$ would result in a probability estimate

$1 - 1.00000000038 = -3.8e - 10 \approx 0$.

What this implies is that a small increment in the estimated parameter, could inflate the probability estimate to either 1 or 0 depending the coefficient. This is further evidenced from the following explanation and the associated figures.

In the left-hand plot of Fig. 5.7, we get a probability estimate of 0.818, with coefficients $\beta_0 = 0$, $\beta_1 = 1$ and $\beta_2 = -1$, at $x = 1$ If we increase the value of the coefficients to $\beta_1 = 2$ and $\beta_2 = -2$ respectively, keeping $beta_0 = 0$, the probability estimate goes up to 0.953, for $x = 1$ remaining same.

We, therefore, need to penalize the weights just like we did in ridge and lasso regression. And, that brings us to regularization of the logistic regression model.

5.2.10 ℓ_2 Regularized Logistic Regression

We had seen earlier the total cost of a model depends on the sum of its *measure of fit* and *measure of magnitude of the coefficients*.

The measure of fit, in logistic regression is its *data likelihood*, i.e., we choose the coefficients that maximize the likelihood $\prod_{i=1}^{n} p(y_i \mid x_i, w)$. We also saw in the

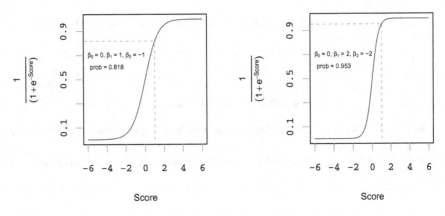

Fig. 5.7   Overfitting in logistic regression as parameters increase in value

earlier section that we do not optimize the data likelihood directly; we optimize the log of the data likelihood, $\ell\ell(w)$, as it makes the math more simple and the convergence behavior, a lot better.

The magnitude of the coefficients is measured by

$$
\begin{aligned}
&\text{Sum of squares } (\ell_2 norm)\ \|w\|_2^2 = \|w_0\|_2^2 + \cdots + \|w_n\|_2^2 \\
&\text{Sum of absolute values } (\ell_1 norm)\ |w|_1^1 = |w_0|_1^1 + \cdots + |w_n|_1^1
\end{aligned}
\tag{5.2.21}
$$

Both of the above penalize large coefficients.

In the ℓ_2 regularized logistic regression, we will select the coefficients w such that we minimize the function

$$
\ell(w) - \lambda \|w\|_2^2
\tag{5.2.22}
$$

In Eq. 5.2.22

$\lambda = 0$: reduces $\max\limits_{w} \ell(w)$ to an unpenalized MLE solution

$\lambda = \infty$: $(\max\limits_{w} \ell(w) - \infty \|w\|_2^2)$ results in a simple model

$0 < \lambda < \infty$: will balance the data likelihood with the magnitude of the coefficients.

As we have seen in regression, λ **is chosen using a validation set (for large datasets) and cross-validation (for smaller datasets).**

A large value of λ will result in a high bias, low variance model (i.e., $\hat{w} = 0$ for $\lambda = \infty$) and, small λ will result in a low bias, high variance model (i.e., MLE will fit high values of $\hat{w}$). As seen in the earlier chapter, λ controls the bias–variance tradeoff.

5.2.11 ℓ_2 Regularized Logistic Regression with Gradient Ascent

The gradient ascent algorithm can be written as

$$\text{while not converged}$$
$$w^{(t+1)} \leftarrow w^{(t)} + \eta \Delta \ell(w^{(t)}) \tag{5.2.23}$$

Total derivative $= \frac{\partial \ell(w)}{\partial w_j} - \lambda \frac{\partial \|w\|_2^2}{\partial w_j}$
The derivative of the ℓ_2 penalty is-

$$\frac{\partial \|w\|_2^2}{\partial w_j} = \frac{\partial}{\partial w_j}(w_0^2 + \cdots + w_j^2 + \cdots + w_n^2) = 2w_j$$

The gradient ascent algorithm for logistic regression with ℓ_2 regularization, can now be written as":

init $w^{(1)} = 0$ (or any number arrived at smartly)

$\quad$ while $\|\Delta \ell(w^{(t)})\| > \epsilon$

$\quad\quad$ for $j = 0, 1, \ldots, n$

$$\frac{\partial \ell(w)}{\partial (w_j)} = \sum_{i=1}^{n} h_j(x_i)[y_i - p(y = 1 \mid x_i, w^{(t)})]$$

$$w_j^{(t+1)} \leftarrow w_j^{(t)} + \eta[\sum_{i=1}^{n} h_j(x_i)[y_i - p(y = 1 \mid x_i, w^{(t)})] - 2\lambda w_j^{(t)}]$$

5.2.12 Writing the Ridge Logistic Regression with Gradient Ascent Application

```
get_data <- function(dataframe, features, label) {
    dataframe["intercept"] = 1
    features = c("intercept", features)
    features_frame = dataframe[features]
    feature_matrix = as.matrix(features_frame)
    label_array = dataframe[label]
    return(list(feature_matrix, label_array))
}
```

```
predict_probability <- function(feature_matrix, weights) {
    link = as.matrix(feature_matrix) %*% (weights)
    probability = 1/(1 + exp(-link))
    return(probability)
}
```

```r
feature_derivative <- function(errors, feature) {
    derivative = (feature) %*% as.matrix(errors)
    return(derivative)
}
```

```r
compute_log_likelihood_gd <- function(feature_matrix, sentiment,
    coefficients, l2_penalty) {
    scores = as.matrix(feature_matrix) %*% (coefficients)
    logexp = log(1 + exp(scores))
    ll = sum((sentiment) * scores - logexp) - l2_penalty * sum(coefficients^2)
    return(ll)
}
```

```r
logistic_regression_gd <- function(feature_matrix, sentiment,
    initial_coefficients, step_size, l2_penalty, tolerance) {

    coefficients = (initial_coefficients)
    converged = FALSE
    k = 0
    lll = compute_log_likelihood_gd(feature_matrix, sentiment,
        coefficients, l2_penalty)

    while (!converged) {
        predictions = predict_probability(feature_matrix, coefficients)
        errors = sentiment - predictions

        for (i in 1:length(coefficients)) {
            if (i == 1) {
                gradient = feature_derivative(errors, feature_matrix[,
                    i])
                coefficients[i] = coefficients[i] + step_size *
                    gradient
            } else {
                gradient = feature_derivative(errors, feature_matrix[,
                    i]) - 2 * l2_penalty * coefficients[i]
                coefficients[i] = coefficients[i] + step_size *
                    gradient
            }
        }
        ll2 = compute_log_likelihood_gd(feature_matrix, sentiment,
            coefficients, l2_penalty)
        if (abs(ll2 - lll) < tolerance) {
            converged = TRUE
        }
        lll = ll2
        k = k + 1
    }
    print(paste0("Gradient ascent converged at iteration:",
        k - 1))
    return(coefficients)
}
```

Now, let us create our feature and target matrices.

```r
feature_matrix <- get_data(review_train_data, pos_neg_words,
                           'sentiment')[[1]]
sentiment <- get_data(review_train_data, pos_neg_words,
                      'sentiment')[[2]]
```

First, we execute our application with $\lambda = 0$—it should give the same solution as the standard MLE.

```
model_lambda_0_coef <- logistic_regression_gd(feature_matrix,
                                              sentiment,
                                              initial_coefficients =
                                                rep(0, ncol(feature_matrix)),
                                              step_size = 1e-4,
                                              l2_penalty = 0,
                                              tolerance = 1e-8)
```

[1] "Gradient ascent converged at iteration: 5453"

```
log_likelihood_with_lambda_0 = compute_log_likelihood_gd(feature_matrix,
                                                         sentiment,
                                                         model_lambda_0_coef,
                                                         l2_penalty = 0)
```

[1] "log-likelihood with lambda equal to 0 is: -7592.6786"

Let us compare our results with the glmnet function in R

```
x = model.matrix(sentiment~., review_train_data)[, -1]
y = review_train_data$sentiment
glmnet_lambda_0 <- glmnet(x, y,
                          alpha=0,
                          lambda = 0,
                          family = 'binomial')
# deviance = -2 * log-likelihood
-deviance(glmnet_lambda_0)/2
```

[1] -7592.679

```
coefs <- data.frame(as.matrix(cbind(model_MLE_coef,
                                    model_lambda_0_coef,
                                    coef(glmnet_lambda_0))
                    )
          )
```

Indeed the results are the same!

Let us explore which are the positive/negative words that our model classified with $\lambda = 0$ (Table 5.1).

```
pos_neg_words[which(model_lambda_0_coef < 0) - 1] # classified as negative words
```

```
[1]  "bad"            "never"       "small"       "stale"
[5]  "not"            "terrible"    "better"      "like"
[9]  "disappointed"
```

Table 5.1 Ridge logistic coefficients calculated by our model and glmnet function in R using lambda = 0

	model_MLE_coef	model_lambda_0_coef	glmnet_lambda_0_coef
(Intercept)	−0.0168938	−0.0168938	−0.0168938
Bad	−1.0129824	−1.0129824	−1.0129825
Never	−0.2459363	−0.2459363	−0.2459370
Small	−0.0446982	−0.0446982	−0.0447002
Stale	−1.3336327	−1.3336327	−1.3336224
Not	−0.5687723	−0.5687723	−0.5687735
Terrible	−1.9840994	−1.9840994	−1.9845799
Good	0.2662022	0.2662022	0.2662033
Great	0.7665887	0.7665887	0.7665918
Healthy	0.3573871	0.3573871	0.3573836
Delicious	1.5100449	1.5100449	1.5100448
Favorite	0.9227286	0.9227286	0.9227287
Love	0.4860345	0.4860345	0.4860346
Glad	1.0279841	1.0279841	1.0279886
Recommended	0.5266714	0.5266714	0.5266765
Variety	0.2865539	0.2865539	0.2865555
Better	−0.2110811	−0.2110811	−0.2110827
Best	1.0968417	1.0968417	1.0968390
Like	−0.1798971	−0.1798971	−0.1798969
Free	0.2776796	0.2776796	0.2776798
Easy	0.9639021	0.9639021	0.9639077
Pleased	1.2841968	1.2841968	1.2842067
Disappointed	−1.6280553	−1.6280553	−1.6280558
Unique	0.7642515	0.7642515	0.7648169

```
pos_neg_words[which(model_lambda_0_coef > 0) - 1] # classified as positive words
```

```
 [1] "good"    "great"   "healthy"     "delicious"  "favorite"
 [6] "love"    "glad"    "recommended" "variety"    "best"
[11] "free"    "easy"    "pleased"     "unique"
```

It seems our application has done a reasonably good job in identifying the positive and negative words! Let us see how our application performs with regularization, i.e., $\lambda = 100$.

```
model_lambda_100_coef <- logistic_regression_gd(feature_matrix,
                                    sentiment,
                                    initial_coefficients =
                                       rep(0,ncol(feature_matrix)),
                                    step_size = 1e-4,
                                    l2_penalty = 100,
                                    tolerance = 1e-8)
```

```
[1] "Gradient ascent converged at iteration: 427"
```

```
log_likelihood_with_lambda_100 = compute_log_likelihood_gd(feature_matrix,
                                                            sentiment,
                                                            model_lambda_100_coef,
                                                            l2_penalty = 100)
```

```
[1] "log-likelihood with lambda equal to 100 is:
-8123.81152"
```

```
glmnet_lambda_100 <- glmnet(x, y, alpha=0, lambda = 100, family = 'binomial')
# log-likelihood is -deviance(glmnet_lambda_100)/2
```

```
[1] "log-likelihood with lambda equal to 100 is:
-8974.93225"
```

```
coefs <- data.frame(as.matrix(cbind(model_lambda_100_coef,
                                    coef(glmnet_lambda_100))
                              )
                   )
-deviance(glmnet_lambda_100)/2
```

```
[1] -8974.932
```

There are some differences in the coefficient values between our model and the glmnet model; however, our model converged at a higher value of log-likelihood, i.e., −8123.8115 than the glmnet model log-likelihood, which converged at a lower value, i.e., −8974.932 (Table 5.2).

Let us check if our model has improved over our MLE model in identifying the positive/negative words

```
pos_neg_words[which(model_lambda_100_coef < 0) - 1]
# classified as negative words
```

```
[1] "bad"      "never"    "stale"    "not"
[5] "terrible" "better"   "like"     "disappointed"
```

```
pos_neg_words[which(model_lambda_100_coef > 0) - 1]
# classified as positive words
```

```
 [1] "small"    "good"    "great"   "healthy"    "delicious"
 [6] "favorite" "love"    "glad"    "recommended" "variety"
[11] "best"     "free"    "easy"    "pleased"    "unique"
```

The word "terrible" has been identified as a negative word.

Now, let us look at the lasso logistic regression application.

Table 5.2 Ridge logistic coefficients calculated by our model and glmnet function in R using lambda = 100

	model_lambda_100_coef	glmnet_lambda_100_coef
(Intercept)	0.0685584	0.0001755
Bad	−0.4681515	−0.0023904
Never	−0.1230193	−0.0007732
Small	0.0000613	−0.0002185
Stale	−0.1944686	−0.0029634
Not	−0.4758842	−0.0010843
Terrible	−0.2296199	−0.0036815
Good	0.2026298	0.0002646
Great	0.5511315	0.0016860
Healthy	0.1762689	0.0008999
Delicious	0.4985100	0.0029903
Favorite	0.4039039	0.0018114
Love	0.3472318	0.0011193
Glad	0.1654889	0.0019955
Recommended	0.1039841	0.0010896
Variety	0.0827232	0.0004390
Better	−0.1273158	−0.0006221
Best	0.5860752	0.0021002
Like	−0.1537878	−0.0005761
Free	0.1479241	0.0006588
Easy	0.3692016	0.0018953
Pleased	0.1982047	0.0025131
Disappointed	−0.4578785	−0.0033429
Unique	0.0661486	0.0017846

5.2.13 *Writing the Lasso Regularized Logistic Regression With Gradient Ascent Application*

In the previous chapter, we have discussed lasso and the coordinate descent algorithm and we will not dwell on the same here.

Instead, a point to note here is that as in ridge regression, in lasso logistic regression we are trying to minimize *(measure of fit* − $\lambda \times$ *(magnitude of the coefficients))*.

The minimization of the sum of the absolute value of the coefficients is dependent on the log-likelihood.

This in turn, is an optimization of the *loglikekihood* of the model and, as before, we will be using the Newton–Raphson technique.

```
get_features <- function(data, features){
  selected_features <- matrix(nrow = nrow(data), ncol = length(features))
  for (i in 1: length(features)){
    selected_features[,i] <- as.numeric(data[[features[[i]]]])
  }
  selected_features
}
```

```
add_constant_term <- function(data_features){
  length <- nrow(data_features)
  combined <- cbind(rep(1, length), data_features)
  combined
}
```

```
construct_features_matrix <- function(features, outputs, data){
  features <- as.list(features)
  data_features <- get_features(data, features)
  output_data <- get_features(data, outputs)
  features_data <- add_constant_term(data_features)
  list(features_data, output_data)
}
```

```
normalize_features <- function(feature_Matrix) {
    norms <- as.numeric(vector(length = ncol(feature_Matrix)))
    normalized_features <- matrix(nrow = nrow(feature_Matrix),
        ncol = ncol(feature_Matrix))
    for (i in 1:ncol(feature_Matrix)) {
        v <- feature_Matrix[, i]
        norms[i] <- sqrt(sum(v^2))
        normalized_features[, i] <- feature_Matrix[, i]/norms[i]
    }
    list(normalized_features, norms)
}
```

```
predict_output <- function(feature_matrix, weights){
  predictions<-feature_matrix[[1]]%*%weights
  predictions
}
```

```
get_ro <- function(feature_matrix, output, weights, i)
{
  prediction <- predict_output(feature_matrix, weights)
  feature_i <- feature_matrix[[1]][, i]
  ro_i <- sum(feature_i * (output - prediction + weights[i] * feature_i))
  return(ro_i)
}
```

```
compute_log_likelihood_lasso <- function(norm_features, output,
    weights, l1_penalty) {
    scores <- as.matrix(norm_features) %*% (weights)
    logexp <- log(1 + exp(scores))
    ll <- sum(output * scores - logexp) - l1_penalty * sum(weights)
    return(ll)
}
```

```
lasso_coordinate_descent_step <- function(i, data_matrix, weights,
    l1_penalty) {
    normalized_features <- normalize_features(feature_Matrix = data_matrix[[1]])
    rho <- get_ro(normalized_features, data_matrix[[2]], weights,
        i)

    if (i == 1) {
        new_weight_i <- rho
    } else if (rho < -l1_penalty/2) {
        new_weight_i <- rho + l1_penalty/2
    } else if (rho > l1_penalty/2) {
        new_weight_i <- rho - l1_penalty/2
    } else {
        new_weight_i <- 0
    }
    return(new_weight_i)
}
```

```
lasso_cyclical_coordinate_descent <- function(data_matrix, initial_weights,
    l1_penalty, tolerance) {
    normalized_features <- normalize_features(feature_Matrix = data_matrix[[1]])
    norms <- normalized_features[[2]]
    k = 0
    converged <- FALSE
    weights <- initial_weights
    lasso_ll1 = compute_log_likelihood_lasso(normalized_features[[1]],
        data_matrix[[2]], weights, l1_penalty = l1_penalty)
    while (!converged) {
        for (i in 1:length(weights)) {
            weights[i] <- lasso_coordinate_descent_step(i = i,
                data_matrix = data_matrix, weights = weights,
                l1_penalty = l1_penalty)
        }
        lasso_ll2 = compute_log_likelihood_lasso(normalized_features[[1]],
            data_matrix[[2]], weights, l1_penalty = l1_penalty)
        if (abs(lasso_ll2 - lasso_ll1) < tolerance) {
            converged = TRUE
        }
        lasso_ll1 = lasso_ll2
        k = k + 1
    }
    weights/norms
}
```

We are now all set to try out our application on the "review" data. But before that we will partition the data into train and test sets.

The features are the pos_neg_words and the response sentiment.

```
features = pos_neg_words
output = "sentiment"
data <- construct_features_matrix(features = features, outputs = output,
    data = review_train_data)
```

```
lasso_model_lambda_0 <- lasso_cyclical_coordinate_descent(data_matrix = data,
                                                          initial_weights
                                                          = rep(0,
                                                              ncol(data[[1]])),
                                                          l1_penalty = 0,
                                                          tolerance = 1e-8)
```

```
lasso_glmnet_lambda_0 = glmnet(x, y,
                               alpha=1,
                               lambda = 0,
                               thresh = 1e-8
                               )
coef <- predict(lasso_glmnet_lambda_0,
                type="coefficients",
                s=0,
                exact = T)
-deviance(lasso_glmnet_lambda_0)/2
```

```
[1] -1326.086
```

```
coefs <- data.frame(as.matrix(cbind(lasso_model_lambda_0,
                                    coef(lasso_glmnet_lambda_0))
                              )
                   )
```

See Table 5.3

```
lasso_model_lambda_5 <- lasso_cyclical_coordinate_descent(data_matrix = data,
                                                          initial_weights
                                                          = rep(0,
                                                              ncol(data[[1]])),
                                                          l1_penalty = 5,
                                                          tolerance = 1e-8)
```

```
lasso_glmnet_lambda_5 = glmnet(x, y,
                               alpha=1,
                               lambda = 5,
                               thresh = 1e-8)
coef <- predict(lasso_glmnet_lambda_5,
                type="coefficients",
                s = 5,
                exact = T)
-deviance(lasso_glmnet_lambda_5)/2
```

```
[1] -1619.75
```

```
coefs <- data.frame(as.matrix(cbind(lasso_model_lambda_5,
                                    coef(lasso_glmnet_lambda_5))
                              )
                   )
```

Table 5.3 Lasso logistic coefficients calculated by our model and glmnet function in R using *lambda* = 0

	lasso_model_lambda_0	lasso_glmnet_lambda_0
(Intercept)	0.4945864	0.4945866
Bad	−0.1657743	−0.1657760
Never	−0.0507874	−0.0507879
Small	−0.0144560	−0.0144573
Stale	−0.2076607	−0.2076611
Not	−0.1043091	−0.1043092
Terrible	−0.2753042	−0.2753039
Good	0.0520220	0.0520220
Great	0.1460993	0.1460992
Healthy	0.0697032	0.0697032
Delicious	0.2495938	0.2495938
Favorite	0.1725760	0.1725760
Love	0.0934323	0.0934324
Glad	0.1883988	0.1883991
Recommended	0.1045560	0.1045562
Variety	0.0461344	0.0461348
Better	−0.0407602	−0.0407598
Best	0.1964706	0.1964707
Like	−0.0345274	−0.0345273
Free	0.0514779	0.0514779
Easy	0.1744155	0.1744156
Pleased	0.2398843	0.2398842
Disappointed	−0.2585203	−0.2585202
Unique	0.1412742	0.1412742

See Table 5.4

As expected, almost all features except the intercept term have been coerced to zero!

Let us have a look at another classification algorithm—Decision Trees.

Table 5.4 Lasso logistic coefficients calculated by our model and glmnet function in R using lambda = 5

	lasso_model_lambda_5	lasso_glmnet_lambda_5
(Intercept)	0.5076892	0.5
Bad	−0.1137689	0.0
Never	0.0000000	0.0
Small	0.0000000	0.0
Stale	−0.0662623	0.0
Not	−0.0790595	0.0
Terrible	−0.1241581	0.0
Good	0.0050981	0.0
Great	0.1090604	0.0
Healthy	0.0000000	0.0
Delicious	0.1723988	0.0
Favorite	0.0934079	0.0
Love	0.0473475	0.0
Glad	0.0188272	0.0
Recommended	0.0000000	0.0
Variety	0.0000000	0.0
Better	0.0000000	0.0
Best	0.1365791	0.0
Like	−0.0071403	0.0
Free	0.0000000	0.0
Easy	0.0888722	0.0
Pleased	0.0676285	0.0
Disappointed	−0.1747628	0.0
Unique	0.0000000	0.0

5.3 Decision Trees

A decision tree is a collection of *decision nodes* connected by branches, extending from the *root node* and terminating at the *leaf nodes*. Attributes are tested at each decision node, and each possible outcome results in a branch. Decision trees are used in classification problems, where the outcome is categorical.

Decision trees are widely used in the medical and finance domains alongwith text classification and spam detection. We, therefore, consider the lending club[2] data set, wherein our dataset consists of 887,379 observations with 74 features. We need to classify whether a borrower can be categorized as "fully paid" or "charged off" in the

---

[2]https://www.kaggle.com/wendykan/lending-club-loan-data, downloaded on June 20, 2017, 12:59 pm IST.

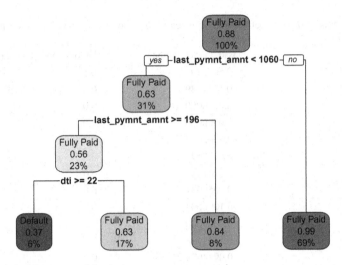

Fig. 5.8 A decision tree model

label, *loan_status* of the data set. To illustrate the point, let us use three predictor variables- *grade:* grade of the loan, *dti:* debt to income ratio, *term:* the term of the loan, *last_pymnt_amnt* : most recent payment.

Figure[3] 5.8 shows a simple decision tree. Each node shows the predicted class, i.e. 'Fully paid' or 'Defaulted'; the predicted probability of payment/default; the percentage of observation in the node.

Given an input, the decision tree model above, should be able to tell us whether an individual is likely to default or fully pay up.

From Fig. 5.8 we can observe that the model selected '*last_payment_amnt* < 1060' as the best feature to split, i.e., if the '*last_payment_amnt*' is not less than 1060, all loans are classified safe and *viceversa*.

The model then figures out that '*last_payment_amnt* >= 196' is the next best feature and if '*last_payment_amnt* >= 196' it is a safe loan and *vice versa*.

Finally, '*dti* >= 22' is the best feature, which results in the subsequent leaf nodes.

We will use the quality metric, classification error in our decision tree algorithm, i.e.,

$$\text{Classification Error} = \frac{\text{number of incorrect predictions}}{\text{total number of observations}} \qquad (5.3.1)$$

---

[3] rpart.plot package was used to plot this figure, author = Stephen Milborrow, title = rpart.plot: Plot rpart Models. An Enhanced Version of plot.rpart, year = 2016, note = R package, url = http://CRAN. R-project.org/package=rpart.plot.

5.3.1 Decision Tree Algorithm

We can now roughly define the decision tree algorithm as follows:

1. Start with an empty tree
2. Select a feature to split the data (that which gives the least error)
3. For each split, consider the following stopping conditions:

   - If the number of observations is less than the minimum specified, make prediction and stop
   - If all the data points belong to a specific label, stop
   - If there are no features to split, stop
   - If it reaches the maximum specified tree depth, stop

4. If none of the stopping conditions are reached, go to step 2 (recurse)

In the above algorithm, the best feature to split is the one with the lowest classification error. In our example, the best feature to start the split happened to be ($last\_payment\_amnt < 1060$). In the second step, the feature ($last\_payment\_amnt \geq 196$) has the lowest classification error and in the third step, the feature (dti) has the lowest classification error.

We stop, when creating a further partition does not reduce classification error or, when the node has too few training observations. Even then, trees built with this stopping criterion tend to overfit training data. To avoid this, a post-processing step called pruning is used to make the tree smaller.

One of the advantages of decision trees is that it gives interpretability to the model by defining the decision rule. In our example, it can be easily interpreted that if $last\_payment\_amnt \geq 1060$, it can be assumed that the loan is fully paid; and so forth.

However, decision trees are **highly prone to overfitting** and one of the ways to restrict overfitting (amongst others) is to have a control over tree depth.

5.3.2 Overfitting in Decision Trees

To understand overfitting due to tree depth, let us fit two decision tree models with different tree sizes. We will then apply the models on test data and evaluate the following:

- **False negatives**: Loans that are safe but predicted as risky. This may result in an opportunity cost of losing a customer.
- **False positives**: Loans that are risky but predicted as safe. These are costly, because it results in disbursing a risky loan.
- **Accuracy**: Overall accuracy of the model.

Table 5.5 Overfitting decreases the accuracy of a complex model with respect to a simple model on unseen data

	False_Positives	False_Negatives	Accuracy	Lift
pred_with_depth_1_train	0	610	0.8806262	0.000172
pred_with_depth_1_test	0	609	0.8807986	
pred_with_depth_6_train	81	263	0.9326810	−0.006081
pred_with_depth_6_test	106	269	0.9266001	

```
train_index <- createDataPartition(y = loan_data$loan_status, p = 0.5)
loan_data_train <- dplyr::slice(loan_data, train_index$Resample1)
loan_data_test <- dplyr::slice(loan_data, -train_index$Resample1)

features <- c("last_pymnt_amnt", "dti", "term", "purpose", "tot_cur_bal",
    "grade")
formula <- as.formula(paste0("loan_status~", paste(features, collapse = "+")))

control_1 <- rpart.control(minsplit = 10, maxdepth = 1)
control_6 <- rpart.control(minsplit = 10, maxdepth = 6)

fit_1 <- rpart(formula, data = loan_data_train, control = control_1)
fit_6 <- rpart(formula, data = loan_data_train, control = control_6)

pred_with_depth_1_train <- predict(fit_1, newdata = loan_data_train,
                 type = "class")
pred_with_depth_1_test <- predict(fit_1, newdata = loan_data_test,
                 type = "class")
pred_with_depth_6_train <- predict(fit_6, newdata = loan_data_train,
                 type = "class")
```

From the results in Table 5.5, it may be observed that the model with tree depth $= 1$ (also known as *decision stump*), performs better than the model with tree depth $= 6$, on unseen data.

5.3.3 Control of Tree Parameters

To prevent overfitting, we control some tree specific parameters which are the following:

- **minsplit**: Defines the minimum number of observations which are required in a node to be considered for splitting. This parameter is used to control overfitting. High values prevent a model from learning relations which might be highly specific to the particular sample selected for a tree. The ideal method to find the correct value of the parameter is by cross-validation.
- **minbucket**: Defines the minimum observations required in a terminal node or leaf and is also used to control overfitting. Lower values should be chosen for imbalanced data because the regions in which the minority class will be in majority will be very small.

- **maxdepth**: This the maximum depth of a tree and is used to control overfitting. Higher tree depth will allow the model to learn relations very specific to a particular sample. This should also be determined using cross-validation.
- **max_features**: Defines the number of features to consider while searching for the best split. As a thumb rule, this can be the square root of the total number of features. Higher values of this parameter may lead to overfitting.

We normally use a stopping criteria to control these parameters and we will be using them in our decision tree algorithm below.

5.3.4 Writing the Decision Tree Application

We know that the prediction at a node is the majority class for all data points at the node. The following function calculates the number of misclassified examples when predicting the majority class, so that we can determine the best feature to split. The function returns the number of misclassified labels.

```
node_error <- function (labels) {
  min(sum(labels == 1), sum(labels == 0))
}
```

The next function will select the best feature for the split by calculating the error of the split for all features. The feature with the lowest error is returned.

```
best_splitting_feature <- function(data, features, target) {
    errors <- sapply(features, function(feature) {
        left_labels <- data[data[feature] == 0, ][[target]]
        right_labels <- data[data[feature] == 1, ][[target]]
        left_error <- node_error(left_labels)
        right_error <- node_error(right_labels)
        error = (left_error + right_error)/length(data)
    })
    return(names(which.min(errors)))
}
```

A leaf is created identifying the positive and negative labels.

```
create_leaf <- function(labels) {
  pos = sum(labels == 1)
  neg = sum(labels == 0)

  list(splitting_feature = NULL,
       left              = NULL,
       right             = NULL,
       is_leaf           = TRUE,
       prediction        = ifelse(pos > neg, 1, 0))
}
```

We are now ready to build our decision tree.
We introduce four stopping conditions as discussed in Sect. 5.3.1

- **Stopping condition 1**: Reached minimum number of observations at node.
- **Stopping condition 2**: All data points in the node belong to the same class

- **Stopping condition 3**: No feature to split on.
- **Stopping condition 4**: Reached the maximum specified tree depth.

While the stopping conditions are not reached, the algorithm, continuously recurses.

```
decision_tree <- function(data, features, target, current_depth = 0,
    max_depth = max_depth, minobs = minobs) {
    remaining_features = features
    target_values = data[[target]]

    if (length(target_values) < minobs) {
        cat("Stopping condition 1: Reached min number of obs at node\n")
        return(create_leaf(target_values))
    }

    if (node_error(target_values) == 0) {
        cat("Stopping condition 2: Data points in node belong to same class\n")
        return(create_leaf(target_values))
    }

    if (length(remaining_features) == 0) {
        cat("Stopping condition 3: All features have been considered\n")
        return(create_leaf(target_values))
    }

    if (current_depth >= max_depth) {
        cat("Stopping condition 4: Reached maximum depth\n")
        return(create_leaf(target_values))
    }

    best_split_feature = best_splitting_feature(data,
        remaining_features, target)

    left_split = data[data[best_split_feature] == 0,
        ]
    right_split = data[data[best_split_feature] ==
        1, ]

    remaining_features = remaining_features[-which(remaining_features ==
        best_split_feature)]

    if (nrow(left_split) == nrow(data)) {
        return(create_leaf(left_split[[target]]))
    }
    if (nrow(right_split) == nrow(data)) {
        return(create_leaf(right_split[[target]]))
    }

    left_tree = decision_tree(left_split, remaining_features,
        target, current_depth + 1, max_depth, minobs)
    right_tree = decision_tree(right_split, remaining_features,
        target, current_depth + 1, max_depth, minobs)

    return(list(is_leaf = FALSE, prediction = NULL,
        splitting_feature = best_split_feature, left = left_tree,
        right = right_tree))
}
```

Prediction of an unseen label is described here.

```
predict_tree <- function (dec_tree, data) {
  if (dec_tree$is_leaf) {
    return(dec_tree$prediction)
  }
  split_feature_value = data[[dec_tree$splitting_feature]]
  ifelse(
    split_feature_value == 0,
    predict_tree(dec_tree$left, data),
    predict_tree(dec_tree$right, data)
  )
}
```

We will apply our application to the lending club loan data set. The target variable is *loan_status*, which consists of 207,723 "fully paid" loans and considered as "safe" loans and, 45,248 "charged off" loans and thus considered "unsafe".

Our data set is **highly imbalanced**, i.e., it consists of 90,496 labels "Fully Paid" and 45,248 labels "Charged Off".

This is an important issue, because an imbalanced dataset may lead to inflated performance estimates, which in turn may lead to false conclusions.

An imbalanced training set may result in a classifier that is biased towards the majority class. When the trained model is applied to a test set that is similarly imbalanced, it would yield an optimistic accuracy estimate. In the extreme case, the classifier might assign every single test case to the majority class, thereby achieving an accuracy equal to the proportion of test cases belonging to the majority class. One of the strategies is to *undersample* the larger class or *oversample* the smaller class.

We will, therefore, undersample the class having the larger number of observations (i.e., where loan_status is fully paid), in order to balance out our dataset, i.e., the labels in our data set will have 45,248 observations for "Fully Paid" and "Charged Off", respectively.

```
loans <- read.csv(paste(file_path, "loan.csv", sep = ""))
safe_loans <- loans[loans$loan_status == "Fully Paid", ]
unsafe_loans <- loans[loans$loan_status == "Charged Off", ]
safe_loans$safe <- 1
unsafe_loans$safe <- 0
safe_loans <- safe_loans[1:nrow(unsafe_loans), ]
```

We will use the predictor variables- "grade", "term", "home_ownership" and "emp_length". We transform them into binary features using the "model.matrix" function.

```
loans <- select(rbind(safe_loans, unsafe_loans),
                grade,
                term,
                home_ownership,
                emp_length,
                safe)

loans_data <- data.frame(loan_status = loans$safe)
loans_data <- cbind(loans_data, model.matrix(~loans$grade - 1))
loans_data <- cbind(loans_data, model.matrix(~loans$term - 1))
```

```
loans_data <- cbind(loans_data, model.matrix(~loans$home_ownership - 1))
loans_data <- cbind(loans_data, model.matrix(~loans$emp_length - 1))
colnames(loans_data) <- c("loan_status",
                          "grade.A",
                          "grade.B",
                          "grade.C",
                          "grade.D",
                          "grade.E",
                          "gradeF",
                          "gradeG",
                          "term.36.months",
                          "term.60.months",
                          "home_ownership.ANY",
                          "home_ownership.MORTGAGE",
                          "home_ownership.NONE",
                          "home_ownership.OTHER",
                          "home_ownership.OWN",
                          "home_ownership.RENT",
                          "emp_length.1year",
                          "emp_length.10+years",
                          "emp_length.2years",
                          "emp_length.3years",
                          "emp_length.4years",
                          "emp_length.5years",
                          "emp_length.6years",
                          "emp_length.7years",
                          "emp_length.8years",
                          "emp_length.9years",
                          "emp_length.<1year",
                          "emp_length.n/a" )
```

Let us look at the structure of our data set.

```
'data.frame':    90496 obs. of  28 variables:
 $ loan_status              : num  1 1 1 1 1 1 1 1 1 1 ...
 $ grade.A                  : num  0 0 0 1 0 0 0 0 0 0 ...
 $ grade.B                  : num  1 0 0 0 0 0 1 1 0 0 ...
 $ grade.C                  : num  0 1 1 0 0 1 0 0 0 1 ...
 $ grade.D                  : num  0 0 0 0 0 0 0 0 1 0 ...
 $ grade.E                  : num  0 0 0 0 1 0 0 0 0 0 ...
 $ gradeF                   : num  0 0 0 0 0 0 0 0 0 0 ...
 $ gradeG                   : num  0 0 0 0 0 0 0 0 0 0 ...
 $ term.36.months           : num  1 1 1 1 1 0 1 1 1 1 ...
 $ term.60.months           : num  0 0 0 0 0 1 0 0 0 0 ...
 $ home_ownership.ANY       : num  0 0 0 0 0 0 0 0 0 0 ...
 $ home_ownership.MORTGAGE: num  0 0 0 0 0 0 0 0 0 0 ...
 $ home_ownership.NONE      : num  0 0 0 0 0 0 0 0 0 0 ...
 $ home_ownership.OTHER     : num  0 0 0 0 0 0 0 0 0 0 ...
 $ home_ownership.OWN       : num  0 0 0 0 0 1 1 0 0 0 ...
 $ home_ownership.RENT      : num  1 1 1 1 1 0 0 1 1 1 ...
 $ emp_length.1year         : num  0 0 0 0 0 0 0 0 0 0 ...
 $ emp_length.10+years      : num  1 1 1 0 0 0 1 0 0 0 ...
 $ emp_length.2years        : num  0 0 0 0 0 0 0 0 0 0 ...
```

```
$ emp_length.3years      : num  0 0 0 1 0 0 0 1 0 0 ...
$ emp_length.4years      : num  0 0 0 0 0 0 0 0 0 1 ...
$ emp_length.5years      : num  0 0 0 0 0 1 0 0 0 0 ...
$ emp_length.6years      : num  0 0 0 0 0 0 0 0 0 0 ...
$ emp_length.7years      : num  0 0 0 0 0 0 0 0 0 0 ...
$ emp_length.8years      : num  0 0 0 0 0 0 0 0 0 0 ...
$ emp_length.9years      : num  0 0 0 0 1 0 0 0 0 0 ...
$ emp_length.<1year      : num  0 0 0 0 0 0 0 0 1 0 ...
$ emp_length.n/a         : num  0 0 0 0 0 0 0 0 0 0 ...
```

Partition our transformed data set into training and test data and, compare our application with the "rpart" function.

```
set.seed(61)
idx <- sample(seq(1, 3), size = nrow(loans_data), replace = TRUE,
    prob = c(0.8, 0.2, 0.2))
train <- loans_data[idx == 1, ]
test <- loans_data[idx == 2, ]
validation <- loans_data[idx == 3, ]
features <- colnames(train[-1])
target <- "loan_status"
```

```
decision_tree_model <- decision_tree(train,
                                     features,
                                     target,
                                     max_depth = 6,
                                     minobs = 10)
```

```
Stopping condition 4: Reached maximum depth
Stopping condition 4: Reached maximum depth
Stopping condition 4: Reached maximum depth
Stopping condition 4: Reached maximum depth
Stopping condition 4: Reached maximum depth
Stopping condition 4: Reached maximum depth
Stopping condition 1: Reached min number of obs at node
Stopping condition 1: Reached min number of obs at node
Stopping condition 4: Reached maximum depth
Stopping condition 1: Reached min number of obs at node
Stopping condition 1: Reached min number of obs at node
Stopping condition 1: Reached min number of obs at node
```

In our code above, we have specified-

- Any decision node can only split if the minimum number of observations in the node is 10
- Maximum tree depth cannot exceed 6 levels after the starting node

We stop when adding a partition does not reduce classification error or, when the node has too few training observations. Even then, trees built with this stopping criterion tend to overfit training data. To avoid this, a post-processing step called pruning is used to make the tree smaller.

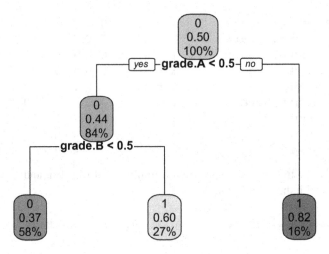

Fig. 5.9 Tree nodes of the trained tree model obtained using rpart

```
pred <- predict_tree(decision_tree_model, test)
confusionMatrix(pred, test$loan_status)[[3]][1]
```

```
 Accuracy
0.6615324
```

```
fit <- rpart(loan_status ~ ., train, method = 'class')
pred <- predict(fit, test, type = 'class')
confusionMatrix(pred, test$loan_status)[[3]][1]
```

```
 Accuracy
0.6592285
```

Indeed, our decision tree application with our defined stopping conditions turns out an slightly better accuracy !

```
rpart.plot(fit, cex = 0.73)
```

From Fig. 5.9 we can observe that the model selected "grade A" as the best feature to split, i.e., if the loan has an "A" grade, all loans are classified safe. The model then figures out that "grade B" is the next best feature to split, i.e., if it is not even "B" grade, the loan is unsafe.

5.3.5 Unbalanced Data

As discussed above, unbalanced data results in a classifier that is biased towards the majority class. Some of the ways to tackle the problem is by

- Restore balance in the data set by undersampling or oversampling.
- Maximize the F1 statistic defined as $\{2 * Precision \times fracRecallPrecision + Recall\}$ using cross-validation.
- Modify the costs of misclassification to prevent bias. In the "tree" function in the *tree* package, the "weights" argument can be used to severely penalize the algorithm for misclassifications of the rare positive cases.
- Use the "cost" argument in "rpart", to define relative costs for misclassifications of true positives and true negatives by setting a high cost for the misclassification of the rare class.

I personally do not favor oversampling/undersampling, as it introduces dependent observations in the dataset and this violates the assumptions of independence.

5.4 Assessing Performance

How do we assess the performance of a classifier model? To understand this we need to know the baseline accuracy of a classifier, i.e., if we do a random guess, how much error can we expect?

It turns out that for binary classifications, i.e., labels having 2 classes, the baseline accuracy will be 0.5, i.e., we have a 50% chance of choosing either label. If the labels have 3 classes, the baseline accuracy will be $\frac{1}{3} = 0.66$ and, in general, the baseline accuracy for any classifier is $\frac{1}{k}$, where k is the number of classes in the label.

These are applicable for balanced data sets where the proportion of labels are equal. For unbalanced data sets, the baseline accuracy is not just choosing the response randomly, but guessing the majority class. Therefore, it will depend on the proportion of each label. The majority class baseline accuracy for an unbalanced data set having a label proportion of 70 and 30% would be $\frac{70}{100} = 0.7$.

So, at the very least, our classifier should better the baseline accuracy.

The output of a classification algorithm can be tabulated in a matrix known as Confusion Matrix. In a binary outcome example, the confusion matrix will have four outcomes

- **True Positives (TP)**: are positive items correctly classified as positive.
- **True Negatives (TN)**: are negative items correctly identified as negatives.
- **False Positives (FP)**: are negative items classified as positive.
- **False Negatives (FN)**: are positives items classified as negative.

The accuracy of the model can be maximized if we have higher values of TP and TN. But we may not be interested in maximizing the accuracy instead, if we attribute a certain cost to FP and FN, we would like to minimize the total cost.

In our loan_data example, we would be more interested to reduce the False Positives, i.e., loans that are risky but predicted as safe, at the cost of missing out on some genuine loan seekers but predicted as risky, i.e., False Negative. Depending on our objective, we can alter the threshold of probability to either increase or decrease the values of the outcome that we seek.

In the area of medicine, a False Positive is a situation when a particular test designed to detect a given condition returns a positive result when the person does not have the given condition. A bigger danger could be a False Negative, wherein in the presence of a given condition the result predicts an absence of the given condition.

It may be appreciated that the presence of False Positives and/or False Negatives can be the determining factors in different domains and, we are sometimes prepared to accept a lower accuracy as long as the FP/FN are within acceptable limits.

We start by defining the confusion matrix which is represented as

Confusion Matrix		Predicted Class	
		Neg	Pos
True Class	Neg	TN	FP
	Pos	FN	TP

From the above matrix, the measures of accuracy can be written as

$$Accuracy = \frac{TP + TN}{TP + FP + TN + FN} \tag{5.4.1}$$

$$\begin{aligned} Classification\ Error &= 1 - Accuracy \\ &= \frac{FP + FN}{TP + FP + TN + FN} \end{aligned} \tag{5.4.2}$$

For imbalanced data sets the F-measure is a better measurement than Accuracy, which is computed using two other performance measures, precision, and recall.

Also as discussed above, sometimes the type of misclassification is important to understand. To measure specific misclassifications, the True Positive Rate (TPR) (also known as Recall or Sensitivity), and True Negative Rate (TNR) (also known as Specificity), are used to determine the performance of the classifier. Sensitivity is the ratio of the number of true positive predictions over all the positive labels present in the data. Specificity is the ratio of true negative predictions over all the negative labels present in the data.

$$Precision = \frac{TP}{TP + FP} \tag{5.4.3}$$

$$Recall\ (\text{Sensitivity, or TPR}) = \frac{TP}{TP + FN} \tag{5.4.4}$$

$$Specificity\ (\text{TNR}) = \frac{TN}{TN + FP} \tag{5.4.5}$$

$$FPR = \frac{FP}{TN + FP} \tag{5.4.6}$$

$$F1 = 2 \times \frac{Precision \times Recall}{Precision + Recall} \tag{5.4.7}$$

Receiver Operating Characteristic curve (ROC), is an important accuracy measure for imbalanced data, where FPR is plotted against TPR. The importance of the ROC curve lies in the fact that, changes in class distribution does not affect the final result as both FPR and TPR happen to be a columnar ratio of the confusion matrix.

While ROC curve is a good visualization aid, a numeric value representing the ROC is the Area Under the ROC Curve (AUC). AUC values lie between 0 and 1, higher the value, better the accuracy.

Let us find the different performance measures for our logistic regression model.

5.4.1 Assessing Performance–Logistic Regression

We will use the training and test sets from our review data and train a ridge logistic regression model with $\lambda = 0.01$. We will then test the model on unseen data.

We will also alter the probability threshold to see how this reduces the number of False Positives.

```
x_train <- model.matrix(sentiment~., review_train_data)[,-1]
y_train <- review_train_data$sentiment

x_test <- model.matrix(sentiment~., review_test_data)[,-1]
y_test <- review_test_data$sentiment

# Ridge logistic with different probability thresholds
ridge_logistic = glmnet(x_train, y_train,
                        alpha=0,
                        lambda = 0.01,
                        thresh = 1e-8)
probs_ridge_logistic <- predict(ridge_logistic,
                        newx = x_test,
                        type = "response",
                        s = 0.01,
                        exact = T)

pred_ridge_logistic = ifelse(probs_ridge_logistic > 0.5, 1, 0)
confusionMatrix(pred_ridge_logistic, y_test)$table
```

```
          Reference
Prediction    0    1
         0 4923 2591
         1 1556 3888
```

```
FP <- confusionMatrix(pred_ridge_logistic, y_test)$table[1,2]
Accuracy = confusionMatrix(pred_ridge_logistic, y_test)$overall[[1]]
```

With probability threshold of 0.5, the number of False
Positives are:
            2591 and accuracy: 0.680

```
pred_ridge_logistic = ifelse(probs_ridge_logistic > 0.4, 1, 0)
confusionMatrix(pred_ridge_logistic, y_test)$table
```

          Reference
Prediction   0   1
         0 2859 878
         1 3620 5601

```
FP <- confusionMatrix(pred_ridge_logistic, y_test)$table[1,2]
Accuracy = confusionMatrix(pred_ridge_logistic, y_test)$overall[[1]]
```

With probability threshold of 0.4, the number of False
Positives are: 878
            and accuracy: 0.653

```
# Calculate AUC ridge logistic
pred_ridge_logistic <- prediction(probs_ridge_logistic, y_test)
auc_ridge_logistic <- performance(pred_ridge_logistic, measure = "auc")
auc_value_ridge_logistic <- auc_ridge_logistic@y.values[[1]]
auc_value_ridge_logistic # 0.7505818
```

[1] 0.7505818

```
# Lasso logistic with different probability thresholds
lasso_logistic = glmnet(x_train, y_train,
                        alpha=1,
                        lambda = 0.01,
                        thresh = 1e-8)
probs_lasso_logistic <- predict(lasso_logistic,
                                newx = x_test,
                                type = "response",
                                s = 0.01,
                                exact = T)

pred_lasso_logistic = ifelse(probs_lasso_logistic > 0.5, 1, 0)
confusionMatrix(pred_lasso_logistic, y_test)$table
```

          Reference
Prediction   0   1
         0 3985 1705
         1 2494 4774

```
FP <- confusionMatrix(pred_lasso_logistic, y_test)$table[1,2]
Accuracy = confusionMatrix(pred_lasso_logistic, y_test)$overall[[1]]
```

Table 5.6 Summary of accuracy based on different probability thresholds for ridge and lasso logistic regression, using lambda = 0.01

Method	Threshold	FP	Accuracy	Threshold	FP	Accuracy	AUC
Ridge logistic	0.5	2591	0.680	0.4	878	0.653	0.7506
Lasso logistic	0.5	1705	0.676	0.4	643	0.625	0.7495

```
At a threshold of 0.5, the number of False Positives
are: 1705
              and accuracy: 0.676
```

```
pred_lasso_logistic = ifelse(probs_lasso_logistic > 0.4, 1, 0)
confusionMatrix(pred_lasso_logistic, y_test)$table
```

```
          Reference
Prediction     0    1
         0  2262  643
         1  4217 5836
```

```
FP <- confusionMatrix(pred_lasso_logistic, y_test)$table[1,2]
Accuracy = confusionMatrix(pred_lasso_logistic, y_test)$overall[[1]]
```

```
At a threshold of 0.4, the number of False Positives
are 643 and accuracy 0.625
```

```
# Calculate AUC lasso logistic
pred_lasso_logistic <- prediction(probs_lasso_logistic, y_test)
auc_lasso_logistic <- performance(pred_lasso_logistic, measure = "auc")
auc_value_lasso_logistic <- auc_lasso_logistic@y.values[[1]]
auc_value_lasso_logistic
```

```
[1] 0.7494858
```

It may be observed from Table 5.6 that lowering the probability threshold from 0.5 to 0.4 drastically reduce the number of False Positives, in both ridge and lasso logistic regression. Both the models have comparable AUC scores and, if we can allow for a 0.03% drop in accuracy, the lasso logistic model fares the best (if False Positives are our concern).

Now, let us plot the ROC curve in Fig. 5.10.

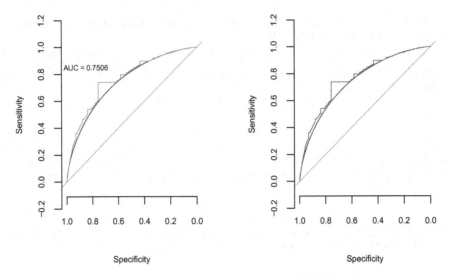

Fig. 5.10 ROC curves: The left plot is the ROC curve for Ridge Logistic and right plot is that for Lasso Logistic. Both the models have been fitted with $\lambda = 0.01$. The very close AUC values are reflected in the respective ROC curves

5.5 Boosting

Boosting is a sequential technique which works on the principle of ensemble, which is based on the technique of combining a set of weak learners to get better prediction accuracy. At any instant t, the model outcomes are weighed based on the outcomes of the previous instant $(t - 1)$. The outcomes which are predicted correctly are given a lower weight and those which are predicted incorrectly, are weighted higher.

Let us try and understand Boosting by an example of credit worthiness for a loan. To predict if an individual is worthy of a loan, we may frame the following rules:

(a) If the length of employment is less than 3 years—it is a risky loan
(b) If the loan amount requested is less than 10,000—it is a safe loan
(c) If the ratio of the borrower's total monthly debt payments to the total debt oblig-ations is greater than 3— it is a risky loan
(d) If the monthly payment owed by the borrower if the loan originates is greater than 1200—the loan is risky.

But, the above rules may not be strong enough individually to classify a safe or a risky loan as they are not "powerful" enough. We therefore call the above rules as "weak learners". To convert the above weak learners into a single strong learner, we will combine the prediction of each weak learner. In the above, example we have defined 4 weak learners of which, 3 are voted as "risky" and 1 is voted as "safe". Therefore, in this case we will consider a loan as risky because we have higher vote for "risky".

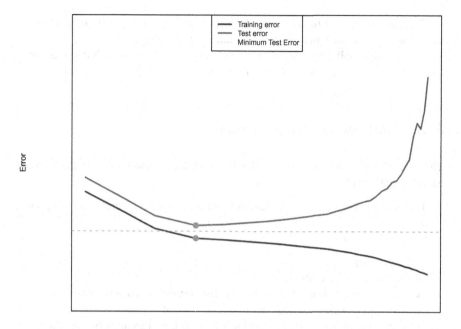

Fig. 5.11 Training and Test Error vs. Model Complexity. The vertical pink dashed line indicates the correct model complexity

To summarize, we can say that simple weak classifiers like shallow decision trees and decision stumps, (including logistic regression with simple features) have low variance and the learning is fast. But how do we find a classifier that is just right?

We go back to our plot of training and test errors with model capacity as shown in Fig. 5.11.

Like every other model, a tree-based model also suffers from the plague of bias and variance. As discussed in Chap. 3, bias is, "how much on an average are the predicted values different from the actual value" and variance is, "how different will the predictions of the model be at the same point if different samples are taken from the same population."

You build a small tree and you will get a model with low variance and high bias. How do you manage to balance the trade off between bias and variance.

Normally, as we increase the complexity of our model, we see a reduction in prediction error due to lower bias in the model. And as we continue to make our model more complex, we end up overfitting our model which will start suffering from high variance.

An ideal model should maintain a balance between these two types of errors. Ensemble learning is one way to manage this bias–variance tradeoff.

The options are to either add more features or increase tree depth or, combine an ensemble of weak classifiers, to arrive at the right complexity.

An ensemble will have classifiers, $f_1(x)$, $f_2(x)$, ..., $f_T(x)$ with corresponding coefficients $\hat{w}_1, \hat{w}_2, \ldots, \hat{w}_T$, which will predict $\hat{y} = sign(\sum_{i=1}^{T} \hat{w}_T f_T(x))$.

5.5.1   AdaBoost Learning Ensemble

This brings us to **AdaBoost** (i.e., Adaptive Boosting),[4] also known as the learning ensemble. Here is how AdaBoost works

1. The base learner takes all the features and assigns equal weights for all points: $\alpha_i = \frac{1}{m}$.
2. For $t = 1, \ldots, T$

   - Learn $f_t(\mathbf{x})$
   - Compute coefficients $\hat{w}_t$
   - Compute prediction error caused by first (previous) learning algorithm.
   - Recompute weights α_i, i.e., mistakes are weighted more.
   - Iterate the above steps till the limit of learning algorithm is reached or, an higher accuracy is achieved.

3. Final model prediction: $\hat{y} = (\sum_{t=1}^{T} \hat{w}_t f_t(x))$

Boosting pays higher focus on examples which have higher errors by the preceding weak rules and combines the outputs from weak learners and creates a strong learner which eventually improves the prediction power of the model.

5.5.2   AdaBoost: Learning from Weighted Data

The **weighted classification error** can be written as

- Total weight of mistakes = $\sum_{i=1}^{m} \alpha_i \Pi(\hat{y}_i \neq y_i)$
- Total weight of all points = $\sum_{i=1}^{m} \alpha_i$
- Weighted error = $\frac{\text{Total weight of mistakes}}{\text{Total weight of data points}}$

Now the best possible weighted error is 0, the worst is 1.0 and for a random classifier it is 0.5.

The formula for computing the coefficient $\hat{w}_t$ is

$$\hat{w}_t = \frac{1}{2}ln(\frac{1 - \text{weighted error}\,(f_t)}{\text{weighted error}\,(f_t)}) \qquad (5.5.1)$$

---

[4]A machine learning algorithm formulated by Yoav Freund and Robert Schapire in 1999.

Table 5.7 Computing the coefficients, $\hat{w}_t$

Is $f_t(x)good$?	weighted error (f_t)	$\frac{1-\text{weighted error}\,(f_t)}{\text{weighted error}\,(f_t)}$	$\hat{w}_t$
Yes	0.1	9	1.098
Random	0.5	1	0
No	0.9	0.11	−1.098

Let us intuitively try and see what is going on. In Table 5.7, we assume a learning classifier to predict correctly/incorrectly and based on some hypothetical weighted errors, we will compute the coefficient $\hat{w}_t$ on training data.

In Table 5.7, we see that the formula assigns a low weighted error to a good classifier and *vice versa*; however, it assigns a weight of 0.5 to a random classifier.

5.5.3 AdaBoost: Updating the Weights

As we seen above in AdaBoost, given an integer T specifying the number of trials, T weighted training sets $s_1, s_2, \ldots, s_T$ are generated in sequence and T classifiers $C_1, C_2, \ldots, C_T$ are built. A final classifier C^* is formed using a weighted voting scheme, i.e., the weight of each classifier depends on its performance on the training set used to build it.

The formula for updating the weights α_i is

$$\alpha_i = \begin{cases} \alpha_i e^{-\hat{w}_t} & if \quad f_t(x_i) = y_i \\ \alpha_i e^{\hat{w}_t} & if \quad f_t(x_i) \neq y_i \end{cases} \tag{5.5.2}$$

Let us again intuitively try and see what is going on. In Table 5.8, we assume a learning classifier to predict correctly/incorrectly and based on some hypothetical weighted errors, we will compute the coefficient $\hat{w}_t$ on training data

Table 5.8 Computing the updated weights, α_i

Is $f_t(x_i) = y_i$?	$\hat{w}_t$	Multiply α_i by	Implication
Yes	1.098	$e^{-1.098} = 0.333$	Decrease importance of x_i, y_i
Yes	0	$e^{-0} = 1$	Keep importance the same
No	1.098	$e^{1.098} = 2.99$	Increase importance of x_i, y_i

5.5.4   AdaBoost Algorithm

One last thing we need to do is to normalize the weights α_i as otherwise, it may cause numerical instability.

We can now finally, summarize the above and define our AdaBoost algorithm

At start, assign same weights to all points: $\alpha_i = \dfrac{1}{m}$

for $t = 1, 2, \ldots, T$

learn $f_t(\mathbf{x})$ with data weights: $\hat{w}_t = \dfrac{1}{2} ln \dfrac{1 - \text{weighted error}(f_t)}{\text{weighted error}(f_t)}$

recompute weights $\alpha_i : \alpha_i = \begin{cases} \alpha_i e^{-\hat{w}_t} & if \quad f_t(x_i) = y_i \\ \alpha_i e^{\hat{w}_t} & if \quad f_t(x_i) \neq y_i \end{cases}$ \hfill (5.5.3)

Normalize the weights $\alpha_i : \alpha_i \leftarrow \dfrac{\alpha_i}{\sum_{j=1}^{m} \alpha_j}$

Predict: $\hat{y} = Sign(\sum_{t=1}^{T} \hat{w}_t f_t(x))$

We will first write our application for weighted decision trees and then move on to write our AdaBoost application.

5.5.5   Writing the Weighted Decision Tree Algorithm

```
intermediate_node_weighted_mistakes <- function(labels_in_node, data_weights){
  total_weight_positive =  sum(data_weights[which(labels_in_node == 1)])

  weighted_mistakes_all_negative = total_weight_positive

  total_weight_negative =  sum(data_weights[which(labels_in_node == 0)])

  weighted_mistakes_all_positive = total_weight_negative
  if (weighted_mistakes_all_positive <= weighted_mistakes_all_negative){
    weight = weighted_mistakes_all_positive
    class_label = +1
  }
  else{
    weight = weighted_mistakes_all_negative
    class_label = 0
  }
  return (list(weight, class_label))
}
```

```
best_splitting_feature <- function (data, features, target, data_weights) {

  errors <- sapply(features, function (feature){
```

```
    left_labels  <- data[data[feature] == 0, ][[target]]
    right_labels <- data[data[feature] == 1, ][[target]]

    left_data_weights = data_weights[data[feature] == 0]
    right_data_weights = data_weights[data[feature] == 1]

    left_weighted_mistakes = intermediate_node_weighted_mistakes(left_labels,
                                                left_data_weights)[[1]]
    right_weighted_mistakes = intermediate_node_weighted_mistakes(right_labels,
                                                right_data_weights)[[1]]

    error = (left_weighted_mistakes + right_weighted_mistakes) /
      (sum(left_data_weights) + sum(right_data_weights))
  })
  return(names(which.min(errors)))
}
```

```
create_leaf <- function(target_values, data_weights){
  leaf = list(splitting_feature = NULL,
              is_leaf           = TRUE
              )
weighted_error = intermediate_node_weighted_mistakes(target_values,
                                                data_weights)[[1]]
best_class     = intermediate_node_weighted_mistakes(target_values,
                                                data_weights)[[2]]
leaf$prediction = best_class
return(leaf)
}
```

```
weighted_decision_tree <- function(data, features,
                                   target,
                                   data_weights,
                                   current_depth = 1,
                                   max_depth = max_depth,
                                   minobs = minobs,
                                   verbose = verbose){
remaining_features = features
target_values = data[[target]]

if(verbose == TRUE){
  cat("----------------------------\n")
  cat(sprintf("Subtree depth = %s (%s data points)", current_depth,
              length(target_values)))
}
if(intermediate_node_weighted_mistakes(target_values,
                                       data_weights)[[1]] <= 1e-15){
  if(verbose == TRUE){
    cat("\n")
    print("Stopping condition 1: Data points in node belong to the same class.")
    return(create_leaf(target_values, data_weights))
  }
}
if (length(target_values) < minobs){
  if(verbose == TRUE){
    cat("\n")
    cat("Stopping condition 2: Reached min number of obsservations
      at node\n")
  }
  return(create_leaf(target_values, data_weights))
```

```r
}
if(length(remaining_features) == 0){
  if(verbose == TRUE){
    cat("\n")
    print("Stopping condition 3: No more features to split")
  }
    return(create_leaf(target_values, data_weights))
}
if(current_depth > max_depth){
  if(verbose == TRUE){
    cat("\n")
    print("Stopping condition 4: Reached maximum depth.")
  }
    return(create_leaf(target_values, data_weights))
}
# If all datapoints are the same, splitting_feature will be NULL; Create leaf
splitting_feature = best_splitting_feature(data, remaining_features, target,
                                           data_weights)
remaining_features = remaining_features[-which(remaining_features ==
                                                 splitting_feature)]

left_split = data[data[splitting_feature] == 0, ]
right_split = data[data[splitting_feature] == 1, ]

left_data_weights = data_weights[which(data[splitting_feature] == 0)]
right_data_weights = data_weights[which(data[splitting_feature] == 1)]

if(verbose == TRUE){
cat("\n")
cat(sprintf("Spliton feature %s (left:%s data points, right:%s datapoints)\n",
            splitting_feature,
            nrow(left_split),
            nrow(right_split)))
}

# Create a leaf node if the split is "perfect"
if(nrow(left_split) == nrow(data)){
  if(verbose == TRUE){
    cat("\nCreating leaf node.\n")
  }
  return(create_leaf(left_split[[target]], data_weights))
  }

if(nrow(right_split) == nrow(data)){
  if(verbose == TRUE){
    cat("\nCreating leaf node.\n")
  }
  return(create_leaf(right_split[[target]], data_weights))
  }

left_tree = weighted_decision_tree(left_split,
                                   remaining_features,
                                   target,
                                   left_data_weights,
                                   current_depth + 1,
                                   max_depth,
                                   minobs,
                                   verbose = verbose)
right_tree = weighted_decision_tree(right_split,
```

```
                                        remaining_features,
                                        target,
                                        right_data_weights,
                                        current_depth + 1,
                                        max_depth,
                                        minobs,
                                        verbose = verbose)

return(list
       (
  is_leaf              = FALSE,
  prediction           = NULL,
  splitting_feature    = splitting_feature,
  left                 = left_tree,
  right                = right_tree)
       )
}
```

```
count_nodes <- function(tree){
  if(tree['is_leaf'] == TRUE){
  return(1)
  }
return(1 + sum(count_nodes(tree$left)) + sum(count_nodes(tree$right)))
}
```

```
predict_tree <- function (dec_tree, data) {
  if (dec_tree$is_leaf) {
    return(dec_tree$prediction)
  }
  split_feature_value = data[[dec_tree$splitting_feature]]
  ifelse(
    split_feature_value == 0,
    predict_tree(dec_tree$left, data),
    predict_tree(dec_tree$right, data)
  )
}
```

```
evaluate_classification_error <- function(tree, data){
  prediction = predict_tree(tree, data)
return(sum(prediction != data[target]) / nrow(data))
}
```

Let us execute our "weighted decision tree" application; we will initialize the weights to 1.

```
data_weights = rep(1, nrow(train))

decision_tree = weighted_decision_tree(train,
                                       features,
                                       target,
                                       data_weights,
                                       max_depth = 4,
                                       minobs = 10,
                                       verbose = TRUE)
```

```
-----------------------------
Subtree depth = 1 (60225 data points)
Split on feature grade.A (left:50737 data points,
right:9488 data points)
-----------------------------
Subtree depth = 2 (50737 data points)
Split on feature grade.B (left:34687 data points,
right:16050 data points)
-----------------------------
Subtree depth = 3 (34687 data points)
Split on feature home_ownership.OTHER (left:34656 data
points, right:31 data points)
-----------------------------
Subtree depth = 4 (34656 data points)
Split on feature grade.C (left:19804 data points,
right:14852 data points)
-----------------------------
Subtree depth = 5 (19804 data points)
[1] "Stopping condition 4: Reached maximum depth."
-----------------------------
Subtree depth = 5 (14852 data points)
[1] "Stopping condition 4: Reached maximum depth."
-----------------------------
Subtree depth = 4 (31 data points)
Split on feature term.36.months (left:3 data points,
right:28 data points)
-----------------------------
Subtree depth = 5 (3 data points)
[1] "Stopping condition 1: Data points in node belong
to the same class."
-----------------------------
Subtree depth = 5 (28 data points)
[1] "Stopping condition 4: Reached maximum depth."
-----------------------------
Subtree depth = 3 (16050 data points)
Split on feature emp_length.n/a (left:15392 data points,
right:658 data points)
-----------------------------
Subtree depth = 4 (15392 data points)
Split on feature home_ownership.NONE (left:15387 data
points, right:5 data points)
-----------------------------
Subtree depth = 5 (15387 data points)
[1] "Stopping condition 4: Reached maximum depth."
-----------------------------
```

```
Subtree depth = 5 (5 data points)
Stopping condition 2: Reached min number of
obsservations
        at node
----------------------------
Subtree depth = 4 (658 data points)
Split on feature term.36.months (left:57 data points,
right:601 data points)
----------------------------
Subtree depth = 5 (57 data points)
[1] "Stopping condition 4: Reached maximum depth."
----------------------------
Subtree depth = 5 (601 data points)
[1] "Stopping condition 4: Reached maximum depth."
----------------------------
Subtree depth = 2 (9488 data points)
Split on feature grade.B (left:9488 data points,
right:0 data points)

Creating leaf node.
```

```
count_nodes(decision_tree)
```

```
[1] 17
```

```
table(predict_tree(decision_tree, test))
```

```
   0    1
8879 6313
```

```
evaluate_classification_error(decision_tree, test)
```

```
[1] 0.337941
```

```
# Accuracy
confusionMatrix(predict_tree(decision_tree, test),
               test$loan_status)$overall[[1]]
```

```
[1] 0.662059
```

Our weighted decision tree application gives a detailed account of what is going on. The total number of leaf nodes are 17 and the classification error on test data is 33.79% and the accuracy 66.2%. We need to tweak the algorithm to improve the accuracy further, which we will look into later.

For now, let us write our AdaBoost application.

5.5.6   *Writing the AdaBoost Application*

For the sake of simplicity, we will stick with decision tree stumps, i.e., training trees
with max_depth = 1.

Recall from the section on Adaboost-

- Start with unweighted data with $\alpha_j = \frac{1}{m}$
- For $t = 1, \ldots, T$
- Learn $f_t(x)$ with data weights α_j
- Compute coefficient $\hat{w}_t$:

$$\hat{w}_t = \frac{1}{2} ln(\frac{1 - \text{weighted error } (f_t)}{\text{weighted error } (f_t)})$$

- Recompute weights α_j:

$$\alpha_i = \begin{cases} \alpha_i e^{-\hat{w}_t} & if \ f_t(x_i) = y_i \\ \alpha_i e^{\hat{w}_t} & if \ f_t(x_i) \neq y_i \end{cases}$$

- Normalize weights α_i:

$$\alpha_i \leftarrow \frac{\alpha_i}{\sum_{j=1}^{m} \alpha_j}$$

It is also to be noted that

- Stump weights ($\hat{w}$) tell us how important each decision stump is while predicting
  using the boosted ensemble.
- Data point weights (α) tell us how important each data point is while training a
  decision stump.

```
AdaBoostStumps <- function(data, features, target, numDTreeStumps,
    minobs = 10, verbose) {
    alpha = rep(1/nrow(data), nrow(data))
    weights = numeric()
    current_DTree_Stump = list()
    target <- "loan_status"
    weight_adjustment <- numeric()
    remaining_features <- features

    for (t in 1:numDTreeStumps) {
        if (verbose == TRUE) {
            print("====================================")
            cat(sprintf("Adaboost Iteration %d \n", t))
            print("====================================")
        }

        this_DTree_Stump = weighted_decision_tree(data, remaining_features,
            target, data_weights = alpha, max_depth = 1, minobs = 10,
            verbose = verbose)
        current_DTree_Stump[[t]] <- this_DTree_Stump
```

```
        splitting_feature = best_splitting_feature(data, remaining_features,
            target, data_weights)
        remaining_features = remaining_features[-which(remaining_features ==
            splitting_feature)]

        predictions = predict_tree(this_DTree_Stump, data)

        Accurate = (predictions == data[target])
        inAccurate = (predictions != data[target])

        weighted_Error = sum(alpha[inAccurate])/sum(alpha)   #0.39975

        weight = 0.5 * log((1 - weighted_Error)/weighted_Error)
        weights[t] <- weight

        weight_adjustment[Accurate] = exp(-weights[t])
        weight_adjustment[inAccurate] = exp(weights[t])

        alpha = alpha * weight_adjustment
        alpha = alpha/sum(alpha)
    }
    return(list(weights, current_DTree_Stump))
}
```

```
predictAdaBoost <- function(weighted_Stumps, curDTreeStumps,
    data) {
    scores = rep(0, nrow(data))
    for (i in 1:length(curDTreeStumps)) {
        predictions = predict_tree(curDTreeStumps[[i]], data)
        predictions = ifelse(predictions == 0, -1, 1)
        scores = scores + weighted_Stumps[i] * predictions
    }
    scores <- ifelse(scores > 0, +1, -1)
    return(scores)
}
```

Let us now execute our "AdaBoostStumps" application and check for accuracy with tree stumps 3 and 5 respectively.

```
adaboostModel <- AdaBoostStumps(train,
                                features,
                                target,
                                numDTreeStumps = 3,
                                minobs = 10,
                                verbose = TRUE
                                )
```

```
[1] "====================================="
Adaboost Iteration 1
[1] "====================================="
---------------------------
Subtree depth = 1 (60225 data points)
Split on feature grade.A (left:50737 data points,
right:9488 data points)
---------------------------
```

```
Subtree depth = 2 (50737 data points)
[1] "Stopping condition 4: Reached maximum depth."
----------------------------
Subtree depth = 2 (9488 data points)
[1] "Stopping condition 4: Reached maximum depth."
[1] "===================================="
Adaboost Iteration 2
[1] "===================================="
----------------------------
Subtree depth = 1 (60225 data points)
Split on feature term.36.months (left:16711 data points,
right:43514 data points)
----------------------------
Subtree depth = 2 (16711 data points)
[1] "Stopping condition 4: Reached maximum depth."
----------------------------
Subtree depth = 2 (43514 data points)
[1] "Stopping condition 4: Reached maximum depth."
[1] "===================================="
Adaboost Iteration 3
[1] "===================================="
----------------------------
Subtree depth = 1 (60225 data points)
Split on feature grade.D (left:49538 data points,
right:10687 data points)
----------------------------
Subtree depth = 2 (49538 data points)
[1] "Stopping condition 4: Reached maximum depth."
----------------------------
Subtree depth = 2 (10687 data points)
[1] "Stopping condition 4: Reached maximum depth."
```

```
weighted_Stumps <- adaboostModel[[1]]
current_DTreeStumps <- adaboostModel[[2]]
pred <- predictAdaBoost(weighted_Stumps,
                        current_DTreeStumps,
                        test
                        )
#Accuracy with tree stumps = 3

confusionMatrix(pred, ifelse(test$loan_status == 0, -1, 1))$overall[[1]]
```

```
[1] 0.6172986
```

```
adaboostModel <- AdaBoostStumps(train,
                                features,
                                target,
                                numDTreeStumps = 5,
```

```
                              minobs = 10,
                              verbose = TRUE
                              )
```

```
[1] "===================================="
Adaboost Iteration 1
[1] "===================================="
----------------------------
Subtree depth = 1 (60225 data points)
Split on feature grade.A (left:50737 data points,
right:9488 data points)
----------------------------
Subtree depth = 2 (50737 data points)
[1] "Stopping condition 4: Reached maximum depth."
----------------------------
Subtree depth = 2 (9488 data points)
[1] "Stopping condition 4: Reached maximum depth."
[1] "===================================="
Adaboost Iteration 2
[1] "===================================="
----------------------------
Subtree depth = 1 (60225 data points)
Split on feature term.36.months (left:16711 data points,
right:43514 data points)
----------------------------
Subtree depth = 2 (16711 data points)
[1] "Stopping condition 4: Reached maximum depth."
----------------------------
Subtree depth = 2 (43514 data points)
[1] "Stopping condition 4: Reached maximum depth."
[1] "===================================="
Adaboost Iteration 3
[1] "===================================="
----------------------------
Subtree depth = 1 (60225 data points)
Split on feature grade.D (left:49538 data points,
right:10687 data points)
----------------------------
Subtree depth = 2 (49538 data points)
[1] "Stopping condition 4: Reached maximum depth."
----------------------------
Subtree depth = 2 (10687 data points)
[1] "Stopping condition 4: Reached maximum depth."
[1] "===================================="
Adaboost Iteration 4
```

```
[1]  "===================================="
----------------------------
Subtree depth = 1 (60225 data points)
Split on feature grade.B (left:44175 data points,
right:16050 data points)
----------------------------
Subtree depth = 2 (44175 data points)
[1] "Stopping condition 4: Reached maximum depth."
----------------------------
Subtree depth = 2 (16050 data points)
[1] "Stopping condition 4: Reached maximum depth."
[1]  "===================================="
Adaboost Iteration 5
[1]  "===================================="
----------------------------
Subtree depth = 1 (60225 data points)
Split on feature grade.E (left:54418 data points,
right:5807 data points)
----------------------------
Subtree depth = 2 (54418 data points)
[1] "Stopping condition 4: Reached maximum depth."
----------------------------
Subtree depth = 2 (5807 data points)
[1] "Stopping condition 4: Reached maximum depth."
```

```
weighted_Stumps <- adaboostModel[[1]]
current_DTreeStumps <- adaboostModel[[2]]
pred <- predictAdaBoost(weighted_Stumps,
                        current_DTreeStumps,
                        test
                        )

#Accuracy with tree stumps = 5
confusionMatrix(pred, ifelse(test$loan_status == 0, -1, 1))$overall[[1]]
```

```
[1]  0.6290811
```

As we increase the number of decision stumps from 3 to 5, our model accuracy on test data goes up from 61.729 to 62.908%.

5.5.7   Performance of our AdaBoost Algorithm

We will consider an 80−20 partition for the training and test data sets respectively. We then train our AdaBoost models from 1 to 30 decision stumps and plot the training error and test error.

In our AdaBoost model, we set verbose to FALSE, to suppress the additional messages on stopping conditions on adaboost iterations.

```
adaboostModel <- AdaBoostStumps(train,
                                features,
                                target,
                                numDTreeStumps = 30,
                                minobs = 10,
                                verbose = FALSE)
weighted_Stumps <- adaboostModel[[1]]
curDTreeStumps <- adaboostModel[[2]]


error_train = numeric()
for(i in 1:30){
  predictions = predictAdaBoost(weighted_Stumps[1:n],
                                curDTreeStumps[1:i],
                                train)
  error_train[i] = 1 - confusionMatrix(predictions,
                                ifelse(train$loan_status == 0, -1, 1)
                                )$overall[[1]]
cat(sprintf("Number of decision stumps: %s, train error = %s\n", i,
        error_train[i]))
}
```

```
Number of decision stumps: 1, train error = 0.39983395599834
Number of decision stumps: 2, train error = 0.39983395599834
Number of decision stumps: 3, train error = 0.386467413864674
Number of decision stumps: 4, train error = 0.386467413864674
Number of decision stumps: 5, train error = 0.374894146948942
Number of decision stumps: 6, train error = 0.374894146948942
Number of decision stumps: 7, train error = 0.360232461602325
Number of decision stumps: 8, train error = 0.374113740141137
Number of decision stumps: 9, train error = 0.359883769198838
Number of decision stumps: 10, train error = 0.369580738895807
Number of decision stumps: 11, train error = 0.357924449979245
Number of decision stumps: 12, train error = 0.370244914902449
Number of decision stumps: 13, train error = 0.357542548775425
Number of decision stumps: 14, train error = 0.357542548775425
Number of decision stumps: 15, train error = 0.357193856371939
Number of decision stumps: 16, train error = 0.357509339975093
Number of decision stumps: 17, train error = 0.358688252386883
Number of decision stumps: 18, train error = 0.358621834786218
Number of decision stumps: 19, train error = 0.358870900788709
Number of decision stumps: 20, train error = 0.358870900788709
Number of decision stumps: 21, train error = 0.358870900788709
Number of decision stumps: 22, train error = 0.358870900788709
Number of decision stumps: 23, train error = 0.358870900788709
Number of decision stumps: 24, train error = 0.358870900788709
Number of decision stumps: 25, train error = 0.358870900788709
Number of decision stumps: 26, train error = 0.358870900788709
Number of decision stumps: 27, train error = 0.358870900788709
Number of decision stumps: 28, train error = 0.358870900788709
Number of decision stumps: 29, train error = 0.358870900788709
Number of decision stumps: 30, train error = 0.358870900788709
```

```
error_test = numeric()
for(i in 1:30){
  predictions = predictAdaBoost(weighted_Stumps[1:i],
                                curDTreeStumps[1:i],
                                test)
  error_test[i] = 1 - confusionMatrix(predictions,
                                      ifelse(test$loan_status == 0, -1, 1)
                                      )$overall[[1]]
  cat(sprintf("Number of decision stumps: %s, test error = %s\n", i,
          error_test[i]))
}
```

```
Number of decision stumps: 1, test error = 0.399157451290153
Number of decision stumps: 2, test error = 0.399157451290153
Number of decision stumps: 3, test error = 0.382701421800948
Number of decision stumps: 4, test error = 0.382701421800948
Number of decision stumps: 5, test error = 0.370918904686677
Number of decision stumps: 6, test error = 0.370918904686677
Number of decision stumps: 7, test error = 0.357951553449184
Number of decision stumps: 8, test error = 0.370787256450764
Number of decision stumps: 9, test error = 0.360057925223802
Number of decision stumps: 10, test error = 0.365126382306477
Number of decision stumps: 11, test error = 0.357161664033702
Number of decision stumps: 12, test error = 0.365784623486045
Number of decision stumps: 13, test error = 0.355581885202738
Number of decision stumps: 14, test error = 0.355581885202738
Number of decision stumps: 15, test error = 0.355055292259084
Number of decision stumps: 16, test error = 0.355055292259084
Number of decision stumps: 17, test error = 0.355713533438652
Number of decision stumps: 18, test error = 0.355779357556609
Number of decision stumps: 19, test error = 0.355845181674566
Number of decision stumps: 20, test error = 0.355845181674566
Number of decision stumps: 21, test error = 0.355845181674566
Number of decision stumps: 22, test error = 0.355845181674566
Number of decision stumps: 23, test error = 0.355845181674566
Number of decision stumps: 24, test error = 0.355845181674566
Number of decision stumps: 25, test error = 0.355845181674566
Number of decision stumps: 26, test error = 0.355845181674566
Number of decision stumps: 27, test error = 0.355845181674566
Number of decision stumps: 28, test error = 0.355845181674566
Number of decision stumps: 29, test error = 0.355845181674566
Number of decision stumps: 30, test error = 0.355845181674566
```

Figure 5.12 plots the classification errors for different ensembles of decision stumps.

The advantages of the AdaBoost algorithm are

- Fast
- Simple and easy to program
- No parameters to tune (except the number of classification trees)
- Can combine with any learning algorithm
- No prior knowledge needed about weak learner

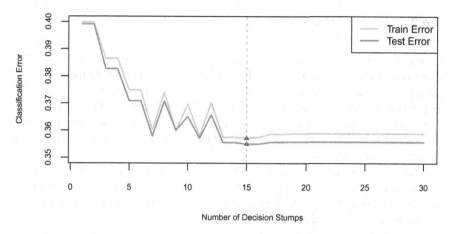

Fig. 5.12 In our AdaBoost model with upto 30 decision stumps, the minimum error is reached with an ensemble of 15 decision stumps

- Can be used with data that is textual, numeric, discrete, etc.
- Can be extended to learning problems well beyond binary classification

The caveats are

- Can fail if weak classifiers are too complex, leading to overfitting
- Can fail if weak classifiers are too weak, leading to underfitting

There are many variants of boosting

5.6 Other Variants

5.6.1 Bagging

The Bagging algorithm (Bootstrap aggregating) by Breiman (1996), votes classifiers generated by different bootstrap samples (replicates). The observations are uniformly sampled with replacement for m instances from the training set. T bootstrap samples $s_1, s_2, \ldots, s_T$ are generated to build T number of classifiers- C_i from each bootstrap sample s_i. The final classifier C^* is built from $C_1, C_2, \ldots, C_T$, whose output is the class predicted most often by the subclassifiers.

For a given bootstrap sample, an instance in the training set has probability $1 - (1 - \frac{1}{m})^m$ of being selected at least once in the m instances randomly selected from the training set. For large m, this is about $1 - \frac{1}{e} = 63.2\%$, which implies that each bootstrap sample contains only about 63.2% unique instances from the training set.

Bagging, like the AdaBoost algorithm also generates a set of classifiers and votes them. *Random Forest* algorithm is an example of Bagging.

5.6.2   Gradient Boosting

Gradient Boosting as the name suggests is adding gradient descent to boosting. The process of gradient boosting involves fitting an ensemble (of trees) in a forward stage-wise manner, like we did in AdaBoost. At each stage, a weak learner is introduced to compensate the shortcomings of existing weak learners. Recall that, in Adaboost, "shortcomings" are identified by high-weight data points. In gradient boosting, they are identified by gradients. Both high-weight data points and gradients tell us how to improve our model.

Freund and Schapire first invented the AdaBoost algorithm in 1996. Breiman, formulated AdaBoost as gradient descent with a special loss function in 1999. Friedman in 2001, generalized AdaBoost to gradient boosting in order to handle a variety of loss functions, beyond classification.

5.6.3   XGBoost

One of the powerful variants of gradient boosting is the *XGBoost* (Extreme Gradient Boosting) algorithm developed by Tianqi Chen. XGBoost employs a number of tricks that make it faster and more accurate than traditional gradient boosting (particularly second-order gradient descent). It is extremely fast and efficient due to the fact that it embraces parallel computation. It is versatile in the sense that it can be for classification, regression, or ranking. It can also extract variable importance and does not require feature engineering like imputating missing values, scaling and normalizing the data. However, it only works with numeric features and leads to overfitting if the hyperparameters are not tuned properly.

Finally, let us work out our loan data using the 'xgboost' (extreme gradient boosting) algorithm in R

```
require(xgboost)
require(Ckmeans.1d.dp)
set.seed(61)
#setting hyperparametrs
param <- list("objective" = "binary:logistic",
              "eval_metric" = "logloss",
              "eta" = 1,
              "max.depth" = 2
)
# xgb.cv is used for cross-validation and finding best value of the
# hyperparameters. Here we will find out the best value of one
# hyperparameter- nrounds (i.e., number of trees).
best_cv <- xgb.cv(param = param,
                  data = as.matrix(train[,features]),
                  label = train$loan_status,
                  nfold = 10,
                  nrounds = 100,
                  verbose = FALSE
                  )
```

```
# What value of nrounds gives the least error
which.min(best_cv$evaluation_log$test_logloss_mean)
```

[1] 37

```
plot(log(best_cv$evaluation_log$test_logloss_mean),
     type = 'l',
     cex.lab = 0.7,
     col = 'darkorange',
     xaxt = 'n',
     yaxt = 'n',
     xlab = 'Number of trees',
     ylab = 'Mean log loss')

axis(1, col = 'black',
     col.axis = 'black',
     cex.axis = 0.7)

axis(2, col = 'black',
     col.axis = 'black',
     cex.axis = 0.7)
```

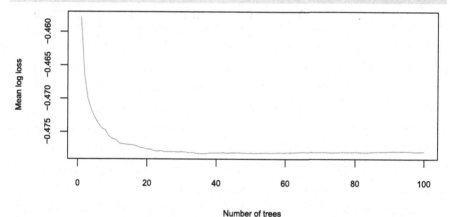

```
# Using nrounds where error is minimum (37 in this case)
final_model <- xgboost(data = as.matrix(train[, features]),
                       label = train$loan_status,
                       params = param,
                       nrounds =
                         which.min(best_cv$evaluation_log$test_logloss_mean),
                       verbose = FALSE
                       )

#Predict with this model
pred <- predict(final_model,
                as.matrix(test[, features])
                )

pred <- ifelse(pred <= 0.5, -1, 1)

#Accuracy
confusionMatrix(pred, ifelse(test$loan_status == 0, -1, 1))$overall[[1]]
```

[1] 0.6618615

```
#Plot importance of variables.
feature_name <- dimnames(train[, features])[[2]]
importance_matrix <- xgb.importance(feature_name,
                                    model = final_model
                                    )
xgb.plot.importance(importance_matrix[1:10, ])
```

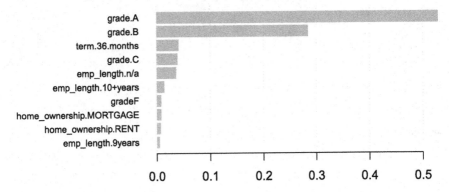

Chapter 6
Clustering

> *Numbers have an important story to tell. They rely on you to give them a voice.*
>
> –Stephen Few

Clustering is the most common form of unsupervised learning, implying that there is no assignment of objects to different classes. Clustering is therefore a machine learning technique to group a set of objects into subsets or clusters. The goal is to create clusters having objects which are similar to each other whereas the objects are dissimilar from objects in the other clusters. In other words, the goal is to minimize the intracluster distances between objects, while maximizing intercluster distances. The **distance measure** thus lies at the heart of clustering.

In clustering, it is the distribution of the data that determines cluster membership whereas in classification, the classifier learns the association between objects and classes from the data.

Some of the applications of clustering can be summarized below

- Finding similar documents—Clustering can discover documents that are conceptually alike in contrast to search-based approaches that are only able to discover whether the documents share many of the same words.
- Document retrieval—is finding documents which are relevant to a particular query.
- Search Optimization and Recommendation System—Clustering can facilitate recommending relevant articles (say, from a scientific journal) to its readers having specific interests.

© Springer Nature Singapore Pte Ltd. 2017
A. Ghatak, *Machine Learning with R*, DOI 10.1007/978-981-10-6808-9_6

k-means is one of the most popular clustering methods because of its simplicity. Starting with a set of randomly chosen initial centers, each input point is assigned to its nearest center; the centers are then recomputed and the input point is again reassigned. This local search, called Lloyd's iteration,[1] continues until the solution does not change between two consecutive rounds. One of the disadvantages of the k-means algorithm is that the final solution is locally optimal, which can be far away from the global optimum.

6.1   The Clustering Algorithm

The clustering algorithm can be defined in the following steps:

1. Assume the number of clusters and initialize the cluster centers.
2. Assign the observations to the closest to the cluster centers by returning the index of the cluster center closest to the observation.
3. Revise the cluster centers as an average of the assigned observations.

The clustering algorithm can be written as

Assume (or smartly determine) number of clusters and initialize cluster centers

$$z_i \leftarrow \underset{j}{argmin} \|\mu_j - x_i\|_2^2 \tag{6.1.1}$$

$$\mu_j = \leftarrow \underset{\mu}{argmin} \sum_{i:z_i=j} \|\mu - x_i\|_2^2$$

Reapeat till convergence

6.2   Clustering Algorithm as Coordinate Descent optimization

It may be observed that the clustering algorithm above is the coordinate descent algorithm defined in Sect. 4.9.2. You may recall that the coordinate descent algorithm is an alternating minimization problem and in clustering, it first minimizes the function

---

[1]Lloyd's algorithm, also known as Voronoi iteration, is named after Stuart P. Lloyd for finding evenly spaced sets of points in subsets of Euclidean spaces.

along one direction, i.e., minimizing z given μ and then along a different direction, i.e., minimizing μ given z.

6.3 An Introduction to Text mining

For the sake of our application, we will consider a data set of 20 newsgroups where each newsgroup's articles are stored in separate folders and each folder consists of documents related to the particular newsgroup. The data set is available at the reuters website.[2]

Before we write the clustering algorithm, we will briefly touch upon some text mining concepts as the data set we will use for clustering is textual.

Quantifying words in text documents has been a focal question in text mining and natural language processing (NLP). One of the ways to find the importance of a word is by measuring the number of times it occurs in the document, known as term frequency (*tf*). However, there are some words which occur many times in a document and yet they are not important, i.e., "the", "an", "of", etc. These words are known as stopwords and we may exclude these words from the document for the sake of our analysis. Another approach to find the importance of a word is by finding the inverse document frequency (*idf*) of the word, which increases the weight of words that are not very common in the documents and decreases the weight of commonly used words.

Both the *tf* and *idf* can be multiplied to give us an importance measuring weight called the *term frequency inverse document frequency* (*tf − idf*). This weight is a statistical measure which evaluates how important a word is to a particular document in a corpus. The importance increases proportionally to the number of times a word appears in a document but decreases by the number of times it appears in the corpus.

6.3.1 Text Mining Application—Reading Multiple Text Files from Multiple Directories

The "20_newsgroups" data set from Reuters consists of 20 folders and each folder contains multiple documents. The first challenge is to read the contents of the documents as separate lines and then strip each line to extract the words.

```
folders <- list.dirs(filepath, recursive = TRUE)[-1]
files <- list.files(folders, recursive = TRUE, full.names = TRUE)
lines <- list()
for (j in files) {
    lines[[j]] <- readLines(j)
}
word_extract <- function(x) unlist(strsplit(x, "[[:space:]]|(?=[.!?*-])",
```

---

[2]http://qwone.com/jason/20Newsgroups/, downloaded on Jul 28, 2017, 6:20 am IST.

```
    perl = TRUE))

doc_words <- list()
for (i in 1:length(lines)) {
    doc_words[[i]] <- word_extract(tolower(gsub(".*?($|'|[^[:punct:]]).*?",
        "\\1", as.character(lines[[i]]))))
}
```

6.3.2   Text Mining Application—Creating a Weighted tf-idf Document-Term Matrix

Each element in the list "doc_words" contains the words from each document; the length of the list is therefore the number of documents, i.e., 11,314 documents.

We number the documents from 1 to 11,314 and create a corpus of words related to each document.

Documents use different forms of words such as "car", "cars", "car's", etc. The goal of stemming is to reduce the derivationally related forms of a word to a common base form—"car".

Stopwords are a list of words that are automatically filtered out in the process of mining a document. Typical stopwords include "a", "and", "is", "but", etc. We can also include our own stopwords to the list.

The usual text transformations are carried out to the corpus, i.e., removing the stopwords, removing any numbers and stemming the words, prior to creating a document term matrix. A document term matrix is a simple triplet matrix which is represented by triplets (i, j, v) of row indices i, column indices j, and values v, respectively. The row indices are the document numbers, the column indices are the words and the values are the weighted $tf - idf$ transformations for each word. For convenience, we normalize the matrix.

Sparsity of a $tf - idf$ matrix refers to the threshold or proportion of relative document frequency of a term, above which the term will be removed. For example, if we set sparse = 0.98 in the argument to "removeSparseTerms", it will remove the terms that are more sparse than 0.98. In the other extreme, if sparse = 0.02, then only the terms that appear in (nearly) every document will be retained.

```
n.docs <- length(doc_words)
names(doc_words) <- paste0("", c(1:n.docs))
my.docs <- VectorSource(doc_words)
my.docs$Names <- names(doc_words)
my.corpus <- Corpus(my.docs)
my.corpus
```

```
<<SimpleCorpus>>
Metadata:  corpus specific: 1, document level (indexed): 0
Content:   documents: 11314
```

```
my.corpus <- tm_map(my.corpus, removeWords,
                    c(stopwords("english"), "replyto", "nntppostinghost",
                      "path", "sender", "address", "email", "mail",
                      "can", "nntp", "just", "edu")
                    )
my.corpus <- tm_map(my.corpus, removeNumbers)
my.corpus <- tm_map(my.corpus, stemDocument)
dtm <- DocumentTermMatrix(my.corpus,
                          control = list(weighting = function(x)
                            weightTfIdf(x, normalize = TRUE)
                            )
                          )
dtm <- removeSparseTerms(dtm, 0.98)
inspect(dtm[1:5, 1:5])
```

```
<<DocumentTermMatrix (documents: 5, terms: 5)>>
Non-/sparse entries: 9/16
Sparsity            : 64\%
Maximal term length: 8
Weighting           : term frequency - inverse document
frequency (normalized) (tf-idf)
Sample              :
    Terms
Docs also        although    america     american    another
1 0.006275525 0.008831778 0.005348454 0.02223823 0.003087606
2 0.007376325 0.001730162 0.000000000 0.00000000 0.004838944
3 0.006564276 0.000000000 0.000000000 0.00000000 0.000000000
4 0.000000000 0.000000000 0.000000000 0.00000000 0.000000000
5 0.000000000 0.000000000 0.000000000 0.00000000 0.000000000
```

6.3.3   Text Mining Application—Exploratory Analysis

Let us explore some of the most frequent words used in the corpus (Fig. 6.1).

```
dtm_matrix <- as.matrix(dtm)
sorted_word_freq <- sort(colSums((dtm_matrix)),
                         decreasing=TRUE
                         )
df <- data.frame(word = names(sorted_word_freq),
                 freq = sorted_word_freq
                 )
```

6.4   Writing the Clustering Application

The 20_newsgroup data set consists of the following topic related folders (each containing multiple text files):

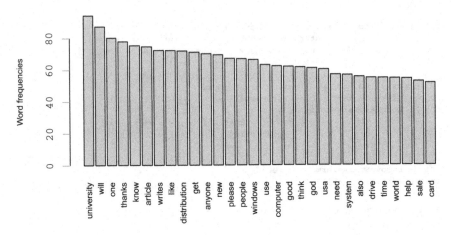

Fig. 6.1   Bar plot of the weighted most frequent words used in the document corpus

1. alt.atheism: 480 files 2. comp.graphics: 584 files

3. comp.os.ms-windows.misc: 591 files

4. comp.sys.ibm.pc.hardware: 590 files 5. comp.sys.mac.hardware: 578 files

6. comp.windows.x: 593 files 7. misc.forsale: 585 files 8. rec.autos: 594 files

9. rec.motorcycles: 598 files

10. rec.sport.baseball: 597 files 11. rec.sport.hockey: 600 files

12. sci.crypt: 595 files

13. sci.electronics: 591 files

14. sci.med: 594 files

15. sci.space: 593 files

16. soc.religion.christian: 599 files

17. talk.politics.guns: 546 files

18. talk.politics.mideast: 564 files

19. talk.politics.misc: 465 files

20. talk.religion.misc: 377 files

Our clustering application will require three functions, namely

1. Read the text in the accompanying folders

2. Allot words to specific documents

3. Define the clusters

From an algorithmic perspective, this can be summarized as

- Calculate the sum total of variance within clusters
- Calculate the Euclidean distance between the data points and the cluster centroids
- Iterate through the data set to find an equilibrium, where the observations do not alter their affiliation for the respective centroids.

Let's get going.

The following function associates the data points with its clusters and calculates the sum of the squared Euclidean distances from the respective cluster centroid.

```
total_within_ss <- function(data, centroids, clusters) {
    sum_o_sqs = list()
    for (i in 1:nrow(centroids)) {
        cluster_data_points = data[clusters == i, ]
        if (any(unique(abs(cluster_data_points)) > 0)) {
            squared_distances = rowSums(t(t(cluster_data_points) -
                centroids[i, ])^2)
            sum_o_sqs[i] = sum(squared_distances)
        }
    }
    sum_o_sqs = Reduce("+", sum_o_sqs)
    return(sum_o_sqs)
}
```

The Euclidean distance for the data points associated with each cluster is calculated and stored in a matrix.

```
euclid_dist <- function(data_matrix, centroids) {
    distanceMatrix <- matrix(NA, nrow = dim(data_matrix)[1],
        ncol = dim(centroids)[1])
    for (i in 1:nrow(centroids)) {
        distanceMatrix[, i] <- sqrt(rowSums(t(t(data_matrix) -
            centroids[i, ])^2))
    }
    return(distanceMatrix)
}
```

This is our k-means application. The first initialization of the centroids is done by sampling the rows of the data matrix. The distance to each centroid is calculated from which the minimum distance of each data point to a cluster determines which cluster does the observation belong.

After the data points have been assigned to their respective clusters, we compute the mean of the data points for each cluster, which determines the coordinates of the new cluster centroid.

For each iteration, the cluster history, centroid history, and the variance (within clusters) history are recorded.

There are two other options available in our application. If the argument "verbose" is set to TRUE, the application will output the number of data points which have changed clusters with each iteration and the sum total variance within clusters, which incidentally, keeps reducing with every iteration. The "nstart" argument is the number of times the algorithm may be repeated. Everytime it is repeated, the initial assignment of cluster centroids changes, which can also lead to differing cluster arrangements, for every nstart.

```
find_k-Means <- function(data, num_centroids, iter, verbose, nstart) {
    for(j in 1:nstart){
        cat(sprintf("Starting k-means with nstart = %d\n***********\n", j))
        cluster_history <- vector(iter, mode="list")
        centroids_history <- vector(iter, mode="list")
        variance_history <- vector(iter, mode = "list")
        set.seed(sample(1:10000, 1, replace=F))
        centroids <- data[sample(nrow(data), num_centroids), ]
```

```
    for(i in 1:iter) {
        distance_to_centroids <- euclid_dist(data, centroids)
        clusters <- apply(distance_to_centroids, 1, which.min)
        centroids <- apply(data, 2, tapply, clusters, mean)
        variance = total_within_ss(data, centroids, clusters)

        cluster_history[[i]] <- clusters
        centroids_history[[i]] <- centroids
        variance_history[[i]] <- variance

        if(i >= 2 & verbose == TRUE){
            num_changed = sum(abs(cluster_history[[i-1]] - cluster_history[[i]]))
            cat(sprintf('Iter no: %d:- %d elements changed their cluster
                        assignment.\n', i-1, num_changed)
                )
            cat(sprintf('Sum of variance within clusters = %f\n',
                        variance_history[[i]])
                )
        }
    }
}
 return(list(clusters = cluster_history,
             centroids = centroids_history,
             sum_cluster_variance = variance_history)
        )
}
```

Let us test our application on the Reuters data set.

Since the data set is composed of 20 different topics, we will initialize the number of centroids to 20. We will also iterate through our application 30 times for each initialization of our cluster centroids and run the application twice for different initializations for the cluster centroids.

```
iters = 30

k-Means_results <- find_k-Means(dtm_matrix,
                                num_centroids = 20,
                                iter = iters,
                                nstart = 2,
                                verbose = T)
```

```
Starting k-means with nstart = 1
***********
Iter no: 1:- 4068 elements changed their cluster
                        assignment.
Sum of variance within clusters = 1390.505180
Iter no: 2:- 5681 elements changed their cluster
                        assignment.
Sum of variance within clusters = 1377.076275
Iter no: 3:- 7130 elements changed their cluster
                        assignment.
Sum of variance within clusters = 1366.827242
Iter no: 4:- 7569 elements changed their cluster
```

assignment.
Sum of variance within clusters = 1360.156089
Iter no: 5:- 6527 elements changed their cluster
     assignment.
Sum of variance within clusters = 1356.088517
Iter no: 6:- 6197 elements changed their cluster
     assignment.
Sum of variance within clusters = 1352.816163
Iter no: 7:- 5739 elements changed their cluster
     assignment.
Sum of variance within clusters = 1349.747091
Iter no: 8:- 5238 elements changed their cluster
     assignment.
Sum of variance within clusters = 1347.480461
Iter no: 9:- 3799 elements changed their cluster
     assignment.
Sum of variance within clusters = 1345.974068
Iter no: 10:- 2656 elements changed their cluster
     assignment.
Sum of variance within clusters = 1344.922904
Iter no: 11:- 2010 elements changed their cluster
     assignment.
Sum of variance within clusters = 1344.293808
Iter no: 12:- 1712 elements changed their cluster
     assignment.
Sum of variance within clusters = 1343.833700
Iter no: 13:- 1823 elements changed their cluster
     assignment.
Sum of variance within clusters = 1343.099974
Iter no: 14:- 2394 elements changed their cluster
     assignment.
Sum of variance within clusters = 1342.165356
Iter no: 15:- 3176 elements changed their cluster
     assignment.
Sum of variance within clusters = 1341.155253
Iter no: 16:- 3787 elements changed their cluster
     assignment.
Sum of variance within clusters = 1340.292693
Iter no: 17:- 3487 elements changed their cluster
     assignment.
Sum of variance within clusters = 1339.779470
Iter no: 18:- 2459 elements changed their cluster
     assignment.
Sum of variance within clusters = 1339.497701
Iter no: 19:- 2184 elements changed their cluster

assignment.
Sum of variance within clusters = 1339.314754
Iter no: 20:- 1491 elements changed their cluster
              assignment.
Sum of variance within clusters = 1339.192158
Iter no: 21:- 1206 elements changed their cluster
              assignment.
Sum of variance within clusters = 1339.111653
Iter no: 22:- 1007 elements changed their cluster
              assignment.
Sum of variance within clusters = 1339.061178
Iter no: 23:- 769 elements changed their cluster
              assignment.
Sum of variance within clusters = 1339.012495
Iter no: 24:- 521 elements changed their cluster
              assignment.
Sum of variance within clusters = 1338.977047
Iter no: 25:- 493 elements changed their cluster
              assignment.
Sum of variance within clusters = 1338.943287
Iter no: 26:- 540 elements changed their cluster
              assignment.
Sum of variance within clusters = 1338.906739
Iter no: 27:- 556 elements changed their cluster
              assignment.
Sum of variance within clusters = 1338.868316
Iter no: 28:- 478 elements changed their cluster
              assignment.
Sum of variance within clusters = 1338.840077
Iter no: 29:- 459 elements changed their cluster
              assignment.
Sum of variance within clusters = 1338.822129
Starting k-means with nstart = 2
****
Iter no: 1:- 11902 elements changed their cluster
              assignment.
Sum of variance within clusters = 1376.232161
Iter no: 2:- 8564 elements changed their cluster
              assignment.

Sum of variance within clusters = 1362.282055
Iter no: 3:- 4740 elements changed their cluster
              assignment.
Sum of variance within clusters = 1354.669879
Iter no: 4:- 2868 elements changed their cluster

```
                              assignment.
Sum of variance within clusters = 1351.026636
Iter no: 5:- 2023 elements changed their cluster
                              assignment.
Sum of variance within clusters = 1348.893252
Iter no: 6:- 1580 elements changed their cluster
                              assignment.
Sum of variance within clusters = 1347.788524
Iter no: 7:- 1048 elements changed their cluster
                              assignment.
Sum of variance within clusters = 1347.139061
Iter no: 8:- 1032 elements changed their cluster
                              assignment.
Sum of variance within clusters = 1346.566164
Iter no: 9:- 906 elements changed their cluster
                              assignment.
Sum of variance within clusters = 1345.945560
Iter no: 10:- 771 elements changed their cluster
                              assignment.
Sum of variance within clusters = 1345.420492
Iter no: 11:- 656 elements changed their cluster
                              assignment.
Sum of variance within clusters = 1345.181179
Iter no: 12:- 417 elements changed their cluster
                              assignment.
Sum of variance within clusters = 1345.039952
Iter no: 13:- 469 elements changed their cluster
                              assignment.
Sum of variance within clusters = 1344.921352
Iter no: 14:- 385 elements changed their cluster
                              assignment.
Sum of variance within clusters = 1344.851656
Iter no: 15:- 264 elements changed their cluster
                              assignment.
Sum of variance within clusters = 1344.809232
Iter no: 16:- 147 elements changed their cluster
                              assignment.
Sum of variance within clusters = 1344.787571
Iter no: 17:- 167 elements changed their cluster
                              assignment.
Sum of variance within clusters = 1344.770232
Iter no: 18:- 156 elements changed their cluster
                              assignment.
Sum of variance within clusters = 1344.740725
Iter no: 19:- 176 elements changed their cluster
```

```
                               assignment.
Sum of variance within clusters = 1344.695779
Iter no: 20:- 219 elements changed their cluster
                               assignment.
Sum of variance within clusters = 1344.627131
Iter no: 21:- 252 elements changed their cluster
                               assignment.
Sum of variance within clusters = 1344.548557
Iter no: 22:- 349 elements changed their cluster
                               assignment.
Sum of variance within clusters = 1344.454185
Iter no: 23:- 420 elements changed their cluster
                               assignment.
Sum of variance within clusters = 1344.362775
Iter no: 24:- 436 elements changed their cluster
                               assignment.
Sum of variance within clusters = 1344.265833
Iter no: 25:- 393 elements changed their cluster
                               assignment.
Sum of variance within clusters = 1344.191612
Iter no: 26:- 213 elements changed their cluster
                               assignment.
Sum of variance within clusters = 1344.168236
Iter no: 27:- 191 elements changed their cluster
                               assignment.
Sum of variance within clusters = 1344.150365
Iter no: 28:- 186 elements changed their cluster
                               assignment.
Sum of variance within clusters = 1344.138358
Iter no: 29:- 96 elements changed their cluster
                               assignment.
Sum of variance within clusters = 1344.133813
```

One drawback of k-means is that it tends to get stuck in a local minimum, which may be observed from the results above. Initialization of the centroids take different values at different runs of the application by using the argument "nstart". This is evident by the sum of variance within clusters, which is 1343.052 after the end of the first run and 1357.365 after the end of the second run.

The number of documents assigned to each cluster is calculated below, which should be the sum total of all documents.

```
table(k-Means_results$clusters[[iters]])
```

1	2	3	4	5	6	7	8	9	10	11	12	13	14	15
291	227	29	21	1960	130	171	78	8	90	6193	194	87	203	766

16	17	18	19	20
226	324	69	130	117

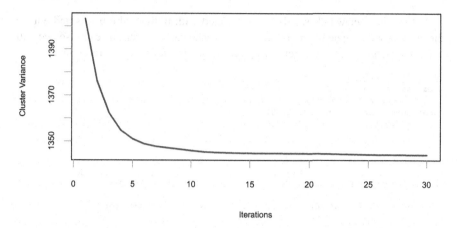

Fig. 6.2 The sum total of variance within the clusters keep reducing as the number of iterations increase. The number of clusters is 20

```
sum(table(k-Means_results$clusters[[iters]]))
```

```
[1] 11314
```

```
plot(x= 1:iters, y = k-Means_results$sum_cluster_variance,
    type ='l',
    col = 'deepskyblue4',
    lwd = 2,
    xlab = 'Iterations',
    ylab = 'Cluster Variance',
    cex.lab = 0.7,
    xaxt = 'n',
    yaxt = 'n')
```

The plot in Fig. 6.2 shows how the sum of the variance within clusters keeps reducing with every iteration.

Let us now test our application with the "k-means" function in R. The attribute '*algorithm*' in the 'k-means' function in R refers to the optimization procedures named after their inventors and we will not get into those details here. Suffice it to say that we are using the algorithm by *Forgy*, (1965).

```
set.seed(61)
centroids <- dtm_matrix[sample(nrow(dtm_matrix), 20), ]
iters = 100
k-means_model <- k-means(dtm_matrix,
                    centroids,
                    iter.max = iters,
                    algorithm = "Forgy")
```

```
k-means_model$tot.withinss
```

```
[1] 1340.33
```

Let us discover which words are associated with individual clusters and equate
the clusters with the newsgroup topics (mentioned earlier). For this exercise, we will
extract the words in each cluster having the highest $tf-idf$ weights (refer Sect. 6.3.1).

```
for (i in 1:20) {
  cat(paste("\n cluster", i, ":", sep = ""))
  sorted_centers <- sort(k-means_model$centers[i, ], decreasing = T)
  cat(names(sorted_centers)[1:10], "\n")
  cat(names(sorted_centers)[11:20], "\n")
}
```

```
  cluster 1:internet frank mike technology institute please thanks fax list access
anyone information phone office university faq service help know quite

  cluster 2:god people article one writes will think like university car
get new know time good right say even now see

  cluster 3:driver drivers card windows ftp video site thanks win version
file bbs looking anybody anyone sound university know mode please

  cluster 4:chip clipper key encryption keys secret government security system house
will public phone bit white clinton communications use systems text

  cluster 5:tin xnewsreader version wrote bill thanks university anyone program group
please get bike know national info post anybody files unix

  cluster 6:dos windows window using system version file memory running win
date disk frank data mode university anyone sale thanks systems

  cluster 7:michael phone programs number line university mike radio usa find
research institute need article writes model internet know technology state

  cluster 8:graphics mode package please thanks help card computer support cards
robert anyone looking bit inc windows video code university newsgroup

  cluster 9:thanks anyone please university looking distribution help computer need info
mac know software advance program information use system usa get

  cluster 10:image files screen color file software thanks source quality program
size earth windows looking display package example graphics university help

  cluster 11:police three continue san due california local came whether john
actually state never another years say way one university organization

  cluster 12:window manager position application accept program size display user want
windows way screen figure set specific whole use may keywords

  cluster 13:james god faith university works someone new state thanks jim
national wanted christian looking say will online know work western

  cluster 14:game team games players baseball hockey season win play year
league jewish toronto runs last university will pittsburgh division first

  cluster 15:test message keith distribution university looks pittsburgh help washington buy
apple data final thanks group home california articleid keywords city

  cluster 16:jim inc god writes article bbs world never distribution nothing
get question control one say group day see car today

  cluster 17:sale offer condition asking excellent price new interested distribution please
best contact usa sell university call college includes software card
```

```
cluster 18:windows file files dos program use help problem thanks run
running win window memory disk using version university screen system

cluster 19:drive card monitor video disk hard mac apple cards system
problem color computer thanks internal university ram anyone ibm use

cluster 20:air space force john back ago technology display anybody turn
years cars distribution wanted used will keywords usa colorado got
```

Referring to Fig. 6.2, we can easily observe that sum total of variance converges at close to 1300. The "k-means" function confirms the same.

Setting k to a high value may not lead to desirable clusters. For example, if we set k = number of data points, it will result in each data point being a separate cluster, which is not a desirable situation.

Let us find out what should be the correct value for k.

6.4.1 Smart Initialization of k-means

A drawback with the k-means algorithm is that it tends to get stuck at the local minima as it depends on the random initialization of the centroids.

A smart initialization of the centroids in k-means is therefore very important to obtain a good solution. This is achieved by the k-means++ initialization algorithm, wherein the cluster centroids are chosen on the basis of the maximum distance from each other.

6.4.2 Writing the k-means++ Application

For the k-means++ application, we will modify our earlier "find_k-Means" function as follows:

```
find_k-MeansPP <- function(data, centroids = centroids, verbose, iter) {
  centroids_history <- vector(iter, mode="list")
  cluster_history <- vector(iter, mode="list")
  variance_history <- numeric()
  for(i in 1:iter) {
    distance_to_centroids <- euclid_dist(data, centroids)
    clusters <- apply(distance_to_centroids, 1, which.min)
    centroids <- apply(data, 2, tapply, clusters, mean)

    variance = total_within_ss(data, centroids, clusters)

    cluster_history[[i]] <- clusters
    centroids_history[[i]] <- centroids
    variance_history <- variance

    if(i >= 2 & verbose == TRUE){
      num_changed = sum(abs(cluster_history[[i-1]] - cluster_history[[i]]))
      cat(sprintf('Iter no %d:- %d elements changed their cluster assignment.
```

```
                        ', i-1, num_changed))
       cat(sprintf('Sum of variance within clusters = %f\n', variance_history))
    }
  }
  return(list(clusters = cluster_history,
                sum_cluster_variance = variance_history,
                centroids = centroids_history,
                iter_no = iter)
          )
}
```

In the following function, we use the probability argument in "sample.int" to find
the index (row number) of the observation which has the maximum distance. Once
we arrive at the coordinates of the cluster center, we then call the "find_k-MeansPP"
function, defined above. This is iterated for the defined number of centroids.

We iterate through this application multiple times using the nstart argument. The
function returns the least within-cluster variance.

```
kmeans_plus_plus <- function(data, num_centroids, iter, nstart) {
  clus_history <- vector(iter, mode="list")
  centroid_history <- vector(iter, mode="list")
  m <- nrow(data)
  centroid_id <- matrix(rep(0,num_centroids), nrow = 1)
  distance_to_centroids <- matrix(numeric(m * (num_centroids - 1)),
                                  ncol = num_centroids - 1)
  best_result <- list(total_withinss = Inf)
  for(i in 1:nstart) {
    cat(sprintf("\nStarting k-means algorithm with smart initialization of
                centroids for nstart = %d\n\n", i))
    p <- rep(1, m)
    for(j in 1:(num_centroids - 1)) {
      centroid_id[j] <- sample.int(m, 1, prob = p)
      distance_to_centroids[, j] <- colSums((t(data) - data[centroid_id[j], ])^2)
      p <- distance_to_centroids[cbind(1:m, max.col(-distance_to_centroids
                                       [, 1:j, drop = FALSE]))]
    }
    centroid_id[num_centroids] <- sample.int(m, 1, prob = p)
    result <- find_kMeansPP(data, centroids = data[centroid_id, ],
                            iter = iter, verbose=T)
    clus_history[[i]] <- result$cluster
    centroid_history[[i]] <- result$centroids
    if(result$sum_cluster_variance < best_result$total_withinss){
      best_result$total_withinss <- result$sum_cluster_variance
      best_result$num_start <- i
      best_result$iter <- result$iter_no
      best_result$clusters <-
        clus_history[[best_result$num_start]][[best_result$iter]]
      best_result$centroids <-
        centroid_history[[best_result$num_start]][[best_result$iter]]
    }
  }
  return(list(least_variance = best_result$total_withinss,
                best_nstart = best_result$num_start,
                best_iter = best_result$iter,
                clusters = best_result$clusters,
                centroids = best_result$centroids))
}
```

Let us execute our *k*-means++ application

```
k-meansPPmodel <- k-means_plus_plus(data=dtm_matrix,
                                     num_centroids = 20,
                                     iter = 25,
                                     nstart = 2)
```

```
Starting k-means algorithm with smart initialization of
                centroids for nstart = 1

Iter no 1:- 19976 elements changed their cluster assignment.
                Sum of variance within clusters = 1376.239874
Iter no 2:- 12816 elements changed their cluster assignment.
                Sum of variance within clusters = 1365.941026
Iter no 3:- 7507 elements changed their cluster assignment.
                Sum of variance within clusters = 1360.900537
Iter no 4:- 4124 elements changed their cluster assignment.
                Sum of variance within clusters = 1357.687071
Iter no 5:- 2881 elements changed their cluster assignment.
                Sum of variance within clusters = 1355.946451
Iter no 6:- 2016 elements changed their cluster assignment.
                Sum of variance within clusters = 1355.122082
Iter no 7:- 1636 elements changed their cluster assignment.
                Sum of variance within clusters = 1354.395641
Iter no 8:- 1706 elements changed their cluster assignment.
                Sum of variance within clusters = 1353.467115
Iter no 9:- 1585 elements changed their cluster assignment.
                Sum of variance within clusters = 1352.358979
Iter no 10:- 1804 elements changed their cluster assignment.
                Sum of variance within clusters = 1351.269253
Iter no 11:- 2145 elements changed their cluster assignment.
                Sum of variance within clusters = 1350.004683
Iter no 12:- 2055 elements changed their cluster assignment.
                Sum of variance within clusters = 1349.106273
Iter no 13:- 1771 elements changed their cluster assignment.
                Sum of variance within clusters = 1348.508597
Iter no 14:- 1641 elements changed their cluster assignment.
                Sum of variance within clusters = 1348.052200
Iter no 15:- 1534 elements changed their cluster assignment.
                Sum of variance within clusters = 1347.568493
Iter no 16:- 1548 elements changed their cluster assignment.
                Sum of variance within clusters = 1346.827767
Iter no 17:- 1446 elements changed their cluster assignment.
                Sum of variance within clusters = 1346.054278
Iter no 18:- 1647 elements changed their cluster assignment.
                Sum of variance within clusters = 1345.337811
Iter no 19:- 1658 elements changed their cluster assignment.
                Sum of variance within clusters = 1344.724617
Iter no 20:- 1373 elements changed their cluster assignment.
                Sum of variance within clusters = 1344.289002
Iter no 21:- 1515 elements changed their cluster assignment.
```

                        Sum of variance within clusters = 1343.740814
Iter no 22:- 1457 elements changed their cluster assignment.
                        Sum of variance within clusters = 1343.251773
Iter no 23:- 1457 elements changed their cluster assignment.
                        Sum of variance within clusters = 1342.758185
Iter no 24:- 1534 elements changed their cluster assignment.
                        Sum of variance within clusters = 1342.275558

Starting k-means algorithm with smart initialization of
                centroids for nstart = 2

Iter no 1:- 3637 elements changed their cluster assignment.
                        Sum of variance within clusters = 1376.081991
Iter no 2:- 3415 elements changed their cluster assignment.
                        Sum of variance within clusters = 1366.094328
Iter no 3:- 3480 elements changed their cluster assignment.
                        Sum of variance within clusters = 1359.706907
Iter no 4:- 2238 elements changed their cluster assignment.
                        Sum of variance within clusters = 1356.597762
Iter no 5:- 1194 elements changed their cluster assignment.
                        Sum of variance within clusters = 1355.003345
Iter no 6:- 976 elements changed their cluster assignment.
                        Sum of variance within clusters = 1353.679757
Iter no 7:- 721 elements changed their cluster assignment.
                        Sum of variance within clusters = 1352.604318
Iter no 8:- 680 elements changed their cluster assignment.
                        Sum of variance within clusters = 1351.544676
Iter no 9:- 685 elements changed their cluster assignment.
                        Sum of variance within clusters = 1349.906577
Iter no 10:- 995 elements changed their cluster assignment.
                        Sum of variance within clusters = 1348.183930
Iter no 11:- 824 elements changed their cluster assignment.
                        Sum of variance within clusters = 1347.293344
Iter no 12:- 530 elements changed their cluster assignment.
                        Sum of variance within clusters = 1346.794625
Iter no 13:- 432 elements changed their cluster assignment.
                        Sum of variance within clusters = 1346.272453
Iter no 14:- 300 elements changed their cluster assignment.
                        Sum of variance within clusters = 1345.900329
Iter no 15:- 217 elements changed their cluster assignment.
                        Sum of variance within clusters = 1345.793406
Iter no 16:- 138 elements changed their cluster assignment.
                        Sum of variance within clusters = 1345.750666
Iter no 17:- 92 elements changed their cluster assignment.
                        Sum of variance within clusters = 1345.712204
Iter no 18:- 24 elements changed their cluster assignment.
                        Sum of variance within clusters = 1345.704662
Iter no 19:- 15 elements changed their cluster assignment.
                        Sum of variance within clusters = 1345.700196
Iter no 20:- 14 elements changed their cluster assignment.

```
                        Sum of variance within clusters = 1345.697690
Iter no 21:- 12 elements changed their cluster assignment.
                        Sum of variance within clusters = 1345.695357
Iter no 22:- 2 elements changed their cluster assignment.
                        Sum of variance within clusters = 1345.694798
Iter no 23:- 1 elements changed their cluster assignment.
                        Sum of variance within clusters = 1345.694646
Iter no 24:- 0 elements changed their cluster assignment.
                        Sum of variance within clusters = 1345.694646
```

It may be observed that the sum of cluster variances is much lower than the *k*-means application with random initialization. The convergence is also much faster. Let us explore the other interesting outputs from our k-meansPPmodel.

```
k-meansPPmodel$least_variance
```

[1] 1342.276

```
k-meansPPmodel$best_nstart
```

[1] 1

```
k-meansPPmodel$best_iter
```

[1] 25

```
table(k-meansPPmodel$clusters)
```

1	2	3	4	5	6	7	8	9	10	11	12	13	14	15
24	313	1	51	40	296	4815	194	188	322	58	3251	140	174	93
16	17	18	19	20										
745	439	2	93	75										

We would like to know, which words are associated with individual clusters, using our application.

```
for (i in 1:20) {
  cat(paste("\n cluster", i, ":", sep = ""))
  sorted_centers <- sort(k-meansPPmodel$centroids[i, ], decreasing = T)
  cat(names(sorted_centers)[1:10], "\n")
  cat(names(sorted_centers)[11:20], "\n")
}
```

```
cluster 1:change data disk windows name computer speed robert tried find
university win manager services write system designed program several xnewsreader

cluster 2:god bible faith hell believe will christians people christian say
jesus peace truth one christ exist love church james life

cluster 3:western soon tin wanted xnewsreader says please university organization lines
also although america american another anyone anything apr area available

cluster 4:peter university department wanted death network looking gun windows file
```

laboratory computer keywords wrote good read version xnewsreader believe engineering

cluster 5:jewish players baseball come bob except somebody mark wondering pretty
sounds present maybe john college past friend list talking day

cluster 6:windows window dos manager version program running problem win memory
use application run using system software thanks screen advance anyone

cluster 7:people article writes one will think like university know time
get right new many now good israel said even government

cluster 8:file files windows program help dos thanks image ftp disk
system need manager color use anybody university looking know version

cluster 9:card video drivers cards windows monitor graphics anyone memory thanks
please system color university bit know version need work get

cluster 10:chip clipper key encryption keys secret government security will system
house public bit phone white communications use text clinton systems

cluster 11:robert bob engineering tin thanks info university andrew xnewsreader computer
buy version anyone speed post board inreplyto inc program good

cluster 12:thanks anyone university please distribution need help use computer car
know looking usa get software info like information problem mac

cluster 13:graphics mode package help please thanks computer support looking code
cards bit anyone software university newsgroup windows image need group

cluster 14:jesus christ god christians christian church paul bible people jews
faith law one say john man name believe jewish religion

cluster 15:list please thanks internet sale send distribution usa anyone bible
interested group day faq know windows info software sorry user

cluster 16:game team games hockey season win play year players baseball
league toronto last runs pittsburgh will university division first think

cluster 17:sale drive offer hard condition monitor disk asking price new
mac please distribution excellent interested usa university best system thanks

cluster 18:difficult money outside find games easy especially line ohio get
says now pay always state might season wait value richard

cluster 19:driver drivers windows ftp card site thanks version looking anybody
win file university video anyone know sound mode bbs please

cluster 20:chris bike dod red needs laboratory thanks name disclaimer article
inc agree anyway writes university distribution now know keywords looking

Let us also look how the words are distributed around the clusters. For better
clarity, we will consider a subset of our data and consider only five clusters. We will
use the "plotcluster" function from the 'fpc' package (Fig. 6.3).

It can be seen that the subset of 100 words from 1000 documents has created
clusters where cluster numbers 2, 3, and 4 are relatively, tightly packed than cluster
number 1.

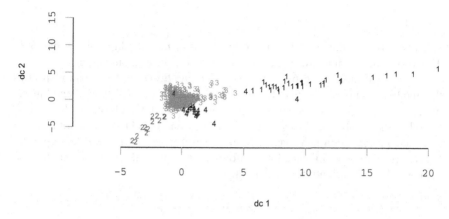

Fig. 6.3 Distribution of data points using 4 clusters

6.4.3 Finding the Optimal Number of Centroids

To settle on the number of clusters, we also need to be clear about how much granularity we would like to have—if we need a rough sketch of the documents, we should settle for a lesser number of clusters however, if we want a better and comprehensive understanding, we should not hesitate to increase the number of clusters. So, selecting the number of clusters is also an art and it depends on the knowledge of the subject matter expert.

Since we are interested in how "tight" the clusters are bound within themselves, it follows that a higher value of k will reduce the variance within clusters. This can be imagined thus—if we have m observations and if we set $k = m$, we will have zero cluster variances. Let us explore this phenomenon by performing an following analysis.

One method to find if the number of clusters k is way too large is to look at the number of members assigned to each cluster as compared to the total number of data points. How many, of our 20 clusters have fewer than words related to an average of $11314/20 = 566$ words per cluster (11314 is the number of documents for 20 subjects and the calculation is a very simple average, because we are not sure how many exact words are present in each of the subject related files).

```
table(k-meansPPmodel$clusters)
```

1	2	3	4	5	6	7	8	9	10	11	12	13	14	15
24	313	1	51	40	296	4815	194	188	322	58	3251	140	174	93
16	17	18	19	20										
745	439	2	93	75										

```
which(table(k-meansPPmodel$clusters) > 566)
```

```
7  12  16
7  12  16
```

Only cluster numbers 7, 12 and 16 have cluster membership greater than 566. This may result from a flaw in the preprocessing of words in our corpus.

Having said this, in Fig. 6.4 we plot the within-cluster variance with respect to the number of clusters. In this plot, we try to look for a pronounced "bend" in the plot, from where the reduction in variance is minimal and it levels of. In other words, we select the number of clusters such that adding another cluster does not result in a substantial reduction in variance. More precisely, the first few clusters upto the "bend" (or "elbow") will add a lot of information (explained variance), but after the "elbow", the gain will not be substantial.

```
k_max <- 50
wcv <- sapply(1:k_max, function(k){k-means(x = dtm_matrix,
                                           k,
                                           nstart = 2,
                                           iter.max = 20 )$tot.withinss
                                  }
             )
wcv
```

```
 [1]  1426.678 1415.079 1406.513 1398.649 1394.327 1386.735 1386.179
 [8]  1377.779 1370.709 1367.612 1361.843 1358.630 1351.142 1349.171
[15]  1340.786 1336.497 1336.002 1337.166 1328.355 1327.607 1323.893
[22]  1315.946 1313.953 1314.177 1314.379 1310.961 1302.936 1299.710
[29]  1298.430 1298.653 1296.795 1292.820 1289.033 1283.606 1287.035
[36]  1287.266 1279.583 1277.944 1277.694 1272.349 1271.528 1267.027
[43]  1264.395 1265.841 1265.227 1262.067 1257.961 1256.304 1254.318
[50]  1254.412
```

```
plot(1:k_max, wcv,
     type="b",
     pch = 20,
     xlab="Number of clusters k",
     ylab="Sum of within-cluster variance",
     cex = 0.7,
     frame = FALSE,
      col = 'deepskyblue4',
     lwd = 1,
     cex.lab = 0.7,
     xaxt = 'n',
     yaxt = 'n')
```

Sometimes however, the "elbow" cannot be unambiguously identified; as in Fig. 6.4; there is a lack of significant change in the variance.

In our plot, the "elbow" is missing as there appears to be a steady gradual drop in variance. In such cases, there is another approach called the Bayesian Inference Criterion for k-means. In this approach, the Bayesian Information Criterion for expectation-maximization is used to determine the optimal number of clusters. A discussion on this topic is beyond the scope of this book.

Suffice it to say that small clusters may also be preferable to a large cluster having a mixed content. But small clusters also has the tendency to overfit.

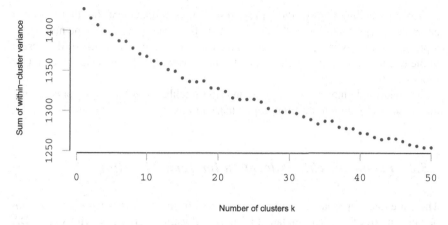

Fig. 6.4 Reduction in within-clusters variance with increasing number of clusters is plotted. We cannot observe an "elbow", from where the drop in variance becomes insignificant

6.5 Topic Modeling

Topic modeling is a process of automatically identifying topics from text documents. So far, we have read the words from different text objects (documents), sanitized the text for special characters, white spaces, etc., removed the stopwords (words which do not carry much information), and created a $tf - idf$ matrix, which is weighted by the frequency of terms in a document and in the corpus of documents. The $tf - idf$ matrix is our representation of the "bag of words" in a numeric format.

The prior probability that a document x_i belongs to a particular topic k can be represented as $p(x_i = k) = \pi_k$. Assuming that the text object i is from topic k, the word x_i will therefore occur with some probability of occurrence. Till now, we have been computing the likelihood of the $tf - idf$ vector to be assigned to a cluster. In topic modeling, we will compute the likelihood of the collection of words in the text object belonging to a topic. In both the cases, the cluster and the topics are treated as distributions.

6.5.1 Clustering and Topic Modeling

In clustering, the basic idea was to group the documents based on some similarity measure. To this effect, we had represented each document by a $tf - idf$ vector representing the weights assigned to the words in the document. Clustering would then result in each word showing up in one of the clusters. In clustering, we have used the $tf - idf$ vector to compute its likelihood to belong to a particular distribution (cluster).

Topic modeling gives us the topics present in each document. In other words, it generates a representation of the documents in the topic space. Since the number of topics associated with the documents is far lesser than the number of words present in the documents, topic modeling can also be viewed as a dimensionality reduction process.

In topic modeling, we would compute the likelihood of the words present in a document, belonging to different topic distributions.

6.5.2   Latent Dirichlet Allocation for Topic Modeling

There are many approaches for obtaining topics from a $tf - idf$ vector namely, non-negative matrix factorization, latent Dirichlet allocation (LDA), etc. However, LDA is one of the most popular topic modeling techniques. The term "Dirichlet" in LDA refers to the fact that topics and words are assumed to follow Dirichlet distributions. Dirichlet distributions provide good approximations to word distributions in documents and are also computationally efficient.

The basic assumption in LDA is that documents are produced from a mixture of topics and the topics generate words, based on their probability distribution. Given a set of documents, LDA tries to figure out the topics, which would create the documents by a matrix factorization technique. Essentially, LDA converts the document-term matrix into two lower dimensional matrices—m_1 and m_2, where m_1 is a document-topics matrix and m_2 is a topic-terms matrix.

As per [Edwin Chen], LDA calculates two probabilities $p_1 = p$(topic t/document d), i.e., the proportion of words in document d that are assigned to topic t and $p_2 = p$(word w/topic t), i.e., the proportion of assignments to topic t over all documents which emanate from word w.

The topic-word assignment is then updated with a new topic having an updated probability $p_1 \times p_2$, assuming that all the existing word-topic assignments except the current word are correct.

Iterating through the above steps, convergence is achieved when the document-topic and topic-term distributions settle down. We then estimate the topic mixtures of each document and the words associated to each topic.

The iterative process is implemented using a technique called **Gibbs sampling**.

6.5.2.1   Gibbs Sampling

Gibbs sampling incorporates a random walk in a way which reflects the characteristics of the distribution. As the starting point of the walk is randomly chosen, the first few steps are discarded and are referred to as the "burnin" period. We then perform say i iterations, taking every say, qth iteration for further use. The reason we do this is to avoid correlations between samples. Different starting points ($nstart = n$) are utilized to carry out independent runs. Each starting point requires a seed to ensure reproducibility. The Gibbs algorithm returns results of the run having the highest posterior probability.

We will not derive the LDA algorithm here and instead work through some examples with data sets available in R packages. As a start, let us examine the "AssociatedPress" data set from the topicmodels package, written by Bettina Gruen and Kurt Hornik. This data set is represented as a DocumentTermMatrix and is a collection of 2246 news articles from an American news agency published in 1988.

Let us first create a topic model using the Gibbs sampling method. We will assume that there are $k = 5$ topics in our data set.

```
data("AssociatedPress")
burnin <- 4000
iter <- 2000
thin <- 500
seed <-list(61, 161)
nstart <- 2
best <- TRUE
k <- 5
lda_model_5 <-LDA(AssociatedPress, k, method='Gibbs',
                control = list(nstart = nstart,
                               seed = seed,
                               best = best,
                               burnin = burnin,
                               iter = iter,
                               thin = thin
                               )

                )
as.matrix(terms(lda_model_5, 10))
```

	Topic 1	Topic 2	Topic 3	Topic 4	Topic 5
[1,]	"percent"	"police"	"i"	"government"	"court"
[2,]	"million"	"people"	"new"	"president"	"state"
[3,]	"year"	"two"	"years"	"soviet"	"federal"
[4,]	"new"	"city"	"bush"	"united"	"law"
[5,]	"billion"	"officials"	"going"	"states"	"department"
[6,]	"company"	"air"	"just"	"party"	"case"
[7,]	"market"	"three"	"dont"	"union"	"office"
[8,]	"last"	"killed"	"first"	"political"	"house"
[9,]	"prices"	"spokesman"	"think"	"military"	"last"
[10,]	"stock"	"miles"	"time"	"official"	"bill"

Now we will create another topic model with $k = 2$.

```
data("AssociatedPress")
burnin <- 4000
iter <- 2000
thin <- 500
seed <-list(61, 161)
nstart <- 2
best <- TRUE
k <- 2
lda_model_2 <-LDA(AssociatedPress,
                  k,
                  method='Gibbs',
```

```
                        control = list(nstart = nstart,
                                       seed = seed,
                                       best = best,
                                       burnin = burnin,
                                       iter = iter,
                                       thin = thin)
                   )
as.matrix(terms(lda_model_2, 10))
```

```
         Topic 1    Topic 2
  [1,]  "percent"  "i"
  [2,]  "new"      "people"
  [3,]  "year"     "two"
  [4,]  "million"  "president"
  [5,]  "last"     "government"
  [6,]  "billion"  "police"
  [7,]  "federal"  "state"
  [8,]  "company"  "soviet"
  [9,]  "york"     "bush"
 [10,]  "first"    "told"
```

With a little bit of thought, we can assign the topics to separate and different subjects. But how do we select the number of topics?

6.5.2.2 Selecting k

As discussed earlier about selecting the number of clusters in a clustering algorithm, selecting the number of topics to create a topic model from an unseen data set is a challenge. As usual, different values for k may be plausible, but higher values of k stands the danger of losing clarity.

Thankfully, there is a statistical measure which can help us determine the optimal number of topics. In R, there is function called "perplexity", which measures how well a probability model predicts a sample. With our LDA model and given the theoretical word distributions represented by the topics, we compare that to the actual topic mixtures, or distribution of words in our documents.

Let us estimate a series of LDA models on the Associated Press data set.

In Fig. 6.5, the model perplexity keeps reducing with the number of topics. From the figure ideally, we may choose the "elbow" to take place with $k = 20$.

For simplicity of understanding, we will consider $k = 2$ to create a two-topic LDA model. The tidytext package provides a method for extracting the per-topic-per-word probabilities, β, from the model (Table 6.1).

```
data("AssociatedPress")
lda_model <- LDA(AssociatedPress, k = 2, control = list(seed = 61))
topics <- tidy(lda_model, matrix = "beta")
```

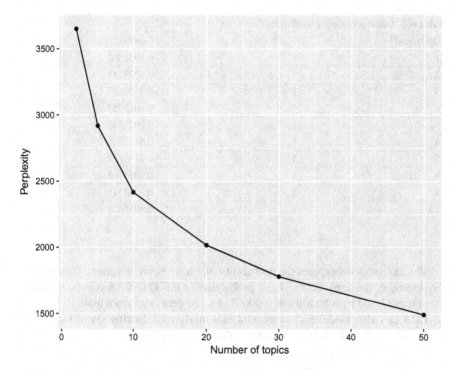

Fig. 6.5 Evaluating LDA Topic models for perplexity using different number of topics

Table 6.1 Word-topic probabilities

Topic	Term	Beta
1	aaron	0.0000297
2	aaron	0.0000114
1	abandon	0.0000246
2	abandon	0.0000512
1	abandoned	0.0001099
2	abandoned	0.0000607
1	abandoning	0.0000218
2	abandoning	0.0000000
1	abbott	0.0000100
2	abbott	0.0000327

Table 6.2 Document-topic probabilities

Document	Topic	Gamma
1	1	0.9992862
2	1	0.5323241
3	1	0.9752807
4	1	0.8017257
5	1	0.9971349
6	1	0.9423526
7	1	0.2732921
8	1	0.9965705
9	1	0.9743715
10	1	0.9066428

The lda_model computes the probability of a term being generated from a topic. For example, the term "aaron" has a probability of 0.0000297 for it to be generated from topic 1 and a probability of 0.0000114 to be generated from topic 2.

LDA can also model each document as a mixture of distribution of topics. The document-topic probabilities, γ can be calculated as follows:

```
prob_doc_topic <- tidy(lda_model,
                       matrix = "gamma"
                       )
```

Table 6.2 tells us that 99.92% of the terms used in document 1 were generated from topic 1 and 27.32% of the terms used in document 7 were generated from topic 1, document 7 mostly comes from topic 2. It may be appreciated that the documents are a mix of two topics.

Let us find out what are the terms used in document 7 (Table 6.3).

```
doc_7 <- tidy(AssociatedPress) %>% filter(document == 7)
sorted_doc_7 <- arrange(doc_7, desc(count))
```

Looks like that document 7 is associated with trade between America and Japan.

Let us explore if topic 2 is indeed about business and trade. For this, we will plot the probabilities associated with the first 15 terms. From the plot below, topic 1 includes words suggesting politics whereas, the words in topic 2 suggest business; indeed our interpretation about document 7 coming from topic 2 was correct (Fig. 6.6).

```
grouped_topics <- topics %>% group_by(topic)

top_terms <- top_n(grouped_topics, 10, beta)

ungrouped_terms <- ungroup(top_terms)

arranged_terms <- arrange(ungrouped_terms)

ordered_terms <- mutate(arranged_terms, term = reorder(term, beta))
```

Table 6.3 Terms in document 7

Document	Term	Count
7	Skins	9
7	Japan	6
7	Trade	5
7	American	3
7	Cites	3
7	Documents	3
7	Export	3
7	Group	3
7	Illegal	3
7	International	3

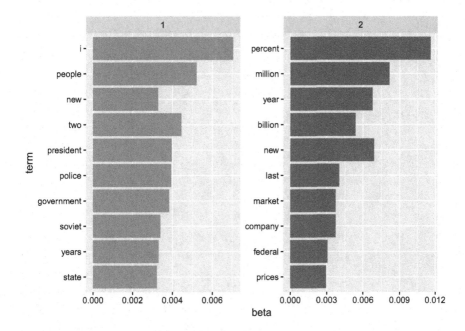

Fig. 6.6 Top 10 term probabilities for two different topics

```
ggplot(ordered_terms, aes(term, beta, fill = factor(topic))) +
  geom_col(show.legend = FALSE) +
  facet_wrap(~ topic, scales = "free") +
  coord_flip()
```

References and Further Reading

Adler J (2012) R in a Nutshell. O Reilly

Afifi A, May S, Clark VA (2012) Practical multivariate analysis. Chapman & Hill, Boca Raton

Bishop CM (2006) Pattern recognition and machine learning. Springer, CA

Bivand RS, Pebesma E, Gormez-Rubio V (2013) Applied spatial data analysis with R. Springer, New York

Casella G, Berger RL (1990) Statistical inference. Wadsworth and Brooks/Cole, Pacific Grove, CA

Chang W (2013) R graphics cookbook. O Reilly

Chen E. What is a good explanation of Latent Dirichlet Allocation. www.quora.com

Cleveland WS (1993) Visualizing data. Hobart Press, Summit, NJ

Conway D, White JM (2013) Machine learning for hackers. O Reilly, India

Cortez P (2014) Modern optimization with R. Springer, New York

Datta BN (2010) Numerical linear algebra and applications. Prentice Hall India Learning Private Limited

Davenport TH, Harris JG (2010) Analytics at work. Harvard Business Publishing, USA

Davison AC, Hinkley DV (1997) Bootstrap methods and their application. Cambridge University Press, Cambridge

Domingos P (2015) The master algorithm. Basic Books, New York

Everitt B, Hothorn T (2011) An introduction to applied multivariate analysis with R. Springer, New York

Fisher RA (1935) The design of experiments. Oliver and Boyd, Edinburgh

Gelman A, Hill J (2009) Data analysis using regression and multilevel/hierarchical models. Cambridge University Press, New York

Ghahramani S (2012) Fundamentals of probability with stochastic processes. Pearson, India

Grus J (2015) Data science from scratch. O Reilly, CA

Hair JF, Black WC, Babin BJ, Anderson RE (2010) Multivariate data analysis. Prentice Hall, NJ

Hastie T, Tibshirani R (1990) Generalized additive models. Chapman & Hall, London

Hastie T, Tibshirani R, Friedman J (2013) The elelements of statistical learning. Springer, New York

Hastie T, Tibshirani R (2015) Statistical learning and data mining III. Palo Alto

Hosmer DW, Lemeshow S (2000) Applied logistic regression, 2nd edn. John Wiley & Sons Inc, New York

Huitema BE (1980) The analysis of covariance and alternatives. Wiley, New York

Hume D (2003) Treatise of human nature. Dover Publications

© Springer Nature Singapore Pte Ltd. 2017
A. Ghatak, *Machine Learning with R*, DOI 10.1007/978-981-10-6808-9

James G, Witten D, Hastie T, Tibshirani R (2013) An introduction to statistical learning. Springer, New York

Jockers ML (2014) Text analysis with r for students of literature. Springer, New York

Knuth DE (1998) The $T_E Xbook$. Addison Wesley, Reading, MA

Kolaczyk ED, Csardi G (2014) Statistical analysis of network data with R. Springer, New York

Kuhn M, Johnson K (2013) Applied predictive modeling. Springer, New York

Larose DT (2005) Discovering knowledge in data. Wiley, Hoboken

Larose DT (2012) Data mining methods and models. Wiley, New Delhi

Lehmann EL (1986) Testing statistical hypotheses. Wiley, New York

Manning C, Raghavan P, Schutze H (2012) Introduction to information retrieval. Cambridge University Press, India

Mardia KV, Kent JT, Bibby JM (1979) Multivariate statistics. Academic Press, London

Markov Z, Larose DT (2007) Data mining the web. Wiley, Hoboken

Miller I, Miller M (2013) Mathematical statistics. Prentice & Hall, India

Mitchell TM (1997) Machine learning. McGraw-Hill, New York

Nolan D, Lang DT (2014) XML and web technologies for data sciences with R. Springer, New York

Nolan D, Lang DT (2015) Data science in R. A case studies approach to computational reasoning. Chapman & Hall, Boca Raton

O'Neil C, Schutt R (2014) Doing data science. O Reilly, CA

Rajaraman A, Ullman JD (2014) Mining massive datasets. Cambridge University Press, New Delhi

Resnik P, Hardisty E (2010) Gibbs sampling for the Uninitiated. CS-TR-4956

Romeijn, Jan-Willem (2017) Philosophy of statistics. The Stanford Encyclopedia of Philosophy

Russel MA (2012) Mining the social web. O Reilly, India

Scott DW (1992) Multivariate density estimation. Wiley, New York, Theory, Practice and Visualization

Segaran T (2007) Programming collective intelligence. O Reilly, CA

Seni G, Elder J (2010) Ensemble methods in data mining. Morgan & Claypool, Chicago

Shores TS (2012) Applied linear algebra and matrix analysis. Springer, India

Strang G (2009) Introduction to linear algebra. Cambridge Press, Wellesley

Therneau TM, Atkinson B (2012) RPART: Recursive partitioning. Maintainer: Brian Ripley, ripley@stats.ox.ac.uk

Wickham H (2009) ggplot2: Elegant graphics for data analysis. Springer, New York

Wickham H (2015) Advanced R. CRC Press, Boca Raton

Wiesberg S (1985) Applied linear regression. Wiley, New York

Williams G (2011) Data mining with rattle and R-The art of excavating data for knowledge discovery. Springer, New York

Winston WL, Albright SC (2012) Practical management science. South-Western CENGAGE Learning, Mason, OH

Witton IH, Frank E, Hall MA (2010) Data mining: practical machine learning tools and techniques. Morgan Kaufman, Burlington

Zucchini W, MacDonald IL (2017) Hidden Markov Models for time series: an introduction using R. CRC Press, Boca Raton

Printed in the United States
By Bookmasters